29TH EDITION

The Good Retirement Guide

EVERYTHING YOU NEED TO KNOW ABOUT HEALTH, PROPERTY, INVESTMENT, LEISURE, WORK, PENSIONS AND TAX

Edited by
Frances Kay and
Allan Esler Smith

The information contained in this book is for general guidance only and does not constitute professional advice. Users should consult with a professional adviser concerning any specific issues, and their impact on any individual or entity, before making any major financial decision.

This 29th edition published in Great Britain in 2015 by Kogan Page Limited

Kogan Page Limited
2nd Floor, 45 Gee Street
London EC1V 3RS
United Kingdom
www.koganpage.com

© Kogan Page, 2013, 2014, 2015

The right of Allan Esler Smith to be identified as the author of Chapter 7 'Scams and Complaints' and Chapter 10 'Starting Your Own Business' has been asserted by him in accordance with the Copyright, Designs and Patents Act 1988.

The right of Kogan Page to be identified as the author of this work has been asserted by them in accordance with the Copyright, Designs and Patents Act 1988.

ISBN   978 0 7494 7338 9
E-ISBN   978 0 7494 7339 6

British Library Cataloguing in Publication Data

A CIP record for this book is available from the British Library.

Typeset by Graphicraft Limited, Hong Kong
Printed and bound in India by Replika Press Pvt Ltd

Contents

16   No one is immortal   345

Chapter One
Looking forward
to retirement...

I'm 65, but if there were 15 months in every year, I'd only be 48.

JAMES THURBER

A recent survey suggests that middle age now begins at 55. This is much later than previously thought (previous studies had pin-pointed the start of middle age as early as 36). Apparently Britons do not see themselves as elderly until they are nudging 70, the survey of 1,000 UK adults aged 50-plus for the *Love to Learn* online learning website states (**www.bbc.co.uk/news/education-19622330**).

According to data from ONS (Office for National Statistics) there are now more adults over 65 than there are under-16s. Rising life expectancy means older people are effectively 'younger', healthier and fitter than previous generations. So it is good to know that this piece of research says that adults in their 50s are upbeat about the benefits of their age group and their upcoming retirement. People have more confidence and experience and are less afraid of making mistakes. This all goes to show that the concept of ageing has changed. It was only a generation ago that people retiring in their 60s considered themselves old. Now 60-year-olds are much younger in attitude and have an active state of mind and positive outlook. It is not over-optimistic to suggest they can look forward to their retirement lasting in excess of a quarter of a century.

Retirement is wonderful and it really doesn't matter when you decide to take the plunge. The actor Peter O'Toole, a month before his 80th birthday in 2012, announced it was time to 'chuck in the sponge' and retire from stage and screen. He believed it was a matter of personal choice when to step down from professional work. Two of the greatest men of modern times ignored the normal retiring age of 65. Winston Churchill was 65 when he first became Prime Minister in May 1940, and he was 70 at the war's end in 1945. Nelson Mandela was 71 when he was released from prison in South Africa in February 1990, and nearly 76 when he was first elected President in 1994. There is a lot to be said for age and experience.

While some of us have the opportunity to retire early, others continue to work into their 70s, usually because they enjoy what they do. So what plans do you have? Buying a copy of the latest edition of *The Good Retirement Guide* is a good first step. This book contains everything you need to know about retirement, and is full of advice and suggestions on planning your future – from finance, pensions, work, home and health, to leisure activities and holidays.

Making the most of your retirement is essential. There are broadly three main groups of retirees:

- *the young retired* aged between 60 and 70, who generally enjoy good health and are keen to pursue an active retirement;
- *the mid retired* aged between 70 and 80 who are established in their retirement, perhaps less energetic than they were, yet still relishing life;
- *the long-term retired* in their 80s and 90s who live independent lives and enjoy themselves, possibly with some input and assistance from others.

Working out how you will manage your life for upwards of 25 years is a challenge. It is often quite difficult to plan a year ahead, let alone a quarter of a century. So much change can happen, much of it outside your control. The two main areas of concern for people coming up to retirement are well documented: finances and health. Retirement is a major lifestyle change but it can be enormously enjoyable. Don't worry about what other people are doing, and what they think – this is not important. You cannot compare your life to someone else's. Seize the opportunity to get rid of anything that isn't useful or needed: retirement can be liberating. No one is in charge of your retirement but you. Take time to work out what is important to you, so that you can spend the majority of your time in whatever way you want. If you prepare for retirement as well as you can, you can then relax and go with the flow.

Some suggestions on retirement planning

- Think about what standard of living you want; how much money you think you'll need; and what sort of social life you wish to enjoy.
- If travel is important to you, make sure your budget allows for this.
- Sign up for a pre-retirement course.
- Work out your finances/pensions/investments with your professional advisor.
- Ask friends or former colleagues who have already retired for their best retirement suggestions.
- Consider where you live – is moving house necessary or desirable?
- Resist the temptation once you've retired to commit yourself to too many new things too early – wait six months to coo how you feel.
- And, most important... read your copy of *The Good Retirement Guide*!

Retirement today is full of opportunity and choice. The 2015 *Guide* is thoroughly updated to reflect recent changes to tax, pensions and opportunities. Planning for retirement can be hard – this book makes it easier.

Pre-retirement courses

Whatever age at which you are due to retire, taking advantage of a pre-retirement course can help you plan well for the next stage in your life. When would be the best time to attend such a course? One or two years before retirement, or earlier? Some people take retirement planning in stages. Some financial decisions, such as those affecting company or personal pension planning, should be taken as early as possible. Others, like whether or not to move house, can wait till later.

Courses are designed to address the main subjects: finances, health, activity, leisure, housing and the implications and adjustments needed to be made when you retire. If your pre-retirement studies stimulate discussion with your partner and others in similar situations, it will have achieved its objective.

Here is a list of some useful websites to look at for those planning retirement:

www.activeageplanning.co.uk;

www.laterlife.com;

www.life-academy.co.uk;

www.res-ltd.net;

www.retirement-courses.co.uk;

www.the-retirement-site.co.uk;

www.sprc.org.uk.

New focus for the retired

As the over-50s are such a large and important section of the population, the amount of information available to retirees is enormous. Here are some useful websites:

- Age UK – Britain's largest charity working with and for older people: **www.ageuk.org.uk.**
- Gov.uk – the UK government website has sections on pensions and retirement planning: **www.gov.uk.**
- National Pensioners Convention – the campaigning voice for UK pensioners: **www.npcuk.org.**
- Retirement Expert – offers expert advice for your retirement: **www.retirementexpert.co.uk.**
- Retirement Links – provides articles and information on all aspects of retirement and pensions: **www.retirementlinks.co.uk.**
- UK Retirement (part of LaterLife) – focuses on planning for your retirement: **www.ukretirement.co.uk.**

Another way to get heaps of advice and information about retirement is to visit The 50 Plus Show. This is Britain's biggest exhibition for the active over-50s and takes place in five locations annually across the UK: Manchester, London, Birmingham, Glasgow and Exeter. See website: **www.50plusshow.com.**

Have fun and enjoy your retirement planning.

Chapter Two
Money in general

Question: Why do retirees count pennies?

Answer: Because they are the only ones who have the time.

Are you worrying about how to finance your retirement? Do you think you will be facing poverty in your old age? Defining poverty surely depends on individual expectations – and money, we know, cannot buy happiness. Indeed, surveys have shown that beyond a certain level wealth can be positively isolating: some very rich people feel comfortable associating only with people as rich as themselves. However, according to a recent study by Liverpool Victoria (LV=), the retirement specialists, a happy retirement can be enjoyed for around £11,000 per year. This involves spending 468 hours on hobbies and 364 hours with grandchildren. The most contented pensioners also spend 21 days on holidays abroad, and live in a detached house with a garden. The 'essential' annual cost of living for a retired person in Britain in 2014 was estimated to be £7,623. Adding the £3,197 cost of the happy retirement that emerged from the survey took the total to £10,820. So next time you feel envious of the latest lottery winner, or the lifestyle of the rich and famous celebrities whose images we see plastered all over the media, remember that the price of happiness in retirement is not very high.

Having said that, what is alarming is that many people approaching retirement do not seek any form of financial advice. Despite the fairly modest aspirations of people when it comes to what they feel they need for a happy retirement – such as spending time with family and friends, which costs very little – it is important that people plan for retirement as early as possible. Everyone should explore all their financial options as retirement approaches. It is essential to know where you are money-wise and not allow your hard-earned funds to retire at the same time as you: your money must continue to work hard for you, so that you have the financial flexibility you need. With the many budget-related decisions that have to be made once you stop working, it is crucial to get these right.

With increasing longevity, retirement is lasting longer, so those of pensionable age desiring the best quality of life for as long as possible must work out how much money they have and what they will actually require to fund their retirement. Whether you are close to giving up work or you are several years away from retirement, the most important thing is to carry out a serious review of your retirement plans. This will help you to work out what options there are for maximizing your future income. Being free of money worries in later life is something well worth investing some time in while you have the opportunity.

The 'This is Money' website (**www.thisismoney.co.uk**) gives top tips for achieving perfect personal finances. If you are approaching retirement take a look at this list of steps to take:

1 Make a will.

2 Pay off debts.

3 Get term life assurance.

4 Fund your company pension to the maximum.

5 Buy a house you can afford.

6 Put six months' worth of outgoings in a cash ISA.

7 Invest any spare money in more ISAs.

8 Find yourself a fee-based financial planner.

Focus on your personal circumstances and look at ways to plan your finances. If, for example, you are coming up to retirement and have a stable job with a strong company, you are fortunate. Should redundancy be a distinct possibility, the right preparation is crucial. Where possible, while still working, everyone should build up a cash emergency fund (provided you have no debts – apart from a mortgage). This means saving roughly enough money for six months' payment of bills and living expenses. You could start an ISA, and save as much as you can.

Should your income be likely to drop, it makes sense to cut debt costs as much as possible. If you have savings, remember that the government guarantees £85,000 per person per UK-regulated financial institution. If you have more than this, you can spread it over multiple accounts. If you have a financial problem that you cannot resolve, there is a free service set up by law with the power to sort out problems between consumers and financial businesses. It is called the Financial Ombudsman Service and there is more information about this in Chapter 6.

To ensure you have a comfortable retirement, you will need to carry out a full financial health check to give you a clear view of your current financial position. Get a state pension forecast, then contact the pension trustees of your current and previous employers. Once you've done that, work out how much income you are likely to need in retirement. Be as realistic as you can: remember to factor in holidays and any debts you might have. If you have lost track of investments or previous pensions, it is worth spending some time to trace these.

The ability to manage your money and know how to budget is important. Don't forget that there are some 'retirement freebies' that are well worth taking advantage of: these include travel concessions, some health benefits and help with fuel bills. It's surprising how much these small things add up to.

The key to managing your retirement well is to know how to make whatever money you have go as far as possible. There are many useful websites brimming with information on retirement issues (some of these are listed at the end of Chapter 1). But if you are keen to budget wisely, there are a number of handy apps to help you balance the books:

- *Account Tracker* (£1.99; iOS). The complexity of managing multiple incomes and outgoings across several accounts often discourages people from budgeting. This five-star-reviewed, very usable app makes it easy.
- *Expensify* (free; iOS and Google Play). Busy people who travel or entertain a lot for work will love this app, which separates your professional expenditure from your personal expenditure so that one doesn't bleed into the other. It logs miles driven and tracks purchases; very useful if you need to file expense accounts on the move.

- *Stockwatch* (£3.99; iOS). This comprehensive app supports 50 exchanges, allowing you to track unlimited stocks, mutuals, futures, etc while out and about. You can customize watch lists and portfolios so that it only shows the sectors you are interested in.

Source: *The Week*, 29 March 2014

Doing the sums

To get an objective view of your financial affairs, draw up a budget showing your income and outgoings. This comprises several lists:

- expected sources of income on retirement;
- essential outgoings;
- normal additional spending (such as holidays and other luxuries).

The following should also be considered:

- possible ways to boost your retirement income;
- spending now for saving later.

You should also try to factor in some of the variables and unknowns, which are much more difficult to estimate. Given the uncertainties in the global markets over recent years, this is not easy. However, the two most important items to consider in retirement planning are tax and inflation. Things like stocks and shares, property prices and energy costs go up as well as down, and all these affect retirement finances. Emergency situations can arise, the most likely being illness, so, if possible, special provisions should be made. The big question (which no one can answer) is how long you, your partner or any dependants might live.

Think about these questions: how will you live in retirement? What items will still represent a significant percentage of your budget? What expenditure will cease to be important? There are probably a number of areas where savings can be made, such as becoming a one-car family, for example. The most practical way forward is to draw up lists of the items that will definitely apply to you and, where possible, write down the expenditure involved. Regard this exercise as no more than a draft. Repeat it as often as necessary, and certainly update it each time you obtain more facts and information.

If retirement is imminent, then doing the arithmetic in as much detail as possible will not only reassure you but also help you plan your future life with greater confidence. There are probably a number of options open to you. Examining the figures written down will highlight the areas of greatest flexibility. One tip, offered by one of the retirement magazines, is to start living on your retirement income some six months before you retire. Not only will you see if your budget estimates are broadly correct, but since most people err on the cautious side when they first retire you will have the bonus of all the extra money you will have saved.

If retirement is still some years ahead, there will be more unknowns and more opportunities. When assessing the figures, take account of your future earnings. Perhaps you should also consider what steps you might be able to take under the pension rules in order to maximize your pension fund. You could also consider whether you should be putting money aside now in a savings plan and/or making other investments. To be on the safe side, assume an increase in inflation. Everyone should, if they possibly can, budget for a nest egg to help cover the cost of any emergencies or special events that may come along.

Possible savings

Once you stop working you should be able to save quite a lot, as a number of expenses will disappear. These include travelling costs to and from work, meals out, business clothes and other work related items. National Insurance contributions (NICs) cease on retirement and, unless you choose to invest in a private plan, your pension payments will also stop. It is important to check (once you retire) what your tax coding is because you may well move to a lower tax bracket. Table 2.1 gives a breakdown of how to estimate where monthly savings can be made.

Extra outgoings

If you are spending more time at home once you retire, your utility bills will increase. You may also find that you spend more on outings, hobbies, and short breaks and holidays (see Table 2.2 for how to estimate monthly costs). Looking ahead, home comforts become increasingly important and you may want to think about paying other people to do some of the jobs that you previously managed yourself. Anticipating such areas of

TABLE 2.1   Breakdown to estimate where monthly savings can be made

Items	Estimated monthly savings
National Insurance contributions	....
Pension payments	....
Travel expenses to work	....
Bought lunches	....
Incidentals at work: eg drinks with colleagues, collections for presents	....
Special work clothes	....
Concessionary travel	....
NHS prescriptions	....
Eye tests	....
Mature drivers insurance policy	....
Retired householders insurance policy	....
Life assurance payments and/or possible endowment policy premiums	....
Other	....
TOTAL	....

NB: You should also take into account reduced running costs if you move to a smaller home; any expenses for dependant children that may cease; other costs such as mortgage payments that may end around the time you retire; and the fact that you may be in a lower tax bracket and may not be liable for National Insurance contributions.

additional expenditure is not being pessimistic – actually it is the surest way of avoiding future money worries. Once you've worked out your retirement income and expenditure in detail you should be able, with a bit of adjustment and compromise, to manage well.

TABLE 2.2 Estimating extra outgoings

Items	Estimated monthly costs
Extra heating and lighting bills	....
Extra spending on hobbies and other entertainment	....
Replacement of company car	....
Private health care insurance	....
Longer or more frequent holidays	....
Life and permanent health insurance	....
Cost of substituting other perks, eg expense account lunches	....
Out-of-pocket expenses for voluntary-work activity	....
Other	....
TOTAL	....

NB: Looking ahead, you will need to make provision for any extra home comforts you might want and, also, at some point, for having to pay other people to do some of the jobs that you normally manage yourself. If you intend to make regular donations to a charity, or perhaps help with your grandchildren's education, these too should be included in the list. The same applies to any new private pension or savings plan that you might want to invest in to boost your long-term retirement income.

Expected sources of income on retirement

Your list will include at least some of the items listed in Table 2.3. Once you have added up these figures, you will need to deduct income tax in order to arrive at the net spending amount available to you.

Many people have difficulty understanding the tax system, and you should certainly take professional advice if you are in any doubt at all. However, if you carefully fill in your expected sources of income and likely tax implications in Tables 2.3 and 2.4, it should give you a pretty good idea of your net income after retirement and enable you to make at least provisional plans.

TABLE 2.3   Expected sources of income

A. Income received _before_ tax	
Basic state pension	....
State graduated pension	....
SERPS/State second pension	....
Occupational pension(s)	....
Stakeholder or personal pension	....
State benefits	....
Investments and savings plans paid gross, eg gilts, National Savings	....
Other incomes (eg rental income)	....
Casual or other pre-tax earnings	....
TOTAL	....
Less: Personal tax allowance and possibly also married couple's allowance	....
Basic-rate tax	....
TOTAL A	....
B. Income received _after_ tax	
Dividends (unit trusts, shares, etc)	....
Bank deposit account	....
Building society interest	....
Annuity income	....
Other (including earnings subject to PAYE)	....
TOTAL B	....
Total A + B	....
Less: Higher-rate tax (if any)	....
Plus: Other tax-free receipts, eg some state benefits, income from an ISA	....
Investment bond withdrawals, etc	....
Other	....
TOTAL NET INCOME	....

TABLE 2.4   Unavoidable outgoings

Items	Estimated monthly cost
Food	....
Rent or mortgage repayments	....
Council tax	....
Repair and maintenance costs	....
Heating	....
Lighting and other energy	....
Telephone/mobile/internet	....
Postage (including Christmas cards)	....
TV licence/Sky/digital subscription	....
Household insurance	....
Clothes	....
Laundry, cleaner's bills, shoe repair	....
Domestic cleaning products	....
Miscellaneous services, eg plumber and window cleaner	....
Car (including licence, petrol, etc)	....
Other transport	....
Regular savings and life assurance	....
HP and other loan repayments	....
Outgoings on health	....
Other	....
TOTAL	....

NB: Before adding up the total, you should look at the 'Normal additional expenditure' list (Table 2.5), as you may well want to juggle some of the items between the two.

Remember too that you may have one or two capital sums to invest, such as:

- the commuted lump sum from your pension;
- money from an endowment policy;
- gains from the sale of company shares (SAYE or other share option scheme);
- profits from the sale of your home or other asset;
- money from an inheritance.

Unavoidable outgoings

No one will have the same list as another, since one person's priority is another's luxury. For this reason, the divide between 'unavoidable outgoings' (see page 13) and 'normal additional expenditure' (see page 15) is likely to vary considerably with each individual. Almost everyone will want to juggle some of the items between the two lists or add their own particular requisites or special enthusiasms. Whatever your own essentials, some of the items listed in Table 2.4 will certainly feature on your list of unavoidable expenses.

Normal additional expenditure

This could include some of the items listed in Table 2.5.

Possible ways of boosting your retirement income

Few people can afford to turn away extra income these days, yet there are really only three possible ways to give your retirement finances a boost: these are from your home, work and investment skills.

Your home

Your home offers several different options: moving somewhere smaller, taking in lodgers or raising money on your home. All the possibilities are explored in greater detail in Chapter 8.

TABLE 2.5 Normal additional expenditure

Items	Estimated monthly cost
Gifts	....
Holidays	....
Newspapers/books/CDs/DVDs	....
Computer (including broadband)	....
Drink	....
Cigarettes/tobacco	....
Hairdressing/beauty treatments	....
Toiletries/cosmetics	....
Entertainment (hobbies, outgoings, home entertaining, etc)	....
Miscellaneous subscriptions, membership fees	....
Gifts, charitable donations	....
Expenditure on pets	....
Garden purchases	....
Other	....
TOTAL	....

NB: For some items, such as holidays and gifts, you may tend to think in annual expenditure terms. However, for the purpose of comparing monthly income versus outgoings, it is probably easier if you itemize all the expenditure in the same fashion. Also, if you need to save for a special event such as your holiday, it helps if you get into the habit of putting so much aside every month (or even weekly).

Work

How about continuing to work? There is plenty of scope here for earning money, even in these difficult times. You could talk to your employer to see what options there are for you to remain with your present organization. Alternatively, retirement for you may offer the chance of setting up on your own. Becoming self-employed or setting up a business may sound attractive but there are start-up costs to be considered. There is a lot more information on work, and how to get it, in Chapters 10, 11 and 12.

Investment

Everyone can try this but if it is unfamiliar territory, what is most important is to get good advice from a trusted professional to help you find the most suitable investment opportunities for you. Chapter 5 sets out the various forms that investment can take.

Money – if you are made redundant

Much of the information in the earlier part of this chapter is equally valid whether you become redundant or retire in the normal way. However, as shown below, there are several key points with regard to redundancy that it could be to your advantage to check.

From your employment

You may be entitled to statutory redundancy pay

Your employer is obliged to pay the legal minimum, which is calculated on your age, length of service and weekly pay. To qualify, you will need to have worked for the organization for at least two years, with no age restriction. Redundancy pay is 1.5 weeks' pay for each year worked if you are over 41 years, up to a maximum of £430 a week.

Ex gratia payments

Many employers are prepared to be more generous. As long as it's not more than £30,000, statutory redundancy pay is not taxable. Any payment over this limit is subject to tax and National Insurance.

Benefits that are not part of your pay

Redundancy may mean the loss of several valuable benefits such as a company car, life assurance and health insurance. Some insurance companies allow preferential rates to individuals who were previously insured with them under a company scheme.

Holiday entitlement

You could be owed holiday entitlement for which you should be paid.

Company pension

Company pension scheme members normally have several choices. See the 'Company pension schemes' section in Chapter 3.

Your mortgage

Your mortgage lender should be notified as soon as possible and might agree to a more flexible repayment system. Check whether your mortgage package includes insurance against redundancy. There is help available from the state if you are claiming benefits, such as income support or income-based Jobseeker's Allowance. Those claiming these benefits could have their interest payments covered for two years if their mortgage is below £200,000. However, no help is available to pay off the capital of your mortgage.

Other creditors/debts

Any creditors that you may have difficulty in paying (electricity, gas, a bank overdraft) should be informed as early as possible in the hope of agreeing easier payment terms. There could be an argument for paying off credit card bills immediately, even if this means using some of your redundancy pay.

Jobseeker's Allowance (JSA)

Even if you are hoping to get another job very soon, you should sign on without delay. Your National Insurance contributions will normally be credited to you. This is important to protect your state pension. To qualify for JSA you need to be under state pension age and must either have paid sufficient Class 1 National Insurance contributions or have a low income. You must also be both available for and actively seeking work.

Current information about JSA and other possible benefits can be found on the government website: **www.gov.uk**. Redundancy Help answers queries on all aspects of redundancy; website: **www.redundancyhelp.co.uk**. The Citizens Advice Bureau also gives redundancy advice; website: **www.adviceguide.org.uk**.

Money left unclaimed

It is estimated that there are over £15 billion worth of unclaimed assets in the UK, and many millions of pounds of unclaimed money is handed over to the Treasury because there are no clues as to whom it belongs. Some funds are in unclaimed benefits and entitlements, others are unclaimed lottery prizes, the remainder is money such as legacies from wills, funds from pensions and insurance policies where there is no next of kin to claim them.

Many people do not know how to begin to trace their money but there are now a number of useful websites to help you:

Experian's Unclaimed Assets Register (UAR): **www.uar.co.uk**.

The Building Societies Association: **www.bsa.org.uk**.

My Lost Account, for lost or dormant bank accounts:
  www.mylostaccount.org.uk.

Which? magazine also gives information and advice on how to track down missing accounts and unclaimed money: **www.which.co.uk**. Also **www.findersuk.com**.

Extra income

There are a number of state benefits and allowances available to help many pensioners on low to middle incomes. Despite just under half of all pensioners being entitled to pension credit – a top-up for people on low incomes – one-third of people don't claim it; 1.8 million pensioners live in poverty yet millions of pounds of pensioner benefits go unclaimed each year. Age UK suggests that many pensioners are unaware of the range of benefits available, think the process too complicated and intrusive, or are simply too proud to claim.

While many of these benefits are 'means tested' some, such as Disability Living Allowance, are not dependent on how poor or how wealthy you are. Many individuals – including over a million pensioners – are not claiming help to which they are entitled and for which in many cases they have actually paid through their National Insurance contributions.

A number of voluntary organizations, benevolent societies and charities also provide assistance to individuals, sometimes in cash or sometimes in the form of facilities, such as special equipment for disabled people. Details are given in the relevant chapters. For further advice and information on benefits check the following websites:

Department for Work and Pensions: **www.dwp.gov.uk**.

Jobcentre Plus: **www.gov.uk** – search 'Benefits'.

Citizens Advice Bureau: **www.citizensadvice.org.uk**.

Age UK: **www.ageuk.org.uk**.

Making your money go further

The following websites cover a broad range of topics relating to your finances and retirement:

www.adviceguide.org.uk;

www.everyinvestor.co.uk;

www.financingretirement.co.uk;

www.moneyadviceservice.org.uk;

www.moneyexpertise.co.uk;

www.moneyweek.com;

www.oscaruk.co.uk;

www.thisismoney.co.uk;

www.which.co.uk.

Useful reading

The following publications are especially for those coming up to retirement and the recently retired:

- *Your Guide to Retirement – Making the Most of Your Money* is a comprehensive guide to help you manage the transition from work to retirement. It is published by the Money Advice Service; website: **www.moneyadviceservice.org.uk**.

- *Wise Guides* – the practical pensioners' handbooks, published by Independent Age; website: **www.independentage.org**.

- *Talking about Retirement*, by Lyn Ashurst. An excellent book for those wanting detailed information about planning their finances, published by Kogan Page. The author is an authority in her field and gives a comprehensive and detailed study of a careful and planned approach to the retirement process, based on about 50 case studies.

For more information and other recommended titles on retirement and associated issues published by Kogan Page, see **www.koganpage.com**.

Chapter Three
Pensions and financing your retirement

It is better to have a permanent income than to be fascinating. **OSCAR WILDE**

On 19 March 2014 in the Budget statement, the prudent among us were given the welcome news that they would be able to make good use of the money they had stored away for their old age. This represented the most far-reaching reform to pensions since 1921. With effect from April 2015, the Chancellor has radically altered the way pensions and savings are taxed and has made sweeping changes to how people can finance their retirement. As we comment in Chapter 5, this Budget headline grabber leaves much of the 'pensions liberation' under consultation at the time of writing this chapter and, therefore, any detailed analysis in this book is not possible and it will be revisited in detail next year. We do, however, have a note of caution about predators that have already started to stalk the industry, offering early pensions 'liberation', and we echo the Pensions Advisory Service's caution 'Don't let your pension become their prey.' The addition of some very sound hints and tips from the Financial Ombudsman Service will also prove invaluable to some of our readers.

In broad terms, until now pensioners had been allowed to take only a small portion of their pension savings each year, for fear that otherwise they might indulge in a wild spending spree and later have to rely on state benefits. The default option for most savers had until then been to purchase an annuity (a type of insurance that provides regular payments for life). The relaxation of these restrictions, which were overprotective, and the flexibility offered as a result, has been welcomed by millions of retiring workers. No one will now have to buy an annuity. People who have worked hard and saved hard all their lives, and done the right thing, are to be trusted with their own finances, which is how it should be. Ensuring a decent income in retirement is vital, yet for years many people have not been able to enjoy much flexibility in regard to their pension savings.

One in seven (14 per cent) of people who retired in 2013 are dependent on their state pension as they have no other income, according to new research from Prudential, the insurance providers. Analysis also revealed that nearly one in five (18 per cent) of those planning to retire this year would be below the poverty line. The Joseph Rowntree Foundation estimates that to be above the poverty line a single pensioner in the UK needs an income of at least £8,254 a year. While the state pension is a valuable source of income for millions of pensioners, it should only represent a part of someone's retirement income, not all of it. It is hoped that government policies will help younger people develop a savings/pension culture, otherwise there will in future be generations of poor pensioners. Perhaps the 'auto-enrolment' of employees, as now started, into pensions with set contributions will move us towards a more sustainable position. The pension crisis has been brewing over decades because so many of us are living longer, yet not saving enough for our old age. People are having to work beyond traditional retirement age in order to finance a good quality of life in retirement. Many women, for example, are staying on longer in employment because husbands and wives may wish to retire at the same time. State pension age (which is rising for both men and women) is becoming an anchor for decisions about when to retire.

NEST, part of the auto-enrolment scheme, is one way for younger people to save for retirement, and the single-tier state pension (of £144 per week) that is planned to come into effect from April 2017 should also help. These changes have been welcomed by the pensions industry. Providing greater clarity at little or no initial extra cost overall will improve the lives of millions and save the government money in the long run. With auto-enrolment in pensions, greater awareness of the need to save, an expectation and desire to work for longer, coupled with housing assets, a skills shortage and equity release (the medium- or high-value property that pensioner households will use to support their retirement) – all these promise to improve the circumstances of those expecting to retire within the next decade. The one unknown (and we don't have our crystal ball here) is how the seismic change in the debt levels carried by many of our young people will influence their saving and pension funding plans. This stems from the average student now being saddled with university tuition fees of over £8,000 per annum compared to less than half of that only a few years ago. Is this a debt time bomb that will never be recoverable – and will parents and grandparents have to step in to assist in a way unheard of before? Time will tell but it is an issue that should be on your radar. The counterbalance could be employers wanting workers to remain in their posts for longer, and a desire among employees to continue working longer. Could today's young be better prepared for retirement and ageing than might previously have been thought?

To avoid a shortfall of income in retirement, the 'This is Money' website (**www.thisismoney.co.uk/pension-plan**) suggests the following ways to finance your future and gives you a useful starting position:

- *In your 20s* you should focus on clearing your debts, open an ISA and save what you can afford.

- *In your 30s* reassess your debts and outgoings, join your company pension scheme and think long term with your investments.

- *In your 40s* if you haven't started saving, do so now. Keep adding to your ISAs and, as your earnings peak, dedicate some to a pension.

- *In your 50s* maximize your contributions, remove risk from your pension investment plan and consider using a SIPP (self-invested personal pension) for greater control.

- *In your 60s* check that all your debts, including mortgage, are in order. Decide how much of your pension you wish to draw down and, most important of all, talk to an IFA (independent financial adviser) before you take any action.

The state pension

State pension age is rising. Those who qualify for a state pension currently start to receive payments in their 60s. The exact age is being equalized for men and women: to 66 for both sexes by 2020, then to 67 by 2028. A look at the *state pension calculator* will give the age at which you will receive it.

The state pension continues to rise annually by whichever is highest – inflation, wage increases or the 2.5 per cent figure – under the 'triple lock' system introduced by the Coalition government. To qualify for a full basic state pension you currently require 30 years' full National Insurance (NI) contributions, rising to 35 years after 2016. For 2014/15 the single-person basic state retirement pension rose by £2.95 per week (from £110.15 to £113.10 – or £5,881 per year). If you're married and both you and your partner have built up state pension, you'll get double this amount – £226.20 per week in 2014/15. But if your partner has not built up their own entitlement, they will still be able to claim a state pension based on your record. The maximum is £67.80 per week.

It then gets more complicated because some people also receive the state second pension, or SERPS, which is the government's earnings-related additional pension. If your income is below a certain level, you can boost it by claiming Pension Credit. This will take your income up to £148.35 per week for a single person and £226.50 per week for a couple (in 2014/15). See further on in this chapter.

The default retirement age of 65 was scrapped in 2011. Employers are no longer allowed to dismiss staff just because they are 65. But as the state pension comes under increasing pressure, it is important to make private pension savings and not rely on the basic state pension to finance your retirement.

Your right to a state pension

Your state pension depends on how long you have worked and the number of National Insurance qualifying years you have. If you reached the state pension age on or after 6 April 2010, you need to have 30 qualifying years for a full basic state pension. If you reached the pension age before April 2010, then a woman normally needed 39 qualifying years, and a man needed 44 qualifying years during a regular working life to get the full state pension. From 2016, you will require 35 years' full NI contributions to qualify for a full state pension. If you are a couple and only one person in a couple qualifies for the basic state pension, then you can still receive top-up state pension payments by using one partner's National Insurance record. For anyone with gaps in their record, you can pay Class 3 voluntary NI contributions.

Points to note, since 6 April 2010:

- married men and female civil partners will also be entitled to a pension based on their wife's or civil partner's record – but their wife or civil partner must have been born on or after 6 April 1950 and have reached state pension age;

- any pension for a wife, husband or civil partner will be payable whether their spouse or civil partner decides to claim or to defer his or her own state pension;

- the earliest date that a male civil partner will be entitled to this is 6 April 2015, because that is the date that a man born on 6 April 1950 reaches pensionable age.

Lived or worked outside Great Britain?

If you have lived in Northern Ireland or the Isle of Man, any contributions paid there will count towards your pension. The same should also apply in most cases if you have lived or worked in an EU country or any country whose social security is linked to Britain's by a reciprocal arrangement. However, there have sometimes been problems with certain countries, so, if you have any doubts, you should enquire what your position is at your pension centre.

Home Responsibilities Protection (HRP)

Since 6 April 2010 Home Responsibilities Protection has been replaced with weekly credits for parents and carers. You can receive these credits for any weeks you are getting Child Benefit for a child under 12, you are an approved foster carer, or you are caring for one or more sick or disabled people for at least 20 hours a week. If you reached state pension age on or after 6 April 2010, any years of HRP you have been awarded before April 2010 will have been converted to qualifying years of credits up to a maximum of 22 years. For more information about the changes introduced by the Pensions Act 2007, see website: **www.gov.uk** – Working, jobs and pensions.

Other situations

If you have been in any of the following situations you will have been credited with contributions (instead of having to pay them):

- you were sick or unemployed (provided you sent in sick notes to your social security office, signed on at the unemployment benefit office or were in receipt of Jobseeker's Allowance);

- you were a man aged 60–64 and not working;
- you were entitled to Maternity Allowance, Invalid Care Allowance or unemployability supplement;
- you were taking an approved course of training;
- you had left education but had not yet started working;
- since April 2000, your earnings had fallen between what are known as the lower earnings limit and the primary threshold, ie between £109 and £149 per week (2013/14).

Married women and widows

Married women and widows who do not qualify for a basic pension in their own right may be entitled to a basic pension on their husband's contributions at about 60 per cent of the level to which he is entitled. Husband and wife are assessed separately for tax and a married woman is entitled to have her section of the joint pension offset against her own personal allowance, instead of being counted as part of her husband's taxable income. For many pensioner couples, this should mean a reduction in their tax liability.

Reduced-rate contributions note: many women retiring today may have paid a reduced-rate contribution under a scheme that was abolished in 1978. Women who were already paying a reduced-rate contribution were, however, allowed to continue doing so. These reduced-rate contributions *do not count* towards your pension and you will not have had any contributions credited to you. If you are still some years away from retirement, it could be to your advantage to cancel the reduced-rate option, as by doing so you may be able to build up a wider range of benefits without paying anything extra. If you are earning above the primary threshold, to get the same extra benefits you would have to start paying extra contributions. For advice, contact your local tax office or see the website: **www.hmrc.gov.uk**.

How your state pension is worked out

Anyone trying to decide whether they can afford to retire should get their state pension forecast from the Pension Service (**www.dwp.gov.uk**). It is worth getting an early estimate of what your pension will be, as it may be possible to improve your NIC record by making additional Class 3 voluntary contributions. See website: **www.gov.uk** – Working, jobs and pensions.

Since April 2011, the basic pension is increased annually by the highest of price inflation, earnings or 2.5 per cent. But if you retire abroad you only get these increases if you live in a European Economic Area (EEA) country, Switzerland or a country with which the UK has a reciprocal agreement that includes state pensions. Due to improvements in service arrangements, you only need to claim a state pension two months before your state pension birthday date. You can check your state pension age using the calculator on the government website: **www.gov.uk** – State pension.

If you do not qualify for a full basic state pension you may be able to pay Class 3 NIC if you have gaps in your National Insurance record. Paying them would mean that years that would not normally be qualifying years would count towards your basic state pension. Your forecast letter will tell you whether or not you can do this. There are time limits for paying Class 3 NIC and you must normally pay them within six years of the end of the tax year for which you are paying.

If you need help deciding whether you need to pay extra contributions, you can obtain help from the National Insurance Contributions Office (**www.hmrc.gov.uk/nic**) or the Pensions Advisory Service (**www.pensionsadvisoryservice.org.uk**). To find out how much pension you are entitled to, you can apply for an online forecast (**www.thepensionservice.gov.uk**).

Additional state pension

If you are (or have been) in employment, you may have been building up an additional state pension, known as the state second pension (S2P). The amount you receive depends on your earnings and your NIC record. There are other means of entitlement to some S2P: for example, if you earn below a certain amount set by the government, if you cannot work through long-term illness or disability, or if you are a carer.

The S2P is not available to the self-employed, for whom the alternative pension choices are either a personal pension or a stakeholder pension. If you are an employee, you are automatically included in S2P unless you decide to contract out, or you are a member of an employer's occupational pension scheme that is contracted out. If you decide to contract out, you stop building up your S2P entitlement and build up a replacement for it in your own pension. You will continue to be contracted out of S2P unless you decide to contract back in.

The end of S2P in 2016 will hit highest earners the hardest. Currently, self-employed workers receive only the basic state pension, as they do not qualify for S2P. However, from 2016 they will be treated the same as employees for the purposes of state pension entitlement. Under the flat-rate pension, anyone with 35 qualifying years of NICs will be eligible for the full £144 per week, and means testing will be abolished.

For more information about contracting out, or if you have any queries regarding the S2P scheme, you can obtain help from this website: **www.gov.uk** – Working, jobs and pensions.

Deferring your pension

The current rules on deferring your pension may not be relevant following pensions liberation but, in the meantime, you don't have to start drawing your pension when you reach state pension age. You can defer it for as little as five weeks. The government will make it worth your while by boosting your income when you do come to take it. Many people prefer to stop working gradually by reducing hours or shifting to part-time work, so you might not need your entire pension straight away. By deferring your state pension, you can have a bigger pension when it does start, or alternatively a lump sum. Your state pension is increased by 1 per cent for each five weeks you defer it, ie an increase of 10.4 per cent per year for each year you defer. But this is only worth considering if you can live without the pension for now. You can continue deferring your pension for as long as you like. The extra money will be paid to you when you eventually decide to claim your pension. The lump sum is worked out as if your deferred pension had been invested and earned a return of 2 per cent more than the Bank of England base rate. If you plan to defer your pension, you should also defer any graduated pension to which you may be entitled – or you risk losing the increases you would otherwise obtain. More information can be found on the Pension Service website: **www.gov.uk** – Working, jobs and pensions.

Adult Dependency Increase

This is an increase in the state pension for a husband, wife or someone who is looking after your children, as long as certain conditions are met.

Since 6 April 2010, you are no longer entitled to claim an Adult Dependency Increase. If you were already entitled to this increase on 5 April 2010 you will be able to keep it until you no longer meet the conditions for the increase, or 5 April 2020, whichever is the first.

Income Support

If you have an inadequate income, you may qualify for Income Support. There are special premiums (ie additions) for lone parents, disabled people, carers and pensioners. A condition of entitlement is that you should not have capital, including savings, of more than £16,000. A big advantage is that people entitled to Income Support receive full help with their rent and should also not have any council tax to pay. See 'Housing Benefit' and 'Council Tax Benefit' in Chapter 8.

Pension Credit

Pension Credit is an income-related benefit for those who have reached the minimum qualifying age and live in Great Britain. You do not need to have paid NIC to get it. There are two parts to Pension Credit.

Guarantee Credit may be paid to you if you have reached the minimum qualifying age. It tops up your income to a guaranteed minimum level (for the year 2014/15 it is £148.35 if you are single, or £226.50 if you have a partner).

Savings Credit is for those who have saved money towards their retirement. You may be able to get it if you are aged 65 or over. You may be able to get Savings Credit as well as Guarantee Credit. You may still get Pension Credit if you live with your grown-up family or own your own home.

If you wish to apply for Pension Credit, you can do so up to four months before the date from which you want to start getting Pension Credit. The longest that Pension Credit claims can be backdated is three months. You do not have to pay tax on Pension Credit. If entitled to it, you may get Savings Credit (for the year 2014/15) of £16.80 per week if you are single or £20.70 per week if you have a partner. The age from which you may get Pension Credit – the qualifying age – is gradually going up to 66 in line with the increase in the state pension age for women to 65 and the further increase to 66 for men and women. To find out when you reach the qualifying age for Pension Credit, visit **www.gov.uk** – State pension.

If you apply for Pension Credit, you may also apply for Council Tax Benefit and Housing Benefit at the same time. The age at which people can get Housing Benefit and Council Tax Benefit for pensioners is also increasing from 60 to 65 between April 2010 and 2020. Housing Benefit is to help people on a low income pay some or all of their rent. Council Tax Benefit is to help people on a low income pay some or all of their council tax. You do not have to pay tax on either of these benefits.

Visit the government website to find out more information: **www.gov.uk** – Heating and housing benefits.

Other sources of help

According to leading charities – Age UK and Elisabeth Finn – an estimated 1.5 million people could claim benefits but the means test puts some people off claiming the top-ups they are entitled to. Every year as much as £5.5 billion of benefits that older people are entitled to go unclaimed, despite many of them struggling to make ends meet. Much needs to be done in terms of raising awareness of welfare benefits available and reducing some of the negative perceptions against claiming when times are tough. Don't be afraid to claim.

For help relating to benefits, Turn2Us (website: **www.turn2us.org.uk**) is a charity set up specifically to identify potential sources of funding for those facing financial difficulty. Individuals can log on to this website for free and in confidence. Also look at Age UK's website, Britain's leading charity for older people: **www.ageuk.co.uk**.

Community Care Grants, Budgeting Loans and Crisis Loans can all help with exceptional expenses if you are facing financial difficulties. These are all dealt with through the government website. See **www.gov.uk** – Jobseeker's Allowance and low income benefits, for the widest range of online government information for the public, covering benefits, financial support, rights, employment, independent living and much more. For information for disabled people, see **www.gov.uk** – Disability benefits.

Early retirement and your state pension

Because some people retire early, they can mistakenly assume it is possible to get an early pension. While the information is correct as regards many employers' occupational pension schemes, as well as for stakeholder and personal pensions, it does not apply to the basic state pension. If you take early retirement before the age of 60, it may be necessary for you to pay voluntary Class 3 NIC to protect your contributions record for state pension purposes. Your local tax office can advise you about NICs.

Other situations

Pensions can be paid to an overseas address, if you are going abroad for six months or more. See website: **www.gov.uk** – Working, jobs and pensions (see section 'State pension if you retire abroad'). If you are in hospital, your pension can still be paid to you and you will receive your pension in full for the duration of your stay, regardless of how long you have to remain in hospital. For advice, contact either the Pension Service or the Citizens Advice Bureau.

Christmas bonus

This is paid shortly before Christmas to pensioners who are entitled to a qualifying benefit. For many years the sum has been £10. The bonus is combined with your normal pension payment for the first week in December.

Advice

The Pension Service provides information to current and future pensioners so that making informed decisions about pension arrangements is straight-forward. If you need help with your retirement plans it can assist you. It will explain what the state will provide when you retire and let you know what pension-related benefits you may be entitled to.

If you have any queries or think you may not be obtaining your full pension entitlement, you should contact the Pension Service as soon as possible. If you think a mistake has been made, you have the right to appeal and can insist on your claim being heard by an independent tribunal. Before doing so, you would be strongly advised to consult a solicitor at the Citizens Advice Bureau or the Welfare Advice Unit of your social security office.

For further information about pensions, there is a booklet full of advice entitled *Pensioners' Guide* obtainable from the Pension Service, part of the Department for Work and Pensions: **www.gov.uk/en/ PensionsandRetirementPlanning**.

Other useful sources of information include:

- The Pensions Advisory Service: **www.pensionsadvisoryservice.org.uk**.
- The Service Personnel and Veterans Agency: **www.veterans-uk.info**.
- Citizens Advice: **www.citizensadvice.org.uk**.

Private pensions

You can save as much as you like towards your pension but there is a limit on the amount of tax relief you can get. The lifetime allowance is the maximum amount of pension savings you can build up over your life that benefits from tax relief. If you build up pension savings worth more than the lifetime allowance you will pay a tax charge on the excess. The rules on pension pots were tightened with effect from 6 April 2014 (the start of the tax year), when the amount that can be saved into a pension each year (known as the annual allowance) and still receive tax relief was cut from £50,000 to £40,000 per year. (There are provisions to use some previous year's unused allowance and if this becomes a potential issue the sums involved would justify specific professional advice.) The limit on the total amount that can be held in pensions by an individual during their lifetime was reduced from £1.5 million to £1.25 million. For those who have taken a break from contributions, there will be the useful option to potentially carry forward up to three years' annual allowance. Those who are in final salary schemes or those with employer, employee and individual pension contributions over two consecutive tax years that combine to over £40,000 will need to be particularly aware of the limits. It would be wise to check with your pension provider when your current 'pension input period' (the accounting period for your pension scheme) ends.

Since April 2014 an 'individual protection' has been in place to honour those funds that exceeded the lifetime limit of £1.25 million. It is important to bear in mind that tax rules and tax reliefs can and do change and their exact value depends on each individual's circumstances.

Pension savings are still one of the most tax-effective investments available because you receive income tax relief on contributions at your highest tax rate and the growth in your pension fund is totally exempt from income tax and capital gains tax. With the sweeping changes coming into effect from April 2015, when savers will be free to withdraw as much or as little of their pension pot as they want, at any time they want, it is an exciting time for prudent pensioners. For further information, see **www.hmrc/pensionschemes**.

Company pension schemes

Types of company pension schemes

The pension that your employer offers may be 'contributory' (you and your employer pay into it) or 'non-contributory', which means that only your employer does. If the scheme offered is a group stakeholder pension scheme, your employer doesn't have to contribute, so you alone may be putting money in. As set out below, there are four main types of company pension: final salary, career average, money purchase and group/personal stakeholder.

Final salary

These are known as a type of defined benefit scheme. You build up a pension at a certain rate – one-sixtieth is quite common – so for each year you've been a scheme member, you receive one-sixtieth of your final salary. In the private sector only 1.3 million workers are in a final salary scheme and few schemes are open to new employees as it is so expensive for employers. More public sector workers (such as teachers, police, NHS and local government workers) pay into a final salary scheme, but this is still only 5.3 million out of 29 million employed people in the UK. If you work for one of the few remaining employers with a final salary scheme, you should join it.

Career average

These are another type of defined-benefit scheme, because the benefit (your pension) is worked out using your salary and the length of time you have been a member of the pension scheme. The pension you receive will be based on an average of your earnings in the time that you're a member of the scheme (often averaged over the last three years before retirement). What you receive will depend on the proportion of those earnings that you get as pension for each year of membership. The most common are one-sixtieth or one-eightieth of your earnings for each year of membership.

The benefits of such schemes are that the pension is based on your length of membership and salary, so you have a fair idea of how much your pension will be before retirement. Also, your employer should ensure that there is enough money at the time you retire to pay you a pension, and you get tax relief on your contributions. Scheme investments grow generally free of income tax and capital gains tax. Your pension benefits are linked to your salary while you are working, so they automatically increase as your pay rises. Your pension income from the scheme will normally increase each year in line with the consumer price index (CPI) instead of the retail price index (RPI). The rationale for this change is that the Department of Work and Pensions (DWP) believe that CPI better reflects the true cost of living. However, there are also potentially significant savings for the DWP, as CPI has historically tracked lower than RPI.

Is there a risk? If a salary-related occupational scheme or the sponsoring employer gets into financial trouble, the Pension Protection Fund can provide some protection. You can normally get a pension of up to 90 per cent of your expected pension, subject to a cap. (See the Pension Protection Fund website for more information: **www.pensionprotectionfund.gov.uk**.)

Money purchase

These are also known as defined-contribution schemes. The money paid in by you and your employer is invested and builds up a fund that buys you an income when you retire. Most schemes offer a choice of investment funds. The amount paid in varies, but the average employer contribution in 2010 to money-purchase schemes was 8 per cent of salary. It helps to think of money-purchase pensions as having two stages, as set out below.

Stage 1. The fund is invested, usually in stocks and shares and other investments, with the aim of growing it over the years before you retire. You can usually choose from a range of funds to invest in. The Pensions Advisory Service (TPAS) has an online investment choices planner to help you decide how to invest your contributions (see **www.pensions-advisoryservice.org.uk/online-planners**).

Stage 2. From April 2015, when you retire you can withdraw your entire fund if you wish. The amount of pension you'll get at retirement will depend on: how much you pay into the fund; how much your employer pays in (if anything); how well your invested contributions perform; the charges taken out of your fund by your pension provider; and how much you wish to withdraw and when. The benefits of money-purchase schemes are that you get tax relief on your contributions; your fund grows generally free of income tax and capital gains tax; you may be able to choose the funds to invest in; and your employer may contribute, if it's a work-based pension.

Group personal/stakeholder

If you've decided on a private pension, you can shop around for either of the above. These are also money-purchase schemes, ie the pension you get is not linked to your salary. Your employer offers access to either a personal or stakeholder plan, which you own, and can take with you if you get a new job. Your employer will choose the scheme provider, deduct the contributions you make from your salary and pay these to the provider, along with employer contributions. There are some differences between them.

Stakeholder pensions must have certain features. Some of these include limited charges; low minimum contributions; flexible contributions; penalty-free transfers; and a default investment fund – ie a fund your money will be invested in if you don't want to choose one yourself. If your employer offers a *group stakeholder* pension, it doesn't have to pay into it.

Personal pensions: these are similar to stakeholder pensions, but they usually offer a wider range of investment choices. If your employer offers a *group personal* pension scheme, it must contribute at least 3 per cent on your behalf. Personal pension charges may be similar to stakeholder pension charges but some are higher. You can compare stakeholder and personal pensions from different providers on the website **www.moneyadviceservice.org.uk**.

Auto-enrolment

The National Employment Savings Trust (NEST), is the not-for-profit, low-cost workplace pension scheme into which employees can be entered. The government introduced this to encourage low- to middle-wage earners to contribute to a personal pension plan. This scheme promises to provide some income for several million people who previously would have had nothing beyond the state pension. As encouragement, employers are given tax breaks if they do not opt out (see **www.nestpensions.org.uk**).

Self-invested personal pensions (SIPPs)

If you want to use a pension to save for your retirement, you don't have to give your money to a fund manager. You can manage your own retirement fund with a self-invested personal pension (SIPP). Most stockbrokers offer SIPP accounts and the good news is that the government is so eager for you to save via a SIPP it will even give you tax back. You can either pay a lump sum to a pension provider or drip feed in monthly amounts. The latter can be made via a scheme into which both you and your employer pay. But instead of your employer directing where your money goes, you get free rein over where it's invested. You can buy a range of asset classes, from stocks to bonds to gold bullion (though you can't buy fine wines). Monthly contributions can be as low as £50. You can pay in amounts equal to 100 per cent of your annual salary up to a current ceiling of £40,000 per year. You can access your SIPP from age 55 and draw down however much you want from April 2015. SIPPs are not suitable for everyone; broadly they are for people with larger pension pots. As SIPPs are fee-based arrangements, the smaller the fund the more expensive they are. If you are someone who finds the idea of investing your own money daunting, a SIPP may not be for you.

For advice on SIPPs talk to your financial adviser or look at the website **www.moneymadeclear.gov.uk**.

Flexible drawdown

As with much of this chapter we will be reading a very different text in the next edition following implementation of the changes announced in the 2014 Budget. In the meantime, the introduction of 'flexible drawdown', effective since 6 April 2011, allows pension investors to take money from their pension as and when they want it. By taking money out of your pension you would, however, be removing it from a tax-free environment, so you would probably leave funds in the pension until you needed them, at which point you could draw out however much you needed. Leaving funds in the pension makes tax-efficient sense because the fund growth is free from UK income and capital gains tax (tax deducted from dividends at source cannot be reclaimed). You will still normally be able to draw tax free up to 25 per cent of your pension when you take retirement benefits.

Some of the requirements you will have to meet to be eligible for flexible drawdown include being over 55 to start drawing a pension; also receiving a secure pension of at least £20,000 per annum. This can include the state pension, final salary pensions and pension annuities. The reason for this requirement is so that even if you draw your entire pension out and spend it, you are unlikely to fall back on means-tested state benefits. Other requirements are if either you or your employer makes contributions to a pension scheme; this could mean that you are prohibited from using flexible drawdown until the start of the tax year after those contributions are made. After you have moved into flexible drawdown, you will be effectively prevented from accruing any more pension benefits, so it is only worth it once you have finished building up pension benefits.

Family pensions

Another change to pension rules is that you now have greater scope to pass on your pension to your heirs. You can now pass on your pension to beneficiaries of your choice as a lump sum, even if you are older than 75 when you die. This will be subject to a 55 per cent tax charge (the tax charge is designed to claw back the tax relief already provided). The government is keeping the current provision, which generally allows you to pass on your pension to a beneficiary as a tax-free lump sum if you die before 75, provided you have not started drawing retirement benefits.

If you have a small pension pot

If the value of your pension rights is below a certain level, it may be possible to give up those rights in exchange for a cash sum. If all your pension savings in all the pension schemes you belong to are worth no more than £30,000 you may be able to take all your pension pots as a lump sum. You can do this even if one or more of your pension pots is worth more than £10,000 or if you've already started to take one of your pensions. If you belong to more than one pension scheme you don't have to take a lump sum from all your schemes. If you are taking a trivial lump sum from more than one of your pension schemes you must take all the trivial lump sums within 12 months of the first lump sum payment. Before 27 March 2014, to qualify for this type of lump sum the value of all your pension savings must have been £18,000 or less.

Minimum retirement age

The minimum age at which you are allowed to take early retirement and draw your pension has been 55 since 6 April 2010. It may be possible to draw retirement benefits earlier if you are in poor health and unable to work.

Becoming self-employed

If, as opposed to switching jobs, you leave paid employment to start your own enterprise, you are allowed to transfer your accumulated pension rights into a new fund. There are two main choices. The most obvious solution is to invest your money with an insurance company, or to take either a personal or a stakeholder pension. An alternative course of action, which might be more attractive if you are fairly close to normal retirement age, is to leave your pension in your former employer's scheme. Before making a decision, take professional advice from your independent financial adviser.

Questions on your pension scheme

If you have a query or if you are concerned in some way about your pension, you should approach whoever is responsible for the scheme in your organization. The questions listed here are simply an indication of some of the key information you may require to plan ahead sensibly.

If you want to leave the organization to change jobs

- Could you have a refund of contributions if you were to leave shortly after joining?
- How much will your deferred pension be worth?
- Should you want to move the transfer value to another scheme, how long would you have to wait from the date of your request? (This should normally be within three to six months.)

If you leave for other reasons

- What happens if you become ill – or die – before pension age?
- What are the arrangements if you want to retire early? Most schemes allow you to do this if you are within about 10 years of normal retirement age, but your pension may be reduced accordingly. Many schemes operate a sliding scale of benefits, with more generous terms offered to those who retire later rather than earlier.

If you stay until normal retirement age

- What will your pension be on your present salary? And what would it be assuming your salary increases by, say, 5 or 10 per cent before you eventually retire?
- What spouse's pension will be paid? Can a pension be paid to other dependants?
- Similarly, can a pension be paid to a partner, male or female?
- What happens if you continue working with the organization after retirement age?
- What are the arrangements if you retire from the organization as a salaried employee but become a retained consultant or contractor?

If you just want information

- Are any changes envisaged to the scheme? For example, if it is a final salary scheme, is there any chance that it might be wound up and a money-purchase scheme offered instead?
- If there were a new money-purchase scheme, would the company be making the same contributions as before or would these be lower in future?
- Is there any risk that benefits – either members' own or those for dependants – could be reduced?
- Is there a possibility that members might be required to pay higher contributions than at present?

Should I transfer my long-lost fund?

- Are there any benefits to transferring old pensions into one new scheme?

  One benefit is the saving on fees. However, you should assess the performance and fees for the new scheme into which you want to transfer the funds. Watch out for transfer charges. These are punitive fees that act as a sneaky deterrent for savers trying to integrate their pensions and keep matters simple.

Beware of predators stalking your pension

Prior to the Budget 2014 announcement about pensions liberation, the Pensions Advisory Service had warned about companies singling out savers and claiming that they can help to cash in a pension early. Until the 2014 Budget announcements about liberation are implemented and understood, the risks from the predators stalking your pension remain. Whilst initially attractive, the sting in the tail is that you could face a tax bill of more than half your pension savings. The Pensions Advisory Service warns that this activity is known as 'pensions liberation fraud' and it is on the increase in the UK. The main warning signs are unsolicited text messages and phone calls, a transfer overseas and seeking to access a pension fund before the age of 55 (access to your pension before the age of 55 can only be achieved in rare circumstances) – and the scammers usual ploy (see Chapter 7 for much more on this) of urgency so that you have no time to think, pause and check it out.

To counter this, always check that any financial adviser is registered with the Financial Conduct Authority (see Chapter 6), obtain a statement about any tax charges and never be rushed into agreeing to a pension transfer. The benefit of dealing with a financial adviser who is registered with the Financial Conduct Authority is that there is a safety net when things go wrong – in the form of the Financial Ombudsman Service – and, if the firm fails and is insolvent the UK safety net, the Financial Services Compensation Scheme, pays up to £50,000 per person per firm (and up to £85,000 per person per institution on savings and deposits). To help you avoid getting tricked in the first place, *The Good Retirement Guide* asked the Financial Ombudsman Service for their top tips to help you fight back against the financial predators trying to separate you from your hard-earned cash and pension. These tips supplement the further hints and tips set out in Chapter 7, and with the combined advice you will have boosted your defence shield – as knowledge and awareness really do give you more power in this arena.

The Financial Ombudsman Service's top tips to fight back against the predators

Co-author of this book Allan Esler Smith worked with David Cresswell two decades ago at the then Investors Compensation Scheme (now the Financial Services Compensation Scheme). Allan undertook the investigations and David looked after communications, and his invaluable hints and tips helped to keep investors safe. David is now Director of Communications and Insight at the Financial Ombudsman Service and his knowledge is second to none. David Cresswell's top five tips for our readers are listed below.

1. Out of the blue

They say you have more chance of being repeatedly struck by lightning than you have of winning the lottery. And yet every day hundreds of us receive e-mails claiming that we've won money from a mysterious foreign country, or that we've been selected by a strange organization for a random prize.

Most of us know better than to fall for this. But, in recent years, fraudsters have invested time and effort into making fake e-mails and letters from official organizations look more convincing. These could be messages from your bank, HMRC or even the ombudsman, all asking for you to confirm your personal details. Recently, we've even seen pleas for help that look like they've been sent to you by friends in trouble who need you to send them cash. Don't fall for them. Watch out for questionable e-mail addresses that are either from personal accounts (Gmail, Hotmail) or other countries (check the letters after the 'dot' – as in '.ru' for Russia) and e-mails or letters that fail to address you by your name.

2. Whose job is it anyway?

Your bank will have its own fraud prevention steps in place to protect you. These will activate if the bank spots suspicious activity on your account, or as soon as you notify it that you think fraud has taken place.

But, what would you do if you received a call from your bank telling you that a fraudster had accessed your account and requesting you to transfer your remaining funds to a 'safer' place or hand over your card to a third party? Watch out – this is a scam! Your bank would never send a courier for your card or ask you to transfer money when it can do this itself. In the most unpleasant form of this scam, you're told there has been an attempted fraud and are asked to call your bank using the number on your card. However, the fraudster stays on the line so it never disconnects. So when you call the (legitimate) number, the fraudster is waiting on the line, impersonating your bank and ready to trick you into transferring your cash.

3. Too much information

Phone or online banking passwords are often the source of much frustration – but they are a necessary hassle in many ways. Your bank will ask you for random letters, numbers or characters from your password. But they will not ask you to confirm your full password on the phone or ask to know your PIN number. If you're asked for this information, this should be a clear warning that something is wrong. If you're struggling to remember a password – or you're worried your existing ones are too simple, try getting creative, like taking the first letter of each word in a line of your favourite song.

Many people are concerned about 'chip and PIN' cards – the ombudsman gets lots of enquiries from people suggesting their card has been cloned. This is extremely unusual. In fact, the most common form of PIN fraud is the most low-tech. Shoulder-surfing – peering over your shoulder at an ATM or when typing in your pin at the local supermarket.

4. Pry before you buy

Every year, the number of things we buy online increases dramatically. Crowded shopping centres and stuffy shops mean many of us are going online and bargain hunting. But sometimes we let down our guard when surfing the web. Websites are always competing to offer you the best possible price and it's tempting to think that 'cheapest is best'.

If you've never used a website before, before you confirm the purchase you should run a quick internet search to check out reviews and see what your fellow consumers are saying. If it seems too good to be true, be sceptical. Regardless, use a form of payment that offers you some protection, such as PayPal or MoneyGram. Alternatively, if you're making a larger payment, your credit card gives you some rights under the Consumer Credit Act if something goes wrong.

5. Look after yourself

The easiest way to spot something untoward with your money is to know your finances inside out. Reading your bank statements and knowing what you've got coming in and going out each month is the best way to avoid any cashflow surprises. Most importantly, trust your instinct. If something doesn't feel right it's probably because it isn't.

Hopefully, these tips will help you keep one step ahead of the scammers. But, if something does go wrong, the most important thing is to keep calm. Contact your bank straight away and it may be able to sort things out. If you don't feel like it's being helpful or you're not sure what it should be doing to help, call the ombudsman – they might be able to help. Financial Ombudsman Service: 0300 123 9123; **www.financial-ombudsman.org.uk**.

Other help and advice

Previous schemes

In addition to understanding your current pension scheme, you may also need to chase up any previous schemes of which you were a member. According to the 'This is Money' financial website, an amazing £1.4 billion is estimated to be forgotten and hidden away in accounts worth less than £5,000. At the moment, around 70,000 people get in touch with the DWP for help in finding a lost pension. Hundreds more queries are fielded by the Pensions Advisory Service.

For free help tracking down a pension, contact the Pension Tracing Service, which assists individuals who need help in tracing their pension rights: **www.gov.uk** – Working, jobs and pensions. Choose the link to 'Workplace and personal pensions'. If you have any queries or problems to do with your pension, there are three main sources of help available to you. These are the trustees of your pension scheme, the Pensions Advisory Service and the Pensions Ombudsman.

Trustees or managers

These are the first people to contact if you do not properly understand your benefit entitlements or if you are unhappy about some point to do with your pension. Pensions managers (or other people responsible for pensions) should give you their names and tell you how they can be reached.

The Pensions Advisory Service

The Pensions Advisory Service provides members of the public with general information and guidance on pension matters and assists individuals with disputes with personal, company and stakeholder pensions. See the Pensions Advisory Service website: **www.pensions-advisoryservice.org.uk**.

Pensions Ombudsman

You would normally approach the ombudsman *only* if neither the pension scheme manager (or trustees) nor the Pensions Advisory Service is able to solve your problem. The ombudsman can investigate: 1) complaints of maladministration by the trustees, managers or administrators of a pension scheme or by an employer; 2) disputes of fact or law with the trustees, managers or an employer. The ombudsman does not, however, investigate complaints about mis-selling of pension schemes, a complaint that is already subject to court proceedings, those that are about a state social security benefit, or disputes that are more appropriate for investigation by another regulatory body. There is also a time limit for lodging complaints, which is normally within three years of the act, or failure to act, about which you are complaining.

There is no charge for the ombudsman's service. The Pensions Ombudsman has now also taken on the role of Pension Protection Fund Ombudsman and will be dealing with complaints about, and appeals from, the Pension Protection Fund. It will also be dealing with appeals from the Financial Assistance Scheme (see below) and the Pensions Ombudsman website: **www.pensions-ombudsman.org.uk**.

If you have a personal pension, the Financial Ombudsman Service (FOS) could help you. Since last year, the maximum award that the Financial Ombudsman can make has increased from £100,000 to £150,000. See website: **www.financial-ombudsman.org.uk**. It is possible you may be referred to the Pensions Ombudsman, but if so you will be informed very quickly.

Protection for pension scheme members

New rules have been introduced to protect pension scheme members in the event of a company takeover or proposed bulk transfer arrangement. There is now also a Pension Protection Fund (PPF) to help final-salary pension scheme members who are at risk of losing their pension benefits owing to their employer's insolvency. Members below the scheme's normal retirement age will receive 90 per cent of the Pension Protection Fund level of compensation plus annual increases, subject to a cap and the standard fund rules. See website: **www.pensionprotectionfund.org.uk**.

There is more help too for members who lost pension savings in a company scheme before the introduction of the Pension Protection Fund. The Financial Assistance Scheme (FAS) offers help to some people who have lost out on their pension. It makes payments to top up scheme benefits to eligible members of schemes that are winding up or have wound up. Assistance is also payable to the survivor of a pension scheme member. It is payable from normal retirement age (subject to a lower age limit of 60 and an upper age limit of 65). See website: **www.pensionprotection-fund.org.uk**.

Another organization that could help is the National Federation of Occupational Pensioners (NFOP). This is an independent organization that exists to help and support those in receipt of a company pension. For more information see the website: **www.nfop.org.uk**.

Pension rights if you continue to work after retirement age

When you reach normal retirement age you will usually stop making contributions into your company pension scheme, even if you decide to carry on working. If your employer wants you to leave, they will have to give you at least six months' notice in writing. If you are facing such a decision, here are some points to bear in mind:

- You can continue working, draw your company pension and put some (or possibly all) of your earnings into a separate scheme.
- You can leave your pension in the fund, where it will continue to earn interest until you retire. In most private schemes you could

expect to receive in the region of an extra 8 per cent for every year that you delay retirement.

- You can leave your pension in the fund, as described above, and additionally contribute to a personal or stakeholder pension, provided your contributions do not exceed the annual allowance (2015) of £40,000.

- Provided your scheme rules allow, you can continue working for your existing employer and draw your pension benefits, as opposed to – as previously – having to defer them until you leave the organization.

Equal pension age

Employers are required to treat men and women equally with regard to retirement and pension issues. They must have a common pension age, and pension schemes must offer the same benefits to their male and female members.

Divorce, separation and bereavement

Divorce

Pension sharing became legally available in respect of divorce or annulment proceedings commenced on or after 1 December 2000. Although women usually benefit most from pension sharing, recent legislative changes equally allow an ex-husband to have a share in his former wife's pension rights. The question of pension sharing is a subject to raise with your solicitor if you are in the process of divorce proceedings. But, however much in favour your legal adviser may be, in the final analysis it is up to the court to decide on what it sees as the fairest arrangement – and pension sharing is only one of several options available.

Divorced wives

If you have a full basic pension in your own right, this will not be affected by divorce. However, if, as applies to many women, despite having worked for a good number of years you have made insufficient contributions to qualify for a full pension, you should contact your pension centre, quoting your pension number and NI number. It is possible that you may be able to obtain the full single person's pension, based on your ex-husband's contributions. Your right to use your ex-husband's contributions to improve or provide you with a pension depends on your age and/or whether you remarry before the age of 60. If you are over 60 when you divorce, then whether you remarry or not you can rely on your ex-husband's contributions. If you remarry before the age of 60, then you cease absolutely being a dependant on your former husband and instead your pension will be based on your new husband's contribution record. The same rules apply in reverse.

Pension sharing

Provisions to enable the court to share occupational or personal pension rights at the time of divorce or annulment came into law on 1 December 2000. The legislation now equally applies to the additional state pension. Sharing, however, is only one option for dealing with pension rights and would not necessarily apply in all cases.

Separated wives

Even if you and your husband have not lived together for several years, from an NI point of view you are still considered to be married. The normal pension rules apply including, of course, the fact that, if you have to depend on your husband's contributions, you will not be able to get a pension until he is both 65 and in receipt of his own pension. If you are not entitled to a state pension in your own right, you will receive the dependant's rate of benefit, which is about 60 per cent of the full rate (or less if your husband is not entitled to a full pension). In such a case, you can apply for Income Support to top up your income. Once you are 60, you can personally draw the wife's pension without reference to your husband.

If your husband dies, you may be entitled to bereavement benefits in the same way as other widows. If there is a possibility that he may have died but that you have not been informed, you can check by contacting the General Register Office website: **www.gro.gov.uk**. The indexes to all birth, marriage and death entries in England and Wales are available from the National Archives website: **www.nationalarchives.gov.uk**.

Widows

There are three important benefits to which widows may be entitled: Bereavement Payment, Bereavement Allowance and Widowed Parent's Allowance. These are all now equally applicable to widowed men or those who have entered a civil partnership. Widows who were already in receipt of the Widow's Pension before it was replaced are not affected by the change and will continue to receive their pension as normal.

Bereavement Payment

This is a tax-free, lump-sum payment of £2,000 to help you when your husband, wife or civil partner has died. To get Bereavement Payment you must usually be under state pension age (currently 65 for men and 60 for women). Even if you are over state pension age, you may be able to get one, if your husband, wife or civil partner was not getting a state pension. The time limit for claiming a Bereavement Payment is 12 months after the person's death. You can fill in a claim form, obtainable from the Pension Service: **www.gov.uk**.

Bereavement Allowance

Bereavement Allowance is paid to widows and widowers between the ages of 55 and 59 inclusive. The standard weekly amount (2014/15) is £108.30. It is normally paid automatically once you have sent off your completed form BB1. In the event of your being ineligible, owing to insufficient NIC having been paid, you may still be entitled to receive Income Support, Housing Benefit or a grant or loan from the social fund. As applies to Widow's Pension, widows who remarry or live with a man as his wife cease to receive Bereavement Allowance. See website: **www.direct.gov.uk/benefits**.

Widowed Parent's Allowance

This is a taxable benefit for widows or widowers who are under state pension age and who have at least one child for whom they are entitled, or treated as entitled, to Child Benefit. The current value (2014/15) is £111.20 per week plus a share of any additional state pension you have built up. The share of additional pension payable will be between 50 and 100 per cent depending on your date of birth. The allowance is usually paid automatically. If for some reason, although eligible, you do not receive the money, you should inform your social security or Jobcentre Plus office. See website: **www.direct.gov.uk**.

Retirement pension

Once a widow reaches 60, she will normally receive a state pension based on her own and/or her late husband's contributions. If at the time of death the couple were already receiving the state retirement pension, the widow will continue to receive her share. An important point to remember is that a widow may be able to use her late husband's NIC to boost the amount she receives. Separate from the basic pension, a widow may also receive money from her late husband's occupational pension, whether contracted in or out of the state scheme. She may also get half of any of his graduated pension.

War widows and widowers

War Widow's or Widower's Pension is a tax-free pension for surviving widows, widowers or civil partners of veterans who died as a result of serving in HM armed forces before 6 April 2005. You may also be able to get extra money or help with funeral costs. The Service Personnel and Veterans Agency will pay War Widow's or Widower's Pension if any of the following applied before 6 April 2005:

- Your husband, wife or partner died as a result of a war injury, or because of a war-risk injury as a merchant seaman.

- Your husband, wife or partner was getting a War Disablement Pension at the rate of 80 per cent or higher and was getting Unemployability Supplement.

- Your husband's, wife's or partner's death was due to, or happened sooner because of, their service with the Polish Forces under British command in the Second World War, or their service with the Polish Resettlement Forces.

- Your husband, wife or partner received, or was entitled to, Constant Attendance Allowance under the War Pension Scheme at the time they died.

- Your husband, wife or partner was a civil defence volunteer or a civilian and their death was due to, or happened sooner because of, a war injury or war service injury they suffered while serving during the Second World War.

If you are a widow, widower or surviving civil partner whose husband, wife or partner left service before 31 March 1973, you can keep your pension if you remarry, form a civil partnership or live with a new partner after 6 April 2005. Otherwise this pension may stop.

If you think you may be entitled to claim War Widow's or Widower's Pension, visit the Service Personnel and Veterans Agency website: **www.veterans-uk.info**.

Chapter Four
Tax

> *The only difference between a tax man and a taxidermist is that the taxidermist leaves the skin.* MARK TWAIN

Shortly after the Budget statement in March 2014, the Office for Budget Responsibility announced that growth in the UK will rise by 2.7 per cent in 2015 with living standards steadily improving too. There was good news for savers and pensioners in that Budget, with the sweeping away of all tax restrictions on access to life savings, the increase in the tax-free limit on all ISAs, the introduction of pensioner bonds with attractive interest rates, and the rise in the total pension savings that people can take as a lump sum. For those planning retirement it couldn't have come at a better time.

Tax planning is, and always has been, essential. Understanding the broad principles of taxation helps you to save money. While you were employed you may have been contributing many thousands of pounds to HM Revenue & Customs (HMRC), but in practice you may have had very little direct contact with the tax system. The accounts department would have automatically deducted – and accounted for – the PAYE on your earnings as a salaried employee. If you were self-employed, or had other money unconnected with your job, you may have had more dealings with your tax office.

The most common types of tax are income tax, NI contributions, capital gains tax and inheritance tax. On reaching retirement you should be able to calculate how much money (after deduction of tax) you will have available to spend: the equivalent, if you like, of your take-home pay. Your tax adviser should be fully conversant with your financial affairs so that he or she can advise in the light of your own circumstances. The following information is based on our understanding of current taxation, legislation and HMRC practice following the 2014 Budget statement. The impact of taxation (and any tax relief) depends on individual circumstances, and professional advice should be sought to ensure you take account of those circumstances and the ever-changing world of tax.

Income tax

This is calculated on all (or nearly all) of your income, after deduction of your personal allowance and, in the case of older married people, of the Married Couple's Allowance. The reason for saying 'nearly all' is that some income you may receive is tax free; types of income on which you do not have to pay tax are listed a little further on in this chapter.

Most income counts, however. You will be assessed for income tax on your pension; interest you receive from most types of savings; dividends from investments; any earnings (even if these are only from casual work); plus rent from any lodgers, should the amount you receive exceed £4,250 per year. Many social security benefits are also taxable. The tax year runs from 6 April to the following 5 April, so the amount of tax you pay in any one year is calculated on the income you receive (or are deemed to have received) between these two dates. Points to note – with effect from 6 April 2014:

- The point at which most people start paying income tax will be the personal allowance of £10,000 (this will increase to £10,500 from 6 April 2015; more on this below).

- The 20 per cent basic-rate tax is payable on further income beyond the personal allowance for income reduced from £32,010 to £31,865 on 6 April 2014 (and then in 2015/16 it reduces again to £31,785).

- The combined effect of the above measures is that the 40p income tax threshold rises from £41,450 in 2013/14 to £42,865 in 2014/15 and then to £42,285 in 2015/16.

- The top rate of 45 per cent is levied on incomes in excess of £150,000.

- From 6 April 2015 the 10 per cent starting rate for savings income is to be cut to zero and the starting rate for tax on savings is increased from £2,880 to £5,000.

Tax allowances

Personal allowance

Your personal allowance is the amount of money you are allowed to retain before income tax becomes applicable. When calculating how much tax you will have to pay in any one year, first deduct from your total income the amount represented by your personal allowance. You should add any other tax allowance to which you may be entitled (see further on in this section). You will not have to pay any income tax if your income does not exceed your personal allowance (or total of your allowances), and you may be able to claim a refund for any tax you have paid, or that has been deducted from payments made to you, during the year.

Calculating your personal allowance since the introduction of independent taxation has become easier. Everyone receives the same basic personal allowance regardless of whether they are male, female, married or single. It does not matter where the income comes from, whether from earnings, an investment, a pension or another source.

The figures for the tax year 2014/15 are as follows:

- Personal allowance for people born after 5 April 1948 is £10,000.

- Personal allowance for people born between 6 April 1938 and 5 April 1948 is £10,500.

- Personal allowance for people born before 6 April 1938 is £10,660.

Married Couple's Allowance

Married Couple's Allowance (for those aged under 75) is no longer applicable. Age-related Married Couple's Allowance (aged 75 and over) for 2014/15 is £8,165. The minimum amount of Married Couple's Allowance is £3,140.

Some important points you should know:

- Married Couple's Allowance is available to people born before 6 April 1935. Tax relief for this allowance is restricted to 10 per cent.

- A widowed partner, where the couple at the time of death were entitled to Married Couple's Allowance, can claim any unused portion of the allowance in the year he or she became widowed.

- Registered blind people can claim an allowance (the Blind Person's Allowance) of £2,230 per year. If both husband and wife are registered as blind, they can each claim the allowance. If you think you would be eligible, you should contact your local tax office with relevant details of your situation. If you were entitled to receive the allowance earlier but for some reason missed out on doing so, you may be able to obtain a tax rebate.

Useful reading

For more detailed information about tax allowances, see HMRC website: **www.hmrc.gov.uk**. The Inland Revenue booklet, IR 121, *Approaching Retirement (A Guide to Tax and National Insurance Contributions)* is also useful.

Same-sex partners

Same-sex couples in a civil partnership are treated the same as married couples for tax purposes. The most important thing to note is that only one property can qualify as their principal home for exemption from capital gains tax (CGT). Against this, there is no CGT to pay on transfer of assets between the couple, and similarly any assets left in a will to each other are free of inheritance tax.

Tax relief

Separate from any personal allowances, you can obtain tax relief on the following:

- a covenant for the benefit of a charity, or a donation under the Gift Aid scheme;
- contributions to occupational pensions, self-employed pension plans and other personal pensions;
- some maintenance payments, if you are divorced or separated and were aged 65 or older at 5 April 2000.

Mortgage interest relief

Mortgage interest relief was abolished on 6 April 2000. The only purpose for which relief is still available is in respect of loans secured on an older person's home to purchase a life annuity. However, to qualify, the loan must have been taken out (or at least processed and confirmed in writing) by 9 March 1999. Borrowers in this situation can continue to benefit from the relief for the duration of their loan. As before, the relief remains at 10 per cent on the first £30,000 of the loan.

Maintenance payments

Tax relief for maintenance payments was also withdrawn on 6 April 2000. Individuals in receipt of maintenance payments are not affected and will continue to receive their money free of income tax. Those who had to pay tax under the pre-March 1988 rules now also receive their payments free of tax. Most individuals paying maintenance, however, face higher tax bills. This applies especially to those who set up arrangements before the March 1988 Budget. While previously they got tax relief at their highest rate, from 6 April 2000 when maintenance relief was withdrawn they no longer get any relief at all. An exception has been made in cases where one (or both) of the divorced or separated spouses was aged 65 or over at 5 April 2000. Those paying maintenance are still able to claim tax relief – but only at the 1999/2000 standard rate of 10 per cent.

Pension contributions

HMRC sets limits on the contributions that individuals can invest in their pension plan and on the pension benefits they can receive. All company and personal pensions are now set under a single tax regime and new rules have been implemented (see Chapter 3 for more information).

For further information on Pension Credit see Chapter 3, or look under 'Pension Credit' on the government website: **www.gov.uk**.

Tax-free income

Some income you may receive is entirely free of tax. It is important to know what income is non-taxable and what can be ignored for tax purposes. If you receive any of the items listed below, you can forget about the tax aspect altogether (for a full list see Citizens Advice Bureau website: **www.adviceguide.org.uk** – taxable and non-taxable income):

- Attendance Allowance;
- Back to Work Bonus;
- Bereavement Payment;
- Child Benefit (NB: Child Benefit cuts have been introduced for families with at least one parent earning £50,000, and axed for those on £60,000);
- child dependency additions;
- Council Tax Benefit;
- Disability Living Allowance and Personal Independence Payment;
- Housing Benefit;
- Industrial Injuries Disablement Pension;
- income-related Employment and Support Allowance;
- Income Support (in some circumstances, such as when the recipient is also getting Jobseeker's Allowance, Income Support benefit will be taxable);
- Social Fund payments;
- Pension Credit;
- all pensions paid to war widows (plus any additions for children);
- pensions paid to victims of Nazism;
- certain disablement pensions from the armed forces, police, fire brigade and merchant navy;
- annuities paid to the holders of certain gallantry awards;
- the £10 Christmas bonus (paid to pensioners);
- the Winter Fuel Payment (paid to pensioners);
- the extra £400 Winter Fuel Payment paid to households with a resident aged 80 and over;
- National Savings Premium Bond prizes;
- winnings on the National Lottery and other forms of betting;
- rental income of up to £4,250 per year from letting out rooms in your home;
- income received from certain insurance policies (mortgage payment protection, permanent health insurance, creditor insurance for loans and utility bills, various approved long-term

care policies) if the recipient is sick, disabled or unemployed at the time the benefits become payable;

- SAYE bonuses;
- all income and dividends received from savings in an individual savings account (ISA);
- all dividend income from investments in venture capital trusts (VCTs).

The following are not income, in the sense that they are more likely to be one-off rather than regular payments. However, as with the above list they are tax free:

- virtually all gifts (in certain circumstances you could have to pay tax if the gift is above £3,000 or if, as may occasionally be the case, the money from the donor has not been previously taxed);
- a redundancy payment up to the value of £30,000;
- a lump sum commuted from a pension;
- a matured endowment policy;
- accumulated interest from a tax-exempt special savings account (TESSA) held for five years;
- dividends on investments held in a personal equity plan (PEP);
- compensation money paid to people who were mis-sold personal pensions;
- compensation paid to those who were mis-sold free-standing additional voluntary contributions (FSAVCs). To qualify for exemption from tax, the money must be paid as a lump sum as opposed to annual payments.

Income tax on savings and investments

Savings

For the tax year 2014/15 the 10 per cent starting rate applies to savings income up to £2,880. For 2015 to 2016 the starting rate for savings income will reduce from 10 per cent to 0 per cent. The maximum amount of an individual's savings income that can qualify for this starting rate is £5,000. Savers who are not liable to pay income tax on their savings income can register to receive interest payments from their bank or building society without tax being deducted. This will increase the number of savers who are not required to pay tax on savings income and represents a good tax-planning opportunity. This is especially the case with a husband and wife (or partners in a civil partnership) on different tax rates.

Investments

For most UK-based equity investments on which you are likely to receive dividends, basic-rate tax will have been deducted before the money is paid to you. If you are a basic-rate taxpayer, the money you receive will be yours in its entirety. If you pay tax at the higher rate of 40 per cent you will have to pay 25 per cent of the net dividend received on the amount received that takes you above the higher rate threshold (£41,865 in 2014/15 and £42,285 in 2015/16) and should allow for this in your budgeting.

Exceptionally, there are one or two types of investment where the money is paid to you gross – without the basic-rate tax deducted. These include NS&I income bonds, capital bonds, the NS&I Investment Account and all gilt interest. (People who prefer to receive gilt interest net can opt to do so.) As with higher-rate taxpayers, you will need to save sufficient money to pay the tax on the due date.

Avoiding paying excess tax on savings income

Banks and building societies automatically deduct the normal 20 per cent rate of tax from interest before it is paid to savers. As a result, most working people, except higher-rate taxpayers, can keep all their savings without having to worry about paying additional tax. While convenient for the majority, a problem is that some 4 million people on low incomes – including in particular many women and pensioners – are unwittingly paying more tax than they need. Those most affected are non-taxpayers (anyone whose taxable income is less than their allowances) who, although not liable for tax, are having it taken from their income before they receive the money.

Non-taxpayers can stop this happening quite simply by requesting their bank and/or building society to pay any interest owing to them gross, without deduction of tax at source. If applicable, all you need do is request form R85 from the institution in question or HMRC Enquiry

Centre, which you will then need to complete. If you have more than one bank or building society account, you will need a separate form for each account. People who have filled in an R85 should automatically receive their interest gross. If your form was not completed in time for this to happen, you can reclaim the tax from your tax office after the end of the tax year in April.

Reclaiming tax overpaid

If you are a non-taxpayer and have not yet completed an R85 form (or forms), you are very likely to be eligible to claim a tax rebate. To claim tax back you will need to fill in HMRC's form R40 Tax Repayment Form. To obtain a claim form and, if relevant, copies of form R85 for you to complete and give to your bank or building society, see the HMRC's website: **www.hmrc.gov.uk/incometax/tax-free-interest.htm.**

Mistakes by HMRC

HMRC does sometimes make mistakes. Normally, if it has charged you insufficient tax and later discovers the error, it will send you a supplementary demand requesting the balance owing. However, under a provision known as the 'Official Error Concession', if the mistake was due to HMRC's failure 'to make proper and timely use' of information it received, it is possible that you may be excused the arrears.

Undercharging is not the only type of error. It is equally possible that you may have been overcharged and either do not owe as much as has been stated or, not having spotted the mistake, have paid more than you needed to previously. So if you have reason to think your tax bill looks wrong, check it carefully. If you think there has been a mistake, write to your tax office explaining why you think the amount is too high. If a large sum is involved it could well be worth asking an accountant to help you, and if HMRC has messed up you may also be able to claim repayment of some or all of the accountant's fees (your accountant will be able to advise you on this).

As part of the Citizen's Charter, HMRC has appointed an independent adjudicator to examine taxpayers' complaints about their dealings with HMRC and, if considered valid, to determine what action would be fair. Complaints appropriate to the adjudicator are mainly limited to the way that HMRC has handled someone's tax affairs. Before approaching the adjudicator, taxpayers are expected to have tried to resolve the matter either with their local tax office or, should that fail, with the regional office.

Genuine mistakes are excused by HMRC but individuals may need to convince officials that they had not been careless in completing their returns, otherwise they could be at risk of incurring a penalty of 30 to 100 per cent of the tax involved, plus the tax owed itself and interest, and potentially HMRC widening its focus on you and your tax affairs.

Important dates to remember: the deadline for filing paper self-assessment forms for the 2014/15 tax year is 31 October 2015. Those filing online will have until 31 January 2016.

Further information

For further information, see HMRC booklet *Code of Practice 1, Putting Things Right: How to complain*, available from tax offices. Contact the Adjudicator's Office for information about referring a complaint. The adjudicator acts as a fair and unbiased referee looking into complaints about HMRC, including the Tax Credit Office, the Valuation Office and the Office of the Public Guardian and the Insolvency Service. See the following websites:

www.adjudicatorsoffice.gov.uk.

The TaxPayers' Alliance campaigns towards achieving a low-tax society: **www.taxpayersalliance.com**.

Tax Help for Older People (TOP) is an independent, free tax-advice service for over-60s whose household income is less than £17,000 per year: **www.taxvol.org.uk**.

Useful tax forms that can help you pay less tax:

- R40. If you want to claim back tax paid on savings and investments, you need to complete this form.
- R85. Getting your interest paid without tax being taken off: if you are not a taxpayer, this form will save you having to claim tax back each year.
- P161. Are you going to be 65 (61 for a woman) in this tax year? Or is your income changing – for example, if state pension and private pensions are due to start. If yes, this form will inform

HMRC of your age and income, allowing it to give you your age allowance and your new tax codes.

- R27. This form helps you to settle the tax affairs of someone who has died. It is worth completing because it often creates a repayment and helps to sort out any final transfer of Married Couples' Allowance. Your solicitor, if you have one, will usually deal with it for you.

- P53. If you have recently taken a lump sum rather than buying an annuity (pension), an enormous amount of tax was deducted before you received it. To claim this back immediately you should complete a P53.

- P45. You should receive one of these when you finish work with an employer. If you start a new job in the same tax year it is important that you give it to your new employer. It will ensure you are given the correct tax code and the right tax is deducted.

- P46. As important as the P45. If you start a new job and you do not have a P45 you must complete a P46. Your employer should prompt you to do this. If not, ask for one. This form also sorts out your tax codes.

- Forms 575 and 18. If you are thinking of transferring some of your Married Couples' Allowance, form 575 allows you to transfer the excess at the end of the tax year. Form 18 allows you to transfer the minimum amount.

Most forms can be obtained via the HMRC website: **www.hmrc.gov.uk**.

NB: HMRC has closed all of its 281 enquiry centres, which gave face-to-face help to 2.5 million people with tax queries. This service has been replaced by a telephone service and home visits. If you have a query you use the HMRC telephone helpline or go online to get your tax query answered.

Source: **www.bbc.co.uk/news/business-21789759**

Tax credits

The amount of tax credits you get depends on how many children you have living with you, whether you work and how many hours you work, if you pay for childcare, if you or any child living with you has a disability, or if you are coming off benefits.

Working Tax Credit

This is an earnings top-up given to low-income workers, including the self-employed. Eligibility is normally restricted to couples and single parents with a low income. The easiest way to check whether you are eligible is via the tax credits calculator on HMRC's website: **www.hmrc.gov.uk/working-tax-credit**, or call 0345 300 3900.

Child Tax Credit

This is a cash payment given to all families with a low household income that have at least one child under 16, or under 20 if in full-time education, and is paid in addition to a basic tax-credit payment. More at **www.gov.uk/child-tax-credit/overview**.

Need to claim

Payment is not automatic. In both cases – Working Tax Credit and Child Tax Credit – you need to complete an application form, available from the above contact points.

Post-war credits

Post-war credits are extra tax that people had to pay in addition to their income tax between April 1941 and April 1946. The extra tax was treated as a credit to be repaid after the war. People who paid credits were given certificates showing the amount actually paid. In 1972 people who could produce at least one of their post-war credit certificates were invited to claim. In cases where the original credit holder has died without claiming repayment and the post-war credit certificate is still available, repayment can be made to the next of kin or personal representative of the estate. Interest is payable on all claims at a composite rate of 38 per cent. The interest is exempt from income tax. All claims should be sent to the Special Post-War Credit Claim Centre at HM Revenue & Customs, HM Inspector of Taxes, PWC Centre V, Ty Glas, Llanishen, Cardiff CF4 5TX.

Tax rebates

When you retire, you may be due for a tax rebate. If you are, this would normally be paid automatically, especially if you are getting a pension from your last employer. You should ask for a P45 form. Then either send it – care of your earlier employer – to the pension fund trustees or, in the event of your receiving only a state pension, to the tax office together with details of your age and the date you retired. Ask your employer for the address of the tax office to which you should write. If the repayment is made to you more than a year after the end of the year for which the repayment is due – and is more than £25 – HMRC will automatically pay you (tax-free) interest. HMRC calls this a 'repayment supplement'.

NB: HMRC says it never sends notifications of a tax rebate by e-mail, or asks you to disclose personal or payment information by e-mail. For more advice and suggestions to protect yourself from scams, see Chapter 7.

Mis-sold PPI

Millions of borrowers have been receiving refunds after being mis-sold payment protection insurance (PPI) with credit cards and personal loans. The route to securing compensation is through first contacting your lender and, if dissatisfied, go straight to the Financial Ombudsman Service, or, if the lender has disappeared or gone bust, the Financial Services Compensation Service can help. Further information on these two excellent organizations is detailed in Chapter 6. You do not need the assistance of a claims firm, who may charge you additional and unnecessary fees. This is good news, as many are receiving cheques for thousands of pounds. Even better, they are being paid 8 per cent interest on the refunds to compensate for being without their money all that time. *But*, while there is no tax to pay on the refund element, which simply returns your own money to you, you have to pay tax on the interest, just as you do on earned interest in a savings account. Some lenders are deducting basic tax at 20 per cent, which non-taxpayers can reclaim, and higher-rate payers must report to the Inland Revenue. The longer someone has been without their money, the higher the interest proportion of it will be.

Capital Gains Tax (CGT)

You may have to pay capital gains tax if you make a profit (or, to use the proper term, 'gain') on the sale of a capital asset. CGT applies only to the actual gain you make. There is an exemption limit of currently £11,000 per year. For married couples, since 6 April 2014 each partner enjoys his or her own annual exemption of £11,000, and from 6 April 2015 this rises by 1 per cent to £11,100. This means that in 2014 a couple can make gains of £22,000 that are free of CGT. However, it is not possible to use the losses of one spouse to cover the gains of the other. Transfers between husband and wife remain tax free, although any income arising from such a gift will of course be taxed.

Any gains you make are taxed at 18 per cent for basic-rate taxpayers and 28 per cent for higher-rate and additional-rate taxpayers. Company owners benefit from further tax breaks, including 'entrepreneurs' relief', which can get relief limits on CGT down to 10 per cent (professional advice should be sought on this; see Chapter 6).

The following assets are not subject to CGT and do not count towards the gains you are allowed to make:

- your main home (but see the note below);
- your car;
- personal belongings up to the value of £6,000 each, such as jewellery, paintings or antiques;
- proceeds of a life assurance policy (in most circumstances);
- profits on UK government loan stock issued by HM Treasury;
- National Savings certificates;
- SAYE contracts;
- building society mortgage cashbacks;
- futures and options in gilts and qualifying corporate bonds;
- personal equity plan (PEP) schemes (now automatically ISAs);
- gains from assets held in an individual savings account (ISA);
- Premium Bond winnings (from 1 August 2014 the £30,000 maximum holding was increased to £40,000 and will be increased again to £50,000 in 2015/16);
- betting and lottery winnings and life insurance policies if you are the original owner;

- gifts to registered charities;
- small part-disposals of land (limited to 5 per cent of the total holding, with a maximum value of £20,000);
- gains on the disposal of qualifying shares in a venture capital trust (VCT) or within the Enterprise Investment Scheme (EIS), provided these have been held for the necessary holding period (see below).

Enterprise Investment Scheme (EIS)

Changes to investment limits and qualifying criteria allow more companies to attract equity investment through the Enterprise Investment Scheme (EIS), venture capital trusts (VCTs) and the Seed Enterprise Investment Scheme. These are complex and tax-efficient investment schemes and carry risk but are outside the scope of this book. Further information can be gained from **www.hmrc.gov.uk**, and professional advice should be sought from a chartered accountant (see Chapter 6).

Your home

Your main home is usually exempt from CGT. However, if you convert part of your home into an office or into self-contained accommodation on which you charge rent, the part of your home that is deemed to be a 'business' may be separately assessed and CGT may be payable when you come to sell it. (CGT would not apply if you simply take in a lodger who is treated as family, in the sense of sharing your kitchen or bathroom.)

If you leave your home to someone else who later decides to sell it, then he or she may be liable for CGT when the property is sold (although only on the gain since the date of death). There may also be inheritance tax implications, so you are strongly advised to consult a solicitor or a chartered accountant. If you own two homes, only one of them is exempt from CGT, namely the one you designate as your 'main residence', although there may be some overlap opportunities and, providing a dwelling home has been your only or main home for a period, the final period of ownership that qualifies for relief can be useful. In the 2014 Budget it was announced that from 6 April 2014 the final period of ownership of a private residence that qualifies for relief was reduced from 36 months to 18 months. HMRC's helpsheet 283, Private Residence Relief, available from **www.hmrc.gov.uk**, provides more information.

Selling a family business

CGT is payable if you are selling a family business, and is 28 per cent for higher-rate and additional-rate taxpayers, but the reduced level of 18 per cent for basic-rate taxpayers. There are a number of CGT reduction opportunities or deferral reliefs allowable. This, however, is a complex area and timing could be vital, so well before either retiring or selling shares you should seek the professional advice of a chartered accountant.

Useful reading

For further information about capital gains tax, see booklet CGT1, *Capital Gains Tax: An Introduction*, available from any tax office. There are also a number of useful help sheets downloadable from the HMRC website: **www.hmrc.gov.uk**.

Inheritance Tax (IHT)

Inheritance tax (IHT) is the tax that is paid on your 'estate'. The tax threshold (the level at which you'll need to pay tax) is set at £325,000 and frozen at this rate until 2019 at the earliest. The threshold amount for married couples and civil partners is £650,000. The value of estates over and above this sum is taxed at 40 per cent.

There is no immediate tax on lifetime gifts between individuals. The gifts become wholly exempt if the donor survives for seven years. When the donor dies, any gifts made within the previous seven years become chargeable and their value is added to that of the estate. The total is then taxed on the excess over £325,000. Chargeable gifts benefit first towards the £325,000 exemption, starting with the earliest gifts and continuing in the order in which they were given. Any unused balance of the £325,000 threshold goes towards the remaining estate.

The £325,000 threshold allows married couples or civil partners to transfer the unused element of their IHT-free allowance to their spouse or civil partner when they die, giving an attractive effective threshold of £650,000. IHT will, however, still be levied at 40 per cent above £325,000 on the estate of anyone who is single or divorced when they die.

The government changed the tax law in April 2012 to encourage donating to charities, and reduced the inheritance tax payable on estates that give at least 10 per cent to charity. The remainder is taxed at 36 per cent against the usual 40 per cent inheritance tax rate. Existing wills can be amended by codicil to include this 10 per cent provision. There is no such benefit to those whose estate falls below the current IHT threshold.

Gifts or money up to the value of £3,000 can be given annually free of tax, regardless of the particular date they were given. Additionally, it is possible to make small gifts to any number of individuals free of tax, provided the amount to each does not exceed £250.

An important consideration relating to IHT is the need to make a will. For further information, see 'Wills', in Chapter 16. If you have already written a will, have it checked by a professional adviser to ensure that you do not give money unnecessarily to HMRC. In view of the recent changes to IHT, check with your professional adviser or HMRC. For assistance see website: **www.gov.uk** – Probate and inheritance tax helpline.

Tax treatment of trusts

There may be inheritance tax to pay when assets – such as money, land or buildings – are transferred into or out of trusts when they reach a 10-year anniversary. There are complex rules that determine whether a trust needs to pay IHT in such situations. This is a particularly complex area, and professional advice from a chartered accountant and/or solicitor is vital and highly recommended. Further information is available on the website: **www.hmrc.gov.uk** – Inheritance tax and trusts.

Independent taxation

Both husband and wife are taxed independently on their own income. Each has his or her own personal allowance and rate band, and both independently pay their own tax and receive their own tax rebates. Couples should note that independent taxation applies equally to both capital gains tax and inheritance tax. Property left to a surviving spouse is, as before, free of inheritance tax.

Self-assessment

Tax return forms are sent out in April, and the details you need to enter on the form you receive in April 2015 are those relating to the 2014/15 tax year. All taxpayers now have a legal obligation to keep records of all their different sources of income and capital gains. These include:

- details of earnings plus any bonus, expenses and benefits in kind received;
- bank and building society interest;
- dividend vouchers and/or other documentation showing gains from investments;
- pension payments, eg both state and occupational or private pensions;
- miscellaneous income, such as freelance earnings, maintenance payments and taxable social security benefits;
- payments against which tax relief can be claimed (eg charitable donations or contributions to a personal pension).

If you are self-employed or a partner in a business, you need to keep, as well as the above list, records of all your business earnings and expenses, together with sales invoices and receipts. All records (both personal and business) should be kept for seven years after the fixed filing date, as you will need these if HMRC enquires into your tax affairs. HMRC can go back six years and raise assessments on careless mistakes, so six years and one extra year's retention is needed. If HMRC believe your errors were deliberate they can go back 20 years. Add in interest on any late tax and further additional penalties of up to 100 per cent of the tax shortfall and you could be facing an eye-watering tax assessment.

Remember that it is your obligation to notify and pay to HMRC any tax due. 'Sorry I didn't realize that I had to pay extra tax on all those dividends I received' or on that offshore bank account that you earned interest on but didn't disclose won't go down well. HMRC will, however, listen carefully to facts that may mitigate any penalty due – and if you are looking at serious amounts of tax due then early discussion with a chartered accountant will assist you in dealing with the unwelcome situation you may find yourself in. You should also check whether any insurance or professional association memberships that you have can provide free tax investigation cover. This is a very useful piece of cover. The *Daily Telegraph* reported in May 2014: 'The number of people being investigated by the taxman has doubled in one year... HM Revenue & Customs made enquiries about the affairs of 237,215 people last year, compared with about 119,000 in 2011/12, figures obtained by *Daily Telegraph* show.' The article went on to explain that simple errors are being targeted and that middle-class professionals such as doctors, lawyers and teachers were being targeted.

Abbey Tax Protection has one of the leading tax consultancy teams in the UK, which is headed by Guy Smith, a former HMRC tax inspector. Indeed, all of Guy's team are ex-tax inspectors and cumulatively have spent over 125 years working for HMRC.

We sought Guy's advice and he confirmed that HMRC's tax investigation activity has stepped up significantly over recent years into both tax evasion, which is illegal, and tax avoidance, which is legal:

> Since the Coalition government came into power, HMRC has been allowed to reinvest efficiency savings of some £1 billion back into tax compliance activity. The result has been an increase in tax yield from investigation work. In 2013/14 alone, HMRC delivered a record amount of £23.9 billion from pursuing tax-investigation-related work, which was up by over £9 billion on the figure just three years earlier. To help bring in the extra tax, 5,463 tax staff have been moved into new compliance roles, with a wide range of trades and professions targeted.

How has HMRC managed to bring in the extra money so quickly? Apart from deploying extra staff and closing tax loopholes to clamp down on tax avoidance, HMRC has an extra trick up its sleeve, as explained by Guy:

> 'Connect' is the name of HMRC's award-winning analytical computer system that houses more information than the British Library. HMRC feeds all of the information it receives from the banks, building societies and other government agencies into Connect, which then brings all of that data together to form an in-depth profile and a spider's web of connections between family members and business associates.
>
> In the past, HMRC received an enormous amount of paper-based information, which was rarely analysed in any detail or matched up to a person's tax record. Tax investigations were usually based purely on entries in a tax return or the figures in a set of accounts. However, HMRC has a far more slick operation now and gets a full picture of the individual or business it is going to investigate, from any bank and building society accounts held, to any properties they own.

Controversially, HMRC has been adding all of its calls to the Tax Evasion Hotline into Connect, so even malicious, unfounded reports from a jealous neighbour, disaffected former employee or jilted lover could form part of the spider's web and part of the risk-assessment process when HMRC is choosing cases for investigation.

If HMRC discovers an error during an investigation, it can reopen other closed years as well. For example, if a careless error is discovered, HMRC can include six years within any settlement negotiations. If a deliberate error is uncovered, HMRC can include up to 20 years in the most serious cases. The behaviour relating to the error also impacts upon the tax penalty HMRC can levy on any additional tax and Class 4 National Insurance, and then there is the interest that HMRC charges as well. Needless to say, tax investigations can prove to be extremely stressful and very expensive.

Guy Smith's advice

- Engage an accountant. Make sure the accountant is a chartered accountant and a member of one of the tax professional bodies. In other words, get an accountant who has passed their exams and has qualifications.

- Keep good records. Although there is an obligation to keep business records, it is always sensible to keep personal records as well. Dividend vouchers and interest certificates will always need to be retained for completing the self-assessment tax return, but it is wise to keep records relating to house moves and monies received from third parties, whether from an inheritance or savings maturity.

- Talk to your accountant. It is always surprising how many people simply give their business records to their accountant and then sign their tax return when it is presented, without asking any questions. The danger is that the accountant may have to make assumptions when preparing the accounts and introduce estimates to get the accounts to balance. If a tax inspector finds estimated or other balancing figures during a tax investigation, it calls into question the accuracy of the business records and can lead to all sorts of problems.

- Get tax investigation insurance cover. Many accountants will offer this type of insurance; specialist providers such as Abbey Tax do too, as well as trade membership bodies such as the Federation of Small Businesses. It is always worth comparing prices and benefits before taking out fee protection insurance, as it is often called.

- Be discreet. HMRC views social media websites so, for example, if your business has had a bad year and made low profits, don't start posting pictures of an expensive foreign holiday on Facebook or a luxury car on Instagram. HMRC also uses Google to zoom in on any home extensions, conservatories and outdoor swimming pools to judge whether someone is living within their means, or understating their income to fund their private lifestyle

Those most likely to be affected by the self-assessment system include anyone who normally receives a tax return, higher-rate taxpayers, company directors, the self-employed and partners in a business. If your only income is your salary from which tax is deducted at source, you will not have to worry about self-assessment. If, however, you have other income that is not fully taxed under PAYE (eg possibly benefits in kind or expenses payments) or that is not fully taxed at source, you need to notify HMRC within six months of the end of the tax year, and you may need to fill in a tax return.

If your financial affairs change, as they sometimes do on retirement (eg if you become self-employed or receive income that has not already been fully taxed), it is your responsibility to inform HMRC and, depending on the amount of money involved, you may need to complete a tax return. The government has recently revised the guidelines, and higher-rate taxpayers will no longer automatically receive a self-assessment form if their affairs can be handled through the PAYE system.

Please note that *self-calculation is optional*. HMRC will continue as before to do the sums for you if you think you are at risk of making a mistake. If you submit a paper return this must be filed by 31 October each year; the deadline for online filing is 31 January the following year.

Further information

See booklets SA/BK4, *Self-Assessment – A General Guide to Keeping Records*; SA/BK6, *Self-Assessment – Penalties for Late Tax Returns*; SA/BK7, *Self-Assessment – Surcharges for Late Payment of Tax*; and SA/BK8, *Self-Assessment – Your Guide*, all obtainable free from any tax office. See website: **www.gov.uk** or HMRC website: **www.hmrc.gov.uk**.

Retiring abroad

A vital question that is often overlooked is the taxation effects of living overseas. There are many examples of people who retired abroad in the expectation of being able to afford a higher standard of living and who returned home a few years later, thoroughly disillusioned. If you are thinking of retiring abroad, do thoroughly investigate the potential effects this will have on your finances in order to avoid unpleasant surprises.

Taxation abroad

Tax rates vary from one country to another: a prime example is VAT, which varies considerably in Europe. Additionally, many countries levy taxes that don't apply in the UK. Wealth tax exists in quite a few parts of the world. Estate duty on property left by one spouse to another is also fairly widespread. There are all sorts of property taxes, different from those in the UK, which – however described – are variously assessable as income or capital. Sometimes a special tax is imposed on foreign residents. Some countries charge income tax on an individual's worldwide income, without the exemptions that apply in the UK.

Apart from the essential of getting first-class legal advice when buying property overseas, if you are thinking of retiring abroad the golden rule must be to investigate the situation thoroughly before you take an irrevocable step, such as selling your home in the UK.

Your UK tax position if you retire overseas

Many intending emigrants cheerfully imagine that, once they have settled themselves in a dream villa overseas, they are safely out of the clutches of the UK tax office. This is not so. You first have to acquire non-resident status. If you have severed all your ties, including selling your home, to take up a permanent job overseas, this is normally granted fairly quickly. But for most retirees, acquiring unconditional non-resident status can take up to three years. The purpose is to check that you are not just having a prolonged holiday but are actually living as a resident abroad. During the check period, HMRC may allow you conditional non-resident status and, if it is satisfied, full status will be granted retrospectively.

Rules

The rules for non-residency are stringent and complex and because of the tax advantage to be gained by becoming non-resident it is apparent that HMRC have been seeking to reduce such opportunities and attacking pre-existing 'understandings'. At a very high level and start point is HMRC's Statutory Residence Test, which states that those seeking to live outside the UK are not allowed to spend more than 182 days in the UK in any one tax year, or to spend more than an average of 90 days per year in the UK over a maximum of four tax years. Even if you are not resident in the UK, some of your income may still be liable for UK taxation and open to attack, so, as with previous suggestions above, professional advice from a chartered accountant should be sought . In the meantime, more information on HMRC's Statutory Residence Test is available at **www.hmrc.gov.uk/international/residence.htm**.

Double tax agreement

A person who is a resident of a country with which the UK has a double taxation agreement may be entitled to exemption or partial relief from UK income tax on certain kinds of income from UK sources, and may also be exempt from UK tax on the disposal of assets. The conditions of exemption or relief vary from agreement to agreement. It may be a condition of the relief that the income is subject to tax in the other country.

It is worth noting that if, as sometimes happens, the foreign tax authority later makes an adjustment and the income ceases to be taxed in that country, you have an obligation under the self-assessment rules to notify HMRC.

Capital gains tax

If you are non-resident the timing of gains may become important. Different rules apply to gains made from the disposal of assets in a UK company and, again, specialist advice should be sought from a chartered accountant.

Inheritance tax

You escape IHT only if: 1) you were domiciled overseas for all of the immediate three years prior to death; 2) you were resident overseas for more than three tax years in your final 20 years of life; and all your assets were overseas.

Even if you have been resident overseas for many years, if you do not have an overseas domicile you will have to pay IHT at the same rates as if you lived in the UK.

Domicile

You are domiciled in the country in which you have your permanent home. Domicile is distinct from nationality or residence. A person may be resident in more than one country, but at any given time he or she can be domiciled in only one. If you are resident in a country and intend to spend the rest of your days there, it could be sensible to decide to change your domicile. If, however, you are resident but there is a chance that you might move, the country where you are living would not qualify as your domicile. This is a complicated area, where professional advice is recommended if you are contemplating a change.

UK pensions paid abroad

If your state pension is your only source of UK income, tax is unlikely to be charged. If you have an occupational pension, UK tax will normally be charged on the total of the two amounts. Both state and occupational pensions may be paid to you in any country. If you are planning to retire to Australia, Canada, New Zealand or South Africa, it would be advisable to check on the up-to-date position regarding any annual increases you would expect to receive to your pension. Some people have found the level of their pension frozen at the date they left the UK, while others have been liable for unexpected tax overseas.

If the country where you are living has a double tax agreement with the UK, as previously explained, your income may be taxed there and not in the UK. The UK now has a double tax agreement with most countries. If your pension is taxed in the UK, you will be able to claim your personal allowance as an offset. Any queries about your pension should be addressed to the International Payments Office, **International Pensions Centre**. For contact details see website: **www.gov.uk** – International Pensions Centre. See Chapter 3 for more information.

Health care overseas

People retiring to another EU country before state retirement age can apply for a form E106, which will entitle them to state health care in that country on the same basis as for local people. This is valid only for a maximum of two and a half years, after which it is usually necessary to take out private insurance cover until state retirement age is reached. More information and advice can be obtained from the website: **www.gov.uk** – Britons living abroad. Thereafter, UK pensioners can request the International Pensions Centre at Newcastle (see under 'UK pensions paid abroad' above) for a form E121, entitling them and their dependants to state health care as provided by the country in which they are living.

Useful reading

- *The Daily Telegraph Tax Guide* by David Genders, published annually by Kogan Page; see website: **www.koganpage.com**.
- *Residents and Non Residents – Liability to Tax in the UK* (IR20) is available from any tax office.
- Leaflet SA29, *Your Social Security Insurance, Benefits and Health Care Rights in the European Community*, contains essential information about what to do if you retire to another EU country, available from any social security or Jobcentre Plus office or website: **www.jobcentreplus.gov.uk**.

Chapter Five
Investing

Saving is a fine thing – especially when your parents have done it for you. WINSTON CHURCHILL

The 2014 Budget was hailed as delivering a savings revolution for many. It included the biggest pension reforms since 1921, and recognized that savers make a vital contribution to the economy and are capable of managing their own financial affairs. While the nation has been attempting to extricate itself from the banking crisis and the recession, many pensioners and savers have been left out in the cold. Money in savings and deposit accounts at banks have been earning virtually no interest and the value of capital sums has been eroded by inflation. Meanwhile, annuity rates have been dragged down by years of record-low interest rates. This has caused real pain to many who have led thrifty lives and saved for old age.

Savings play a critical role in the way that the whole economy works. The more encouragement people have to save, the better it is for new investment, future growth, greater productivity and higher living standards. The jump in the annual limit of how much can be held in an ISA is for savers most welcome news, as is the flexibility to switch their funds between cash or shares. These changes put the onus on pension savers to make sensible decisions about how to invest and provide for their retirement.

Successful investing has never been easy but for those who are interested in saving for retirement, and for the long term, the principles remain the same: keep the costs down; shelter as much money from the tax office as you can; buy assets when they are cheap and sell when they are expensive. To be a successful investor you have to be disciplined. You need to decide on a strategy, allocate your money to your investment accordingly, then stick with that through the ups and downs that the markets will inevitably bring. Since no one is able to predict the future, a sensible approach to investment is to split your money between assets that behave in different ways.

But there's a big difference between 'saving' and 'investing'. Investing is for the long term. It's money you can put away for your retirement, and in the long run it should grow more rapidly than in a savings account. If you are saving for a shorter-term goal, perhaps in less than five years, then you're looking to get the most interest paid on your money. Here are some tips for starters:

- *Don't let your emotions ruin you.* Approach investing calmly and never panic. If the market crashes don't rush to dump everything. At the other end of the spectrum, overconfidence is also a threat.

- *Don't invest and forget.* Regularly reviewing your portfolio is essential. A six-monthly check should suffice. Being disciplined increases the chance of improved investment performance. Don't be afraid to rebalance should it be necessary.

- *Don't invest without understanding the risks.* Beware of investing by label: funds don't always do what they say on the tin.

- *It's risky to take no risk.* To grow your money you need to beat inflation and add a bit on top. Diversify: spread your risk, don't over-invest in one firm or sector, and invest globally not just in your home market.

- *Be contrary.* Have confidence to buy unpopular assets. Buy at a point of maximum pessimism, when prices are low and when volumes are low. Boom and bust have never been abolished; the same goes for stock market cycles.

- *Don't invest in myths.* There is a myth, for instance, that when times are tough you should avoid smaller domestic companies because they suffer more than larger global businesses. Being overcautious could mean missing out on some decent gains.

- *Be critical.* A critical, sceptical mind is key to investing skill. Form your own opinion and never go along with something just because 'an expert says so'.

- *Don't risk investing money you can't afford to lose.* When told by a friend that he was being kept awake at night because of his investments, JP Morgan, the founder of the investment bank, reportedly advised him 'to sell down to the sleeping point'.

- *Pick a strategy and stick with it.* Find a strategy that you are comfortable with and don't chop and change (but don't forget the six-monthly reviews).

- *Start small then scale up.* The small investor can invest in any sector they like. Aim to find good firms at low prices. Study your target firms and understand why they are successful. Once you're comfortable with your strategy then gradually increase the amounts traded.

Thanks to the internet, investors have unprecedented opportunity to access information and advice. Here are some useful websites you could look at:

The Motley Fool: **www.fool.co.uk**.

Henry Tapper: **www.henrytapper.com**.

Ethical Money: **www.ethicalmoney.org**.

Money Advice Service: **www.moneyadviceservice.org.uk**.

Money Facts: **www.moneyfacts.co.uk**.

Money Supermarket: **www.moneysupermarket.com**.

Money Saving Expert: **www.moneysavingexpert.com**.

This is Money: **www.thisismoney.co.uk**.

Which?: **www.which.co.uk**.

Since everyone has different financial aims, there is no one-size-fits-all approach to investing. In very simple terms, there are four different types of investment you could consider:

- *Cash investments*: made into a bank account or cash ISA. These are generally short term and offer easy access to your money, and lower risk so the potential returns are much less than other types of investment. Your money is secure, but it could lose value due to tax and inflation.

- *Bonds and gilts*: effectively, an IOU from the government or big companies. When you buy one you are lending money that earns an agreed fixed rate of interest. Government bonds (called gilts) are backed by the state and are as good as guaranteed. Corporate bonds carry greater risk but offer the possibility of improved returns.

- *Investing in property*: directly as a buy-to-let investor or indirectly through certain investment funds carries more risk. Property prices go down as well as up, and it can take time to sell property. Be sure to seek advice beforehand and, even better, don't do anything without reading *Successful Property Letting: How to make money in buy-to-let*, by David Lawrenson.

- *Shares*: sometimes referred to as 'equities', this basically means putting money on the stock market. You can do this by buying shares in individual companies or by investing through a professionally managed investment fund, such as a unit trust.

While you were working, you probably had an emergency fund equal to at least three months' take-home pay. In retirement you may not need such a big fund. Work out what you need to have put away for a rainy day; once you have this sum set aside, you could consider investing for higher potential returns.

Sources of investable funds

If you are looking at investment options from your resources, possible sums of quite significant capital include:

- *Commuted lump sum from your pension*: one-quarter of your pension can be taken as a tax-free lump sum. The remainder can be taken as cash, subject to the ordinary rates of income tax.

- *Insurance policies*: designed to mature on or near your date of retirement. These are normally tax free.

- *Profits on your home*: if you sell it and move to smaller, less expensive accommodation. Provided this is your main home, there is no capital gains tax to pay.

- *Redundancy money, golden handshake or other farewell gift from your employer*: you are allowed £30,000 redundancy money free of tax. The same is usually true of other severance pay up to £30,000. But there can be tax to pay if, however worded, your employment contract indicates that these are deferred earnings.

- *Sale of SAYE and other share option schemes*: the tax rules vary according to the type of scheme, and since the rules are liable to change with each Budget statement, further information should be sought on the HMRC website: **www.hmrc.gov.uk**.

General investment strategy

Investments differ in their aims, their tax treatment and the amount of risk involved. If you are taking the idea of investing seriously, the aim for most people is to acquire a balanced portfolio. This could comprise a mix of investments variously designed to provide some income to supplement your pension and also some capital appreciation to maintain your standard of living in the long term. Except for annuities and National Savings and Investments, which have sections to themselves, the different types of investment are listed by groups, as follows: variable interest accounts, fixed interest securities, equities and long-term lockups. As a general strategy, mix and match your investments so they are spread across several groups.

Annuities

Until the 2014 Budget this used to be one of the biggest decisions that most people approaching retirement had to make: cashing in their pension and buying an annuity. The headline grabber on Budget day was probably the biggest shake-up to the savings and pension market in the last four decades. At the time of writing, much of the 'pensions liberation' remains under consultation and, therefore, any detailed analysis in this book is not possible. In brief, the Chancellor announced that it would no longer be necessary to buy an annuity, giving the individual power to manage their own payments if they choose. In conjunction with the removal of the requirement to buy an annuity there will be a relaxation of the rules governing drawdown and commutation, and lower tax charges on withdrawals above the limits. Although restrained by further clarifying information, the terms mentioned above and further context on the existing position are set out below.

Presently, when you buy an annuity, you hand over a lump sum (usually your pension fund, although you can first withdraw up to 25 per cent of it as a tax-free lump sum) to an insurance company in return for a regular, guaranteed income for the rest of your life. Under the current rules the earliest age you can do this is 55. This income is taxable if it exceeds your personal allowance. If you are retiring today, low annuity rates probably make you wince. That doesn't mean you should necessarily ignore them. Once you have bought your annuity, the income you receive is effectively free of investment risk. That has been transferred to your provider. There is little danger of running out of money, as your provider has to pay you for as long as you live.

When you approach retirement your pension company will contact you about purchasing an annuity and will outline the recently announced changes and options available to you. They will provide you with a quotation, which will tell you the amount of money you have in your 'pension pot', the amount of tax-free lump sum you are entitled to take, and the level of income you will receive each month (should you convert your pension fund to an annuity with them). Check you are getting the correct allowance and that you have the right tax code. This tells the pension company how much tax to deduct, but there is no guarantee that it will be right. For more information, see **www.incometaxcalculator.com**. Specialist help for older people is available from **www.taxvol.org.uk**.

You need to do some research to make sure which type of annuity is best for you and how the Chancellor's 2014 Budget announcements have developed. You only get one chance to purchase an annuity, and once you have done so there is no going back. The benefit of shopping around is that you could very well receive more money by doing so. Each annuity provider will have different rates dependent on its own under-writing criteria and your own position. Research shows that by shopping around you may be able to increase the amount of income you receive by up to 20 per cent. Choosing an annuity is a decision that should not be taken without the help of a specialist financial adviser who has experience in this field.

The gender gap closed in December 2012, from which point insurers are no longer allowed to take gender into account when fixing annuity rates. Rates for men will get worse and won't improve much for women either.

Types of annuities

There are several different kinds of annuities.

The most basic is a *level annuity*. This pays you a fixed income for the rest of your life. If you die, the income usually stops. And – crucially – it will not change if prices rise. So in an inflationary world, your purchasing power will fall every year. For example, if inflation averages 4 per cent per year, the purchasing power of your annuity income will halve in 18 years.

To avoid this you could buy an *increasing annuity*. Here, the amount of income you receive will rise in line with inflation each year, or by a set percentage. And if you are worried about your insurance company keeping a large chunk of your pension fund should you die after only a few years of retirement, you could buy a *guaranteed annuity*. So if you bought a five-year guarantee, and you died after two years, your nominated beneficiary (your spouse perhaps) would receive annuity income for another three years.

Another option is a *joint-life annuity* where your partner can receive some or all of your pension income if you die before them. If you want to take a bit more of a risk, you could choose an *investment-linked annuity*. Here you start with an initial level of income while your fund is invested in an insurance company's with-profits fund. If the fund makes a profit, your income goes up. If it loses money, however, your income goes down.

Your health can also have a significant impact. If you are a smoker or have an illness, you may be eligible for an *enhanced annuity* or *impaired life annuity*. These pay a higher annual income than a standard annuity. In short, the annuity provider is betting that you won't live as long, so it can afford to pay you more.

It pays to shop around

Presently there are a wide range of annuities available and everyone is entitled to shop around for the best one for their circumstances; how this situation will develop following the 2014 Budget is yet to be seen. This is known as the OMO (open market option). In other words, you don't have to take the offer from your existing pension provider – you are free to go to any provider. Figures show that fewer than half of people shop around. Failing to do so is a huge mistake, particularly since annuity rates have fallen in recent years. The reasons for the fall in rates are due to people living longer. Insurance companies have to keep paying incomes for longer. Second, falling interest rates make it harder to generate a source of funds to pay annuity income. Currently there is a gap of around 20 per cent between the best and the worst annuity rates – so don't just take the first offer that comes your way.

Other options

If you don't want to buy an annuity because of low rates, there are a number of strategies you can use. One is known as *phased retirement*. This is where you set up a series of annuities and drawdowns with 25 per cent tax free lump sums. You will get a lower starting income but if you think annuity rates are going to rise it might be worth considering.

Another possible option is *fixed-term annuities*. Here you set up an annuity for a fixed period (say 5 or 10 years). You get paid an income for the fixed term but at the end of the period you have a guaranteed pot of money to reinvest again. As with phased retirement, your income will be lower than from a standard annuity.

Alternatives to annuities

Income drawdown is an alternative to buying an annuity at retirement. Instead of purchasing a guaranteed income from an insurance company, pension savings remain invested and a percentage can be 'drawn down' each year. There are two types: 'capped' imposes limits on how much you can withdraw; the other – 'flexible' – puts no limits on withdrawals. These products came into force in April 2011, replacing an unsecured pension or an alternatively secured pension; at the same time the government removed the requirement to buy an annuity by age 75. The catch is that you presently need at least £20,000 in other sources of guaranteed income, such as state pension and annuities, to qualify, but the 2014 Budget announced that this would be reduced to £12,000. As there are certain risks, financial advice is essential before making a decision. One good piece of news is that the income drawdown rules were changed in the April 2014 Budget. The limit had been restored to 120 per cent in the April 2013 Budget (previously limited to 100 per cent) of what you would get from the equivalent annuity. The limit will now be increased to 150 per cent. This change will attract more pensions to drawdown, experts predict, as one of the advantages is that drawdown can be used to minimize your tax bill in several ways (see 'How To Choose an Annuity' by Phil Oakley and Tim Bennett, *The Week PROSPER* – **www.theweek.co.uk**).

Small pension pots

Presently up to two pension pots with a value less than £2,000 can be taken as a lump sum; the limit increased following the 2014 Budget to £10,000 and will apply to three pension pots.

Tax

It is important in all of the above plans to consider carefully the tax implications. Income tax on optional annuities is relatively low, as part of the income is allowed as a return on capital that is not taxable. Pension-linked annuities are fully taxable.

Another 2014 Budget headline grabber was the remarkable announcement that will shake up the pensions industry like nothing before on the future taxation (subject to consultation) of withdrawals of pension pots. It was announced that withdrawals will be taxed at the marginal rates of the pensioner rather than at the flat rate of 55 per cent as previously. So just think about it – if you are a basic-rate taxpayer working part-time in your retirement years and perhaps receiving some state pension you could just draw down some of your 'pension pot' to keep within the basic-rate tax band and avoid having to take a pension that forces you into paying higher-rate tax at this stage in your life. The big pension payment can just wait until you give up that part-time job. It will be interesting to see how this new regime will work, but it could shake up the pension industry and perhaps see people 'switch' to ISA savings to fund their retirement. Some concerns exist about the lack of discipline in accessing supposed 'pension pots' and whether people will 'tap in and blow it all'. Time will tell.

How to obtain an annuity

The annuity market is large and there is a vast choice of products. A helpful free booklet is Martin Lewis's (Money Saving Expert.com) *Guide to Annuities* sponsored by Annuity Direct Limited (published March

2013). See: Martin Lewis's website: **www.moneysavingexpert.com** or Annuity Direct: **www.annuitydirect.co.uk**.

Other useful websites include:

Annuity Advisor: **www.annuity-advisor.co.uk**.

Annuity Bureau: **www.annuity-bureau.co.uk**.

Hargreaves Lansdown: **www.h-l.co.uk/pensions**.

Origen Annuities: **www.origenfsannuities.co.uk**.

William Burrows: **www.williamburrows.com**.

You can also buy an annuity direct from an insurance company or via an intermediary, such as an independent financial adviser (IFA). See Chapter 6; you can also consult these professional advice websites:

Unbiased.co.uk: **www.unbiased.co.uk**.

The Institute of Financial Planning: **www.financialplanning.org.uk**.

Personal Finance Society (PFS): **www.findanadviser.org**.

Telegraph Retirement Service: **www.telegraph.co.uk/retire**.

National Savings & Investments (NS&I)

NS&I Savings Certificates, of which there are two types (fixed interest and index linked), are free of tax. They do not pay much interest but any tax-free investment is worth considering. For non-taxpayers who invest in NS&I products there is no need to complete an HM Revenue & Customs (HMRC) form to receive money in full, as this is automatic. See the website: **www.nsandi.com**.

The main NS&I investments are:

- *Easy-access savings accounts*: this is an easy way to build up your savings, with instant access to your money and the option to save regularly by standing order.

- *Income Bonds*: a safe and simple way of earning additional income every month. They pay fairly attractive, variable, tiered rates of interest, increasing with larger investments. Interest is taxable, but paid in full without deduction of tax at source. There is no set term for the investment.

- *Fixed Interest Savings Certificates*: lump-sum investments that earn guaranteed rates of interest over set terms. There are two terms: two years and five years. For maximum benefit, you must hold the certificates for five years.

- *Index-Linked Savings Certificates*: inflation-beating tax-free returns guarantee that your investment will grow in spending power each year, whatever happens to the cost of living. Certificates must be retained for either three or five years. Interest is tax free.

- *Children's Bonus Bonds*: these allow you to invest for a child's future in their own name – and there's no tax to pay on the interest or bonuses. Interest rates are fixed for five years at a time, plus a guaranteed bonus. These are tax free for parents and children and need not be declared to HMRC.

- *New from January 2015*: NS&I will offer the Pensioner Bonds, two fixed-rate 'market leading' savings bonds for people aged 65 and over. At the time of writing, rates are still to be set, but the one-year bond is expected to pay around 2.8 per cent and the three-year bond 4 per cent. Supply is limited, with up to £10 billion being made available. Pensioners are allowed to save a maximum of £10,000 in each bond, offering a total of £20,000. Interest on the bonds will be taxed in line with all other savings income at the individual's personal tax rate.

- *Premium Bonds*: one of Britain's most popular savings products, the maximum amount that can be saved into Premium Bonds will jump from £30,000 to £50,000 some time in 2015, and the number of £1 million prizes handed out every month doubled from 1 to 2 in August 2014. Over 21 million people hold Premium Bonds, and tax-free prizes are paid out every month. Many savers love the reliability of Premium Bonds, which are backed by the government-supported National Savings & Investments.

Complaints

If you have a complaint about any NS&I product, you should raise this with the Director of Savings. Should the matter not be resolved to your satisfaction it can be referred to the Financial Ombudsman Service; see website: **www.financial-ombudsman.org.uk**.

Variable interest accounts

You can save in a wide range of savings accounts with banks, building societies, credit unions and National Savings & Investments (NS&I) – already mentioned. With around 54 million current accounts in the UK, banks and building societies frequently introduce new accounts with introductory bonuses, to attract new customers. Although keeping track may be time-consuming, all advertisements for savings products must now quote the annual equivalent rate (AER). AER provides a true comparison, taking into account the frequency of interest payments and whether or not interest is compounded.

NB: The over-50s are being advised to show added caution when signing up to a savings account, particularly if it is tailored to their age. By looking only at over-50s products, savers would be ignoring over 93 per cent of the market. There are around 43 different variable-rate bank accounts available for the over-50s in the UK, offered by 22 different providers
Source: *The Mature Times* – **www.maturetimes.co.uk**.

Definition

Other than the interest-bearing current accounts described above, these are all 'deposit'-based savings accounts of one form or another, arranged with banks, building societies, the National Savings & Investments Bank, and some financial institutions that operate such accounts jointly with banks. The accounts include instant-access accounts, high-interest accounts and fixed-term savings accounts. Some institutions pay interest annually; others – on some or all of their accounts – will pay it monthly. Although you may get a poor return on your money when interest rates drop, your savings will nearly always be safe. Should the bank or building society get into serious financial difficulty, up to £85,000 of your money will be 100 per cent protected under the Financial Services Compensation Scheme. See website: **www.fscs.org.uk**.

Access

Access to your money depends on the type of account you choose: you may have an ATM card and withdraw your money when you want; you may have to give a week's notice or slightly longer. If you enter into a term account, you will have to leave your money deposited for the agreed specified period. In general, the longer the period of notice required, the better the rate of interest earned.

Sum deposited

You can open a savings account with as little as £1. For certain types of account, the minimum investment could be anything from £500 to about £5,000. The terms tend to vary depending on how keen the institutions are to attract small investors.

Tax

With the exception of tax-free cash ISAs and of the National Savings and Investments Bank, where interest is paid gross, tax is deducted at source. However, you must enter the interest on your tax return and, if you are a higher-rate taxpayer, you will have additional liability. Basic-rate taxpayers pay 20 per cent on their bank and building society interest. Higher-rate taxpayers pay 40 or 45 per cent. Non-taxpayers can arrange to have their interest paid in full by completing a certificate (R85, available from HMRC or the bank) that enables the financial institution to pay the interest gross. If you largely rely on your savings income and believe you are or have been paying excess tax, you can reclaim this from HMRC. For further information, see 'Income tax on savings and investments' in Chapter 4.

Choosing a savings account

There are two main areas of choice: the type of savings account and where to invest your money.

Instant-access savings account

This attracts a relatively low rate of interest, but it is both easy to set up and very flexible, as you can add small or large savings when you like and can usually withdraw your money without any notice. It is an excellent temporary home for your cash if you are saving in the short term. However, it is not recommended as a long-term savings plan.

High-interest savings account

Your money earns a higher rate of interest than it would in an ordinary savings account. However, to open a high-interest account you will need to deposit a minimum sum, which could be £500 to £1,000. Although you can always add to this amount, if your balance drops below the required minimum your money will immediately stop earning the higher interest rate. Terms vary between providers. Usually interest is only paid yearly, and you can only withdraw yearly.

Fixed-term savings account

You deposit your money for an agreed period of time, which can vary from a few months to over a year. In return for this commitment, you will normally be paid a superior rate of interest. As with high-interest accounts, there is a minimum investment: roughly £1,500 to £10,000. If you need to withdraw your money before the end of the agreed term, there are usually hefty penalties. If interest rates are still low, your money may be better invested elsewhere.

Equity-linked savings account

This offers a potentially better rate of return, as the interest is calculated in line with the growth in the stock market. Should the market fall, you may lose the interest, but your capital should normally remain protected. The minimum investment varies from about £500 to £5,000 and, depending on the institution, the money may need to remain deposited for perhaps as much as five years.

ISA savings

See later in this chapter, page 98.

Information

For banks, enquire direct at your nearest high-street branch. You can also investigate other banks and building societies to see whether they offer better terms. Look at as many as you can since the terms and conditions may vary quite widely. The Building Societies Association offers information and advice on savings and types of accounts and much more. See its website: **www.bsa.org.uk**.

The safety of your investment

Investors are protected by the legislative framework in which societies operate and, in common with bank customers, their money (up to a stated maximum) is protected under the Financial Services Compensation Scheme. See website: **www.fscs.org.uk**.

Complaints

If you have a complaint against a bank or building society, you can appeal to the Financial Ombudsman Service (FOS) to investigate the matter, provided the complaint has already been taken through the particular institution's own internal disputes procedure – or after eight weeks if the problem has not been resolved – and provided the matter is within the scope of the ombudsman scheme. Generally speaking, the FOS can investigate complaints about the way a bank or building society has handled some matter relating to its services to customers. See website: **www.financial-ombudsman.org.uk**.

Fixed interest securities

Fixed interest securities pay interest at a rate that does not change with any external variable. The coupon payments are known in advance. Coupons are almost always all for the same amount and paid at regular intervals, regardless of what happens to interest rates generally. There are two risks with fixed income securities: credit risk and interest rate risk.

Credit risk is one of the main determinants of the price of a bond. The price of a debt security can be explained as the present value of the payments (of interest and repayment of principal) that will be made. Credit risk is an issue for lenders such as banks, ie losses to the bank. So correlation with the bank's other lending is what matters, not correlation with debt available in the market.

Interest rate risk is simply the risk to which a portfolio or institution is exposed because future interest rates are uncertain. Bond prices are interest-rate sensitive, so if rates rise the present value of a bond will fall sharply. This can also be thought of in terms of market rates: if interest rates rise, then the price of a bond will have to fall for the yield to match the new market rates. The longer the duration of a bond, the more sensitive it will be to movements in interest rates.

If you buy when the fixed rate is high and interest rates fall, you will nevertheless continue to be paid interest at the high rate specified in the contract note. However, if interest rates rise above the level when you bought, you will not benefit from the increase. Generally these securities give high income but only modest, if any, capital appreciation. The securities include high-interest gilts, permanent interest-bearing shares, local authority bonds and stock exchange loans, debentures and preference shares.

Gilt-edged securities

Definition

Gilts, or gilt-edged securities, are bonds issued by the UK government that offer the investor a fixed interest rate for a predetermined, set time, rather than one that goes up or down with inflation. The 10-year gilt yield is now around 2.0 per cent and seemed to bottom out around August 2012. If thinking of buying gilts, diversify your portfolio.

Buying gilts is best done when interest rates are high and look likely to fall. When general interest rates fall, the value of the stock will rise and can be sold profitably. When buying or selling, consideration must be given to the accrued interest that will have to be added to or subtracted from the price quoted. Gilts are complicated by the fact that you can either retain them until their maturity date, in which case the government will return the capital in full, or sell them on the London Stock Exchange at market value.

Yields are low, and while bank interest rates remain at 2014 levels things are not likely to improve.

Index-linked gilts

Index-linked gilts are government-issued bonds – glorified IOUs – that you can buy to obtain a guaranteed rate of return over inflation. In previous years they have performed well, but if you are buying them now you will be doing so at a premium and it is likely you will suffer capital losses as their value falls back, even while your income remains above inflation. However, if you are less worried about preserving your capital and require inflation-linked income, then these can still be useful in a balanced portfolio.

Tax

Gilt interest from whatever source is paid gross. Gross payment means that you must allow for a future tax bill before spending the money. Recipients who prefer to receive the money net of tax can ask for this to be arranged. A particular attraction of gilts is that no capital gains tax is charged on any profit you may have made, but equally no relief is allowed for any loss.

How to buy

You can buy gilts through banks, building societies, a stockbroker or a financial intermediary, or you can purchase them through Computershare Investor Services; see website: **www.computershare.com**. In all cases, you will be charged commission.

Assessment

Gilts normally pay reasonably good interest and offer excellent security, in that they are backed by the government. You can sell at very short notice, and the stock is normally accepted by banks as security for loans, if you want to run an overdraft. Index-linked gilts, which overcome the inflation problem, are generally speaking a better investment for higher-rate taxpayers – not least because the interest paid is very low.

Gilt plans

This is a technique for linking the purchase of gilt-edged securities and with-profit life insurance policies to provide security of capital and income over a 10- to 20-year period. It is a popular investment for the commuted lump sum taken on retirement. These plans are normally obtainable from financial intermediaries.

Permanent interest-bearing shares (PIBS)

These are a form of investment offered by some building societies to financial institutions and private investors as a means of raising share capital. They have several features in common with gilts: they pay a fixed rate of interest that is set at the date of issue; this is likely to be on the high side when interest rates generally are low and on the low side when interest rates are high. The interest is usually paid twice yearly; there is no stamp duty to pay or capital gains tax on profits. Despite the fact that PIBS are issued by building societies, they are very different from normal building society investments. They are generally rated as being in the medium- to high-risk category, so professional advice should be taken first. In the event of any losses, PIBS are not covered by the Financial Services Compensation Scheme.

Equities

These are all stocks and shares, purchased in different ways and involving varying degrees of risk. They are designed to achieve capital appreciation as well as give you some regular income. Most allow you to get your money out within a week. Millions of people in the UK invest in shares. Equity securities usually provide steady income as dividends but they fluctuate with the ups and downs in the economic cycle. Investing has never been easier with the growing number of internet-based trading facilities. Equities include ordinary shares, unit trusts, open-ended investment companies (OEICs) (see below), investment trusts and real estate investment trusts (REITs).

Equities probably provide the greatest potential for income that can beat inflation over the medium to long term. Dividend yields on many equity funds are currently in excess of 3–4 per cent per annum.

Unit trusts and OEICs

Definition

Unit trusts and open-ended investment companies (OEICs, a modern equivalent of unit trusts) are forms of shared investments, or funds, which allow you to pool your money with thousands of other people and invest in world stock markets. The advantages are that they are simple to understand, you get professional management and there are no day-to-day decisions to make. Additionally, every fund is required by law to have a trustee (called a 'depository' in the case of OEICs) to protect investors' interests.

Unit trusts have proved incredibly popular because your money is invested in a broad spread of shares and your risk is reduced, but they are rapidly being replaced by the OEIC (pronounced 'oik'). The minimum investment in some of the more popular funds can be as little as £25 per month or a £500 lump sum. Investors' contributions to the fund are divided into units (shares in OEICs) in proportion to the amount they have invested. Unit trusts and OEICs are both open-ended investments. As with ordinary shares, you can sell all or some of your investment by telling the fund manager that you wish to do so. The value of the shares you own in an OEIC, or units in a unit trust, always reflects the value of the fund's assets. The key differences between the two are:

- *Pricing*: when investing in unit trusts, you buy units at the offer price and sell at the lower bid price. The difference in the two prices is known as the spread. To make a return, the bid price must rise above the offer before you sell the units. An OEIC fund contrastingly has a single price, directly linked to the value of the fund's underlying investments. All shares are bought and sold at this single price. An OEIC is sometimes described as a 'what you see is what you get' product.

- *Flexibility*: an OEIC fund offers different types of share or sub-fund to suit different types of investor. The expertise of different fund management teams can be combined to benefit both large and small investors. There is less paperwork as each OEIC will produce one report and accounts for all sub-funds.

- *Complexity*: unit trusts are, legally, much more complex, which is one of the reasons for their rapid conversion to OEICs. Unit trusts allow an investor to participate in the assets of the trust without actually owning any. Investors in an OEIC buy shares in that investment company.

- *Management*: with unit trusts, the fund's assets are protected by an independent trustee and managed by a fund manager. OEICs are protected by an independent depository and managed by an authorized corporate director.

- *Charges*: unit trusts and OEICs usually have an upfront buying charge, typically 3–5 per cent, and an annual management fee of between 0.5 and 1.5 per cent. It is possible to reduce these charges by investing through a discount broker or fund supermarket, but this means acting without financial advice. Charges on OEICs are relatively transparent, shown as a separate item on your transaction statement.

Investment trusts

Over the past decade investment trusts beat unit trusts in eight of nine key sectors. One of the biggest benefits that investment trusts offer is to income investors. While open-ended funds must pay out all the income they receive, investment trusts can hold some back in reserve. This allows them to offer a smoother and more certain return. There are four major advantages that an investment trust has over a unit trust:

- *Cost.* The initial charges on unit trusts typically range from 4 to 6 per cent but there is also the annual fee costing in the region of 1.5 to 2 per cent. An investment trust also levies annual fees, but on average they are lower because most investment trusts don't pay commission to financial advisers.

- *Gearing.* Like other companies, investment trusts are fairly free to borrow for investment purposes. Unit trusts, however, are usually restricted by regulation. But when markets are rising and the trust is run well, gearing will deliver superior returns.

- *Size.* Investment trusts tend to be smaller than unit trusts on average, and so are less unwieldy and more focused on their investment objectives. To grow beyond their initial remit, they need permission from shareholders. Many also have a fixed life expectancy. Conversely, unit trusts are called 'open ended' because they can expand and contract to meet demand ('Big' is not always beautiful.)

- *Discounts.* Because their shares are listed and traded freely (unlike a unit trust), investment trusts can end up with a market capitalization that is greater than (at a 'premium'), or lower than (at a 'discount') its assets under management (the 'net asset value', or NAV). If the discount narrows after you buy, you'll make a small gain on top of any increase in the trust's NAV.

How to obtain

Units and shares can be purchased from banks, building societies, insurance companies, stockbrokers, specialist investment fund providers and independent financial advisers, directly from the management group and via the internet. Many of the larger firms may use all these methods. For a list of unit trusts, investment trusts and OEICs the Investment Management Association (IMA) website gives information: **www.investmentfunds.org.uk**. Or you can look at the following:

> **www.thisismoney.co.uk/investing**;
>
> **www.moneyweek.com**;
>
> **www.moneysupermarket.com**;
>
> **www.investment-advice.org.uk**;
>
> **www.investorschronicle.co.uk**.

For further information on investment advice, see Chapter 6.

Tax

Units and shares invested through an ISA have special advantages (see 'Individual savings account', below). Otherwise, the tax treatment is identical to that of ordinary shares.

Assessment

Unit trusts and OEICs are an ideal method for smaller investors to buy stocks and shares: less risky and easier. This applies especially to tracker funds, which have the added advantage that charges are normally very low. Some of the more specialist funds are also suitable for those with a significant investment portfolio.

Complaints

Complaints about unit trusts and OEICs are handled by the Financial Ombudsman Service (FOS). It has the power to order awards of up to £100,000. Before approaching the FOS, you must first try to resolve the problem with the management company direct via its internal complaints procedure. If you remain dissatisfied, the company should advise you of your right to refer the matter to the FOS; see website: **www.financial-ombudsman.org.uk**.

The safety of your investment

Investors are protected by the legislative framework and, in common with bank customers, their money (up to a stated maximum) is protected under the Financial Services Compensation Scheme (FSCS); see website: **www.fscs.org.uk**.

Ordinary shares listed on the London Stock Exchange

Definition

Public companies issue shares as a way of raising money. When you buy shares and become a shareholder in a company, you own a small part of the business and are entitled to participate in its profits through a dividend, which is normally paid six monthly. It is possible that in a bad year no dividends at all will be paid. However, in good years, dividends can increase very substantially. The money you invest is unsecured. This means that, quite apart from any dividends, your capital could be reduced in value – or if the company goes bankrupt you could lose the lot. The value of a company's shares is decided by the stock market. The price of a share can fluctuate daily, and this will affect both how much you have to pay if you want to buy and how much you will make (or lose) if you want to sell.

See the London Stock Exchange website, **www.londonstockexchange. com**, to find a list of brokers in your area that would be willing to deal for you. The securities department of your bank or one of the authorized share shops will place the order for you, or you can do it online. Whichever method you use, you will be charged both commission and stamp duty, which is currently 0.5 per cent. Unless you use a nominee account (see below), you will be issued with a share certificate that you or your financial adviser must keep, as you will have to produce it when you wish to sell all or part of your holding. It is likely, when approaching a stockbroker or other share-dealing service, that you will be asked to deposit money for your investment up front or advised that you should use a nominee account. This is because of the introduction of several new systems, designed to speed up and streamline the share-dealing process.

There are three types of shares that are potentially suitable for small investors:

- *Investment companies* invest in the shares of other companies. They pool investors' money and so enable those with quite small amounts to spread the risk by gaining exposure to a wide portfolio of shares, run by a professional fund manager. See the Association of Investment Companies website: **www.theaic.co.uk**.

- *Real estate investment trusts (REITs)* pool investors' money and invest it for them collectively in commercial and residential property. They offer individuals a cheap, simple and potentially less risky way of buying shares in a spread of properties, with the added attraction that the funds themselves are more tax efficient, as both rental income and profits from sales are tax free within the fund. Also, if wanted, REITs can be held within an ISA or self-invested personal pension (SIPP). It is recommended that professional advice is taken before investing.

- *Convertible loan stocks* give you a fixed guaranteed income for a certain length of time and offer you the opportunity to convert them into ordinary shares. While capital appreciation prospects are lower, the advantage of convertible loans is that they usually provide significantly higher income than ordinary dividends. They are also allowable for ISAs.

Tax

All UK shares pay dividends net of 10 per cent corporation tax. Basic-rate and non-taxpayers have no further liability to income tax. Higher-rate 40 per cent taxpayers must pay further income tax that works out at 25 per cent of the net dividend received. Since April 2014 investors in London's alternative investment market (AIM) no longer pay 0.5 per cent stamp duty on transactions. Investors are allowed to hold AIM stocks in their individual savings accounts.

Assessment

Although dividend payments generally start low, in good companies they are likely to increase over the years and so provide a first-class hedge against inflation. Good advice is critical, as this is a high-risk, high-reward market.

Individual savings account (ISA)

Definition

About 14 million people put money into ISAs each year. Since ISAs were introduced 15 years ago they have proved wildly popular because of the tax breaks, as you do not pay any tax on the interest or the profits you make. Savers who use cash ISAs can build up their nest eggs three times faster than those who put them in instant access accounts. If you're looking to get the most interest paid on your savings, a cash ISA is about the best bet. ISAs are very popular forms of investment as all income and gains generated in the account are tax free, and they stay tax free, year after year. It is important to shop around for the best rates and take full advantage of your annual allowance. There are two types of ISA: cash ISAs, and stocks and shares ISAs.

Since 1 July 2014, everyone can put up to £15,000 into a new, simpler type of tax-free savings account. In this new account, savers will be able to move their money easily between the stock market and regular high-street deals in a bid to get the best possible return from their nest eggs. ISAs can be held in any mix of cash and stocks and shares – and entirely in cash if desired. The rules covering switching ISAs have also been relaxed. For the first time, savers can now transfer the previous years' funds from stocks and shares ISAs into cash ISAs.

'Peer to peer' loans are now eligible to hold in ISAs. These are loans made by individuals, via websites such as Zopa, to borrowers in return for regular interest, at rates much better than are available on normal savings accounts.

Bonds – IOUs issued by companies and governments and traded on the stock market – are also eligible to be included irrespective of how close they are to being repaid.

Tax

ISAs are completely free of all income tax and capital gains tax. You should be aware that a 20 per cent charge is levied on all interest accruing from non-invested money held in an ISA that is not specifically a cash ISA.

Assessment

ISAs offer a simple, flexible way of starting, or improving, a savings plan. For further information on the various forms of ISAs, see these websites:

www.thisismoney.co.uk/investing;

www.moneyweek.com;

www.moneyadviceservice.org.uk;

www.moneysavingexpert.com;

www.moneysupermarket.com;

www.investment-advice.org.uk;

www.investorschronicle.co.uk;

www.investmentfunds.org.uk;

www.telegraph.co.uk/isas.

How to invest for your grandchild

Children's savings account

All you need to set this up is the child's birth certificate. The interest on money deposited by grandparents isn't subject to tax, and interest rates are currently as high as 6 per cent.

Junior ISA

You can't open a junior ISA for your grandchild – that's one for the parents – but you can make contributions up to the ISA's annual limit. The government has raised the allowance for junior ISAs and child trust funds from £3,720 to £4,000. Junior ISAs are available to all children born on or after 3 January 2011, or born before September 2002, or are under 18 and do not have a child trust fund. The fund is locked until the child is 18 when they get control of the money.

Child trust funds

Children born after December 2010 are not eligible for a child trust fund. However, accounts set up for eligible children will continue to benefit from tax-free investment growth. Withdrawals will not be possible until the child reaches 18.

Children's Bonds

Unlike the lottery of Premium Bonds – which require a minimum investment of £100 – Children's Bonds offer a guaranteed rate of return, with only a £25 minimum investment; the best five-year deal currently pays 2.5 per cent.

Stakeholder pension

For really long-term saving, pay into a stakeholder pension. Your grandchild takes control at 18, but can only access the money aged 55. Tax relief applies so the government will top up a payment of £2,880 to the limit of £3,600.

SOURCE: *Sunday Telegraph*

Useful reading

How the Stock Market Works, by Michael Becket of the *Daily Telegraph*, published by Kogan Page; see website: **www.koganpage.com**.

Long-term lock-ups

Certain types of investment, mostly offered by insurance companies, provide fairly high guaranteed growth in exchange for your undertaking to leave a lump sum with them or to pay regular premiums for a fixed period, usually five years or longer. The list includes life assurance policies, investment bonds and some types of National Savings Certificates.

Life assurance policies

Definition

Life assurance can provide you with one of two main benefits: it can either provide your successors with money when you die or it can be used as a savings plan to provide you with a lump sum (or income) on a fixed date. There are three basic types of life assurance: whole-life policies, term policies and endowment policies:

- *Whole-life policies* are designed to pay out on your death: you pay a premium every year and, when you die, your beneficiaries receive the money. The insurance holds good only if you continue the payments. If one year you did not pay and were to die, the policy could be void and your successors would receive nothing.

- *Term policies* involve a definite commitment. As opposed to paying premiums every year, you elect to make regular payments for an agreed period, for example until such time as your children have completed their education, say eight years. If you die during this period, your family will be paid the agreed sum in full. If you die after the end of the term (when you have stopped making payments), your family will normally receive nothing.

- *Endowment policies* are essentially savings plans. You sign a contract to pay regular premiums over a number of years and in exchange receive a lump sum on a specific date; this could be from 10 to 25 years. Once you have committed yourself, you have to go on paying every year (as with term assurance). There are heavy penalties if you decide that you no longer wish to continue.

An important feature of endowment policies is that they are linked to death cover. If you die before the policy matures, the remaining payments are excused and your successors will be paid a lump sum on your death. The amount of money you stand to receive, however, can vary hugely, depending on the charges and how generous a bonus the insurance company feels it can afford on the policy's maturity. Over the past few years, payouts have been considerably lower than their earlier projections might have suggested. Aim to compare at least three policies before choosing.

Both whole-life policies and endowment policies offer two basic options: with profits or without profits:

- *Without profits*: sometimes known as 'guaranteed sum assured'. The insurance company guarantees you a specific fixed sum, you know the amount in advance and this is the sum you – or your successors – will be paid.

- *With profits*: you are paid a guaranteed fixed sum plus an addition, based on the profits that the insurance company has made by investing your annual or monthly payments. The basic premiums are higher and the profits element is not known in advance.

- *Unit linked*: a refinement of the 'with profits' policy, in that the investment element of the policy is linked in with a unit trust.

Premiums can normally be paid monthly or annually, as you prefer. The size of premium varies enormously, depending on the type of policy you choose and the amount of cover you want. As a generalization, higher premiums tend to give better value, as relatively less of your contribution is swallowed up in administrative costs. You may be required to have a medical check if large sums are involved. More usually, you fill in and sign a declaration of health. If you make a claim on your policy and it is subsequently discovered that you gave misleading information, your policy could be declared void and the insurance company could refuse to pay. Many insurance companies offer a better deal if you are a non-smoker. Some also offer more generous terms if you are teetotal. Women generally pay less than men of the same age because of their longer life expectancy.

How to obtain

Policies are usually available through banks, insurance companies, independent financial advisers (IFA) and building societies. Be careful with the small print: terms and conditions that sound very similar may obscure important differences that could affect your benefit. To be sure of choosing the policy best suited to your requirements, consult an IFA. For help in finding an IFA in your area, see Chapter 6, and the following websites:

www.unbiased.co.uk;

www.financialplanning.org.uk;

www.findanadviser.org.

Disclosure rules

Advisers selling financial products have to abide by a set of disclosure rules, requiring them to give clients certain essential information before a contract is signed. They present potential clients with two 'key facts' documents: 'About our services', describing the range of services and the type of advice on offer; and 'About the cost of our services'. IFAs must offer clients the choice of paying fees or paying by commission. For further information consult the Association of British Insurers (ABI) website: **www.abi.org.uk**. See also Chapter 6.

Tax

Under current legislation, the proceeds of a qualifying policy – whether taken as a lump sum or in regular income payments – are free of all tax. If, as applies to many people, you have a life insurance policy written into a trust, there is a possibility that it could be hit by inheritance tax rules affecting trusts if the sum it is expected to pay out is above the (2014/15) £325,000 IHT threshold. The best advice is to check with a solicitor.

Assessment

Life assurance is a sensible investment, whether the aim is to provide death cover or the benefits of a lump sum to boost your retirement income. It has the merit of being very attractive from a tax angle, though you are locked into a long-term commitment. So choosing the right policy is very important. Shop around, take advice and, above all, do not sign anything unless you are absolutely certain that you understand the small print.

Complaints

Complaints about life assurance products, including alleged mis-selling, are handled by the Financial Ombudsman Service (FOS). Before approaching the FOS, you first need to try to resolve a dispute with the company direct. See the website: **www.financial-ombudsman.org.uk**.

The Financial Services Compensation Scheme (FSCS) is the compensation fund of last resort for customers of authorized financial services firms. If a firm becomes insolvent or ceases trading, the FSCS may be able to pay compensation to its customers. See the website: **www.fscs.org.uk**.

Alternatives to surrendering a policy

If you wish to terminate an endowment policy before the date of the agreement, and avoid the punitive costs, you could sell the policy for a sum that is higher than its surrender value. See the Association of Policy Market Makers website: **www.apmm.org**. For those looking for investment possibilities, second-hand policies could be worth investigating. Known as traded endowment policies (TEPs), they offer the combination of a low-risk investment with a good potential return. A full list of appropriate financial institutions and authorized dealers that buy and sell mid-term policies is obtainable from the Association of Policy Market Makers. It can also arrange for suitable policies to be valued by member firms, free of charge.

Bonds

The London Stock Exchange operates a retail bond platform designed to make trading corporate bonds as easy as trading listed shares. Since March 2011 nearly £1.7 billion has been raised by companies in the market. Bonds generally offer less opportunity for capital growth; they tend to be lower risk as they are less exposed to stock market volatility; but they have the advantage of producing a regular guaranteed income. The three main types of bonds are:

- *Gilts*: (government bonds) explained earlier in this chapter, are the least risky. They are secured by the government, which guarantees both the interest payable and the return of your capital in full if you hold the stocks until their maturity.

- *Corporate bonds*: these are fairly similar to gilts except that you are lending to a large company, rather than owning a piece of it, as you do with an equity. The company has to repay the loan at some point, known as the bond's redemption date. It will pay out the 'face value' of the bond and the company also has to pay interest on the loan, known as the 'coupon'. After they are issued, bonds trade in the secondary market, just like shares. Bond prices are driven by two main factors: interest rates and credit risk. Most bonds have a fixed income; the longer the time to maturity, the more sensitive the bond is to changes in interest rates.

One reason to hold bonds is for income. Should corporate profits stall, companies might have to cut dividends. But unlike dividends, bond coupons can't be suspended, so your income is more predictable. The main risks to bonds are rising interest rates and credit risk. With market interest rates at rock-bottom levels, they can only go up over time. If this happens then fixed income investments such as bonds will look very unattractive. To hedge against these you should diversify: buy a portfolio of different maturity date bonds and spread your corporate bond companies across different industry sectors. In general, the higher the guaranteed interest payments, the less totally secure the company in question.

- *Investment bonds*: these are different in that they offer potentially much higher rewards but also carry a much higher degree of risk. If you are thinking of buying bonds, expert advice is very strongly recommended.

Investment bonds

Definition

This is the method of investing a lump sum with an insurance company, in the hope of receiving a much larger sum back at a specific date – normally a few years later. All bonds offer life assurance cover as part of the deal. A particular feature of some bonds is that the managers have wide discretion to invest your money in almost any type of security. The risk/reward ratio is, therefore, very high. They can produce long-term capital growth but can also be used to generate income.

While bonds can achieve significant capital appreciation, you can also lose a high percentage of your investment. An exception is guaranteed equity bonds, which, while linked to the performance of the FTSE 100 or other stock market index, will protect your capital if shares fall. However, while your capital should be returned in full at the end of the fixed term (usually five years), a point not always appreciated is that, should markets fall, far from making any return on your investment you will have lost money in real terms. Your capital will have fallen in value, once inflation is taken into account; and you will have lost out on any interest that your money could have earned had it been on deposit.

All bond proceeds are free of basic-rate tax, but higher-rate tax is payable. However, higher-rate taxpayers can withdraw up to 5 per cent of their initial investment each year and defer the higher-rate tax liability for 20 years or until the bond is cashed in full, whichever is earlier. Although there is no capital gains tax on redemption of a bond (or on switching between funds), some corporation tax may be payable by the fund itself, which could affect its investment performance. Companies normally charge a front-end fee of around 5 per cent plus a small annual management fee, usually not related to performance.

Tax

Tax treatment is complicated, as it is influenced by your marginal income tax rate in the year of encashment. For this reason, it is generally best to buy a bond when you are working and plan to cash it after retirement.

Offshore bonds

It has been suggested that offshore bonds are the new pensions, with a recent surge of interest in offshore bonds from high earners looking for an alternative to pensions for their retirement savings. These can provide significant tax savings for investors because up to 5 per cent of capital can be withdrawn while deferring higher-rate tax for up to 20 years, with no immediate tax to pay.

Offshore bonds are an insurance 'wrapper' around a portfolio of investments, which receive tax advantages by allowing you to defer the tax on the growth of the investments. Capital growth in an onshore bond is taxed at 20 per cent, whereas offshore bond capital grows tax free. While basic-rate taxpayers have no more tax to pay when they cash in an onshore investment bond, higher-rate taxpayers must pay a further 20 per cent and top-rate taxpayers must pay 30 per cent. With offshore bonds there is no tax to pay until you encash the bond, when higher-rate taxpayers will pay the entire 40 per cent and the top-rate payers will be liable for 50 per cent.

Charges for offshore bonds are high: typically 0.3 to 1 per cent up front plus £400 to 0.25 per cent per year, depending on how much is invested. Adviser commission on top means the bonds are generally best for investments greater than £100,000 and held for more than five years. In comparison with pensions, these schemes are being increasingly recommended for retirement savings for higher-rate taxpayers who use their ISA and capital gains allowance, and no longer benefit from higher-rate tax relief.

Investor protection

Since 1 April 2013, the Prudential Regulation Authority (PRA) ensures the stability of financial services firms and is part of the Bank of England. It regulates around 1,700 financial firms. The Financial Conduct Authority (FCA) is now the City's behavioural watchdog. The Bank of England has also gained direct supervision for the whole of the banking system through its powerful Financial Policy Committee (FPC), which can instruct the two new regulators. Another change occurred with the Retail Distribution Review (RDR), which came into effect in January 2012, requiring all financial advisers to set out their charges explicitly, so you will know how much they cost you (see Chapter 6).

Investment businesses must adhere to a proper complaints procedure, with provision for customers to receive fair redress, where appropriate. Unsolicited visits and telephone calls to sell investments are for the most part banned. Where these are allowed for packaged products (such as unit trusts and life assurance), should a sale result the customer will have a 14-day cooling-off period (or a seven-day 'right to withdraw' period if the packaged product is held within an ISA and the sale follows advice from the firm). The cooling-off period is to give the customer time to explore other options before deciding whether or not to cancel the contract.

A single ombudsman scheme

The single statutory Financial Ombudsman Service (FOS) provides a 'one-stop shop' for dissatisfied consumers and covers complaints across almost the entire range of financial services and products – from banking services, endowment mortgages and personal pensions to household insurance and stocks and shares. The list equally includes unit trusts and OEICs, life assurance, FSAVCs and equity release schemes. A further advantage is that the FOS applies a single set of rules to all complaints. The Financial Ombudsman Service also covers the consumer-credit activities of businesses with a consumer-credit licence issued by the Office of Fair Trading. Consumer credit activities now covered by the ombudsman range from debt consolidation and consumer hire to debt collecting and pawnbrokers.

For further information on complaints, scams and how to protect yourself, see Chapter 7 and see also Chapter 6 for hints and tips from the Financial Ombudsman Service.

Chapter Six
Professional advisers

"No one wants advice – only corroboration.   JOHN STEINBECK

Would you be able to obtain good financial advice if you had unlimited funds in order to do so? In the 2014 Budget, the Chancellor allocated £20 million to help people access impartial advice, following the bold move to liberate some 13 million defined contribution pensionholders from the obligation of purchasing an annuity. Doubtless some people will still opt for the certainty of income provided by annuities, but it is expected that many will take advantage of the freedom to cash in their lump sum at the age of 55. It is to be hoped that the funds designated by the government for acquiring unbiased financial advice will be sufficient to help those who need it. Obtaining good-quality financial advice has always been essential for savers and the newly retired, but as a result of the recent changes it is now even more important.

Choosing an independent financial adviser (IFA)

The role of IFAs has become more important since the number of investment, mortgage, pension protection and insurance products has multiplied and financial decision making has become increasingly complicated. An IFA is the only type of adviser who is able to select from all the investment policies and products on offer in the marketplace. It is his or her responsibility to make sure you get the right product for your individual needs.

IFAs must assess whether customers are at risk of overcommitting themselves or taking some other risk that might jeopardize their security,

This means they have to gain a full understanding of your circumstances and requirements before helping to choose any financial products. You should ask your adviser a number of questions including – most important – by whom they are regulated. All IFAs must be authorized and regulated by the Financial Conduct Authority and are obliged to offer what is termed 'suitable advice'.

Professional advice is essential if you don't feel confident about doing the research yourself when looking for complex financial products. It's worth paying an adviser to ensure you get it right. Common areas where you might want expert help include:

- annuities (pensions);
- endowments;
- financial and tax planning and structuring;
- investments;
- mortgages;
- pensions and pension transfers.

Advisers are legally divided into one of two types:

- *Independent financial advisers*: IFAs are unbiased and can advise on, and sell, products from any provider right across the market. They are obliged to give 'best advice'.

- *Restricted advisers*: they can be found in high-street banks or have chosen to specialize in particular providers' products or specific areas of advice. Their 'restricted' status means they can only sell and advise on a limited range of products, or from a limited number of firms.

Since 31 December 2012, independent and restricted advisers have to charge a fee for investment, pension and endowment advice rather than accepting commission. You can pay up front for the adviser's time, rather like an accountant or solicitor, or you can agree a commission-like fee that is deducted from the money you invest in a product purchased through them. Don't worry about asking up front what the cost will be – it is vital – so just take a deep breath and ask the question so that you can compare different IFAs.

There are other advisers who deal with mortgage, tax or debt advice. Mortgage brokers advise on mortgage products, which are fast-changing.

Tax accountants are usually unavoidable if you are self-employed, but some small-business owners can look after their own accounts and tax (more on this in Chapter 10). As a business grows it will probably benefit from professional tax and accounts advice and this becomes all the more vital if you have complicated tax affairs or need advice on inheritance tax. Debt advisers are the people you will need if you have serious debt problems.

When choosing an IFA, there are usually four main considerations: respectability, suitability, price and convenience. The best way to ensure decent advice is to establish credentials and qualifications. As a basic safeguard, check that an individual is a member of a recognized institution. If you are thinking of using a particular adviser, do you already know him or her in a professional capacity? If not, ask family or friends whom they would recommend. You should certainly check on the adviser's reputation, ideally talking to some of his or her existing clients. Do not be afraid to ask for references. Most reputable professionals will be delighted to assist, as it means that the relationship will be founded on a basis of greater trust and confidence. Whilst trust and long-term standing are important, do also remember to get absolute clarity on the fee basis.

When choosing an IFA:

- To check whether your IFA is registered, see the FCA's Central Register website: **www.fca.org.uk**.

- To find an IFA near you, look at the Unbiased.co.uk website: **www.unbiased.co.uk**, which has a network of 15,000 IFAs.

- You could look at a new site, VouchedFor: **www.vouchedfor.co.uk**, which hosts reviews of IFAs and checks that they are from genuine clients.

- Or try Find an Adviser at **www.findanadviser.org**, with a network of 7,000 IFAs.

Other websites worth checking are:

Ethical Investment Research Service (EIRIS):
www.yourethicalmoney.org.

Institute of Financial Planning: **www.financialplanning.org.uk**.

MyLocalAdviser: **www.mylocaladviser.co.uk**.

The Personal Finance Society (PFS): **www.thepfs.org**.

Top questions to ask for finding an IFA

Are you independent or restricted?

An independent financial adviser will be able to search the whole market and must be entirely unbiased to call him/herself independent.

How long have you been established?

Look for an IFA business that has been established for at least three years.

Are you authorized?

The Financial Conduct Authority monitors firms to check whether they are qualified. Before you meet any IFA, search the FCA's website: **www.fca.org.uk**.

What qualifications do you have?

The FCA requires all IFAs to pass Level 4 qualifications. The adviser also needs to have an annual Statement of Professional Standing issued by an FCA accredited body, which should be displayed in their office. For a full list of IFA qualifications see Unbiased website: **www.unbiased.co.uk/qualifications**.

SOURCE: www.moneysaving expert.com

Since January 2013 the Prudential Regulation Authority (PRA) ensures the stability of financial services firms and is part of the Bank of England (see **www.bankofengland.co.uk**). The Financial Conduct Authority (FCA) is the City's behavioural watchdog (see **www.fca.org.uk**). It polices firms' conduct to ensure consumers are protected. It ensures that your financial adviser meets certain standards regarding how they give you advice.

> ### Tips for when you meet your IFA
>
> - *Always ask, 'how much do you charge?'* Remember the deep breath first, of course, and check if you are paying by the hour and whether the price includes VAT.
>
> - *Don't be afraid to haggle.* Especially if you are seeing a number of IFAs. At least try to ask for a reduction in fees or a rebate on commission (if they're advising on insurance or mortgages).
>
> - *Before you go, fill out a fact find.* Advisers must collect information about you so they can properly assess your situation. Ask for this form to be sent to you to fill out beforehand. It can save you both time and money.
>
> - *Get it in writing.* Be sure to get their recommendations in writing. Read them through carefully, and if you don't understand, ask.
>
> - *Final checks.* The decision is your alone. You do not have to do what they tell you. Make sure their advice is really right for you.

For your protection

The Financial Services Compensation Scheme (FSCS) is the body that can pay you compensation if your financial services provider goes bust. FSCS is independent. The financial services industry funds FSCS and the compensation it pays. It does not charge anyone for using its services. There are limits to how much compensation it pays, and these are different for different types of financial products. To be eligible for compensation, the financial services firm must have been authorized by the Financial Services Authority (FSA). See website: **www.fscs.org.uk**.

Despite the safeguards of the Financial Services Act, when it comes to investment – or to financial advisers – there are no cast-iron guarantees. Under the investor protection legislation, all practitioners and/or the businesses they represent offering investment or similar services must be authorized by the FCA or, in certain cases, by a small number of designated professional bodies that themselves are answerable to the FCA. A basic question, therefore, to ask anyone offering investment advice or products is: are you registered and by whom? Information is easily checked via the Financial Conduct Authority website: **www.fca.org.uk**.

OTHER TYPES OF ADVISERS

Accountants

Accountants are specialists in matters concerning taxation. Many accountants can also help with raising finance and offer support with the preparation of business plans. Additionally, they may be able to advise in a general way about pensions and your proposed investment strategy. Most accountants, however, do not claim to be experts in these fields. If you need help in locating a suitable accountant, any of the following should be able to advise:

> Association of Chartered Certified Accountants (ACCA), website: **www.accaglobal.com**.

> Institute of Chartered Accountants in England and Wales (ICAEW): website: **www.icaew.co.uk**.

> Chartered Accountants Ireland (for both N Ireland and the Republic of Ireland: **www.charteredaccountants.ie**.

> Institute of Chartered Accountants of Scotland (ICAS): website: **www.icas.co.uk**.

Complaints

Anyone with a complaint against an accountancy firm should contact the company's relevant professional body for advice and assistance – see ACCA, ICAEW, CAI or ICAS, above.

Banks

Banks provide comprehensive services, in addition to the normal account facilities. These include investment, insurance and tax-planning services, as well as how to draw up a will. Other more specialized banks such as Hoare's, Coutts and overseas banks are all part of the UK clearing system and can offer a very good service. The main banks are listed below with their websites; if you prefer to call into your local branch, a specialist adviser should be able to assist you:

Barclays Bank plc: **www.barclays.co.uk**.

Co-operative Bank: **www.co-operativebank.co.uk**.

HSBC: **www.hsbc.co.uk**.

Lloyds TSB: **www.lloydstsb.com**.

NatWest (part of the RBS group): **www.natwest.com**.

RBS (Royal Bank of Scotland): **www.rbs.co.uk**.

Santander: **www.santander.co.uk**.

Complaints

The Financial Conduct Authority regulates the way that banks and building societies do business with you. If you have a complaint about a banking matter, you must first try to resolve the issue with the bank or building society concerned. If you remain dissatisfied, you can contact the Financial Ombudsman Service; see website: **www.financial-ombudsman.org.uk**.

Insurance brokers

The insurance business covers a very wide area, from straightforward policies – such as motor or household insurance – to rather more complex areas, including life assurance and pensions. Whereas IFAs specialize in advising on products and policies with some investment content, brokers primarily deal with the more straightforward type of insurance, such as motor, medical, household and holiday insurance. Some brokers are also authorized to give investment advice. A broker will help you to choose the policies best suited to you, assist with any claims, remind you when renewals are due and advise you on keeping your cover up to date.

An essential point to check before proceeding is that the firm the broker represents is regulated by the FCA. A condition of registration is that a broker must deal with a multiplicity of insurers and therefore be in a position to offer a comprehensive choice of policies. Generally speaking, you are safer using a larger brokerage with an established reputation. Also, before you take out a policy, it is advisable to consult several brokers in order to get a better feel for the market.

The British Insurance Brokers' Association represents nearly 2,200 insurance broking businesses and will help you find an insurance broker. See website: **www.biba.org.uk**.

Complaints

The Association of British Insurers (ABI) represents some 400 companies providing all types of insurance from life assurance and pensions to household, motor and other forms of general insurance. About 90 per cent of the worldwide business done by British insurance companies is handled by members of the ABI. For information on insurance products see website: **www.abi.org.uk**.

Occupational pension advice

If you are (or have been) in salaried employment and are a member of an occupational pension scheme, the normal person to ask is your company's personnel manager or pensions adviser or, via him or her, the pension fund trustees. Alternatively, if you have a problem with your pension you could approach your trade union, since this is an area where most unions are particularly active and well informed. If you are in need of specific help, a source to try could be The Pensions Advisory Service – for information on state, company, personal and stakeholder pensions, and for help with problems or complaints about pensions, see website: **www.pensionsadvisoryservice.org.uk**.

As with most other financial sectors, there is also a Pensions Ombudsman. You would normally approach the ombudsman if neither the pension scheme trustees nor the Pensions Advisory Service are able to solve your problem. Also, as with all ombudsmen, the Pensions Ombudsman can only investigate matters that come within its orbit. These are: complaints of maladministration by the trustees, managers or administrators of a pension scheme or by an employer; and disputes of fact or law with the trustees, managers or an employer. The Pension Ombudsman is also the Pension Protection Fund Ombudsman. See website: **www.pensions-ombudsman.org.uk**.

Another source of help is the Pension Tracing Service, which can provide individuals with contact details for a pension scheme with which they have lost touch. There is no charge for the service. See website: **www.direct.gov.uk/pensions**.

Four other organizations that are interested in matters of principle and broader issues affecting pensions are:

- National Association of Pension Funds, which is committed to ensuring that there is a sustainable environment for workplace pensions; website: **www.napf.co.uk**.

- The Pension Income Choice Association publishes a useful directory of retirement advisers and brokers; website: **www.pica.org**.

- The Pensions Regulator, for information about work-based pensions; website: **www.thepensionsregulator.gov.uk**.

- The National Federation of Occupational Pensioners (NFOP) for those in receipt of a company pension; website: **www.nfop.org.uk**.

Solicitors

Solicitors are professional advisers on subjects to do with the law or on matters that could have legal implications. Their advice can be invaluable in vetting any important document before you sign it. Often the best way to find a suitable lawyer (if you do not already have one) is through the recommendation of a friend or other professional adviser, such as an accountant. If you need a solicitor specifically for a business or professional matter, organizations such as your local Chambers of Commerce, small business associations, your professional institute or trade union may be able to put you in touch with someone in your area who has relevant experience.

Two organizations to contact for help are: The Law Society, website: **www.lawsociety.org.uk**; and Solicitors for Independent Financial Advice (SIFA), which is the trade body for solicitor financial advisers: **www.sifa.co.uk**.

Complaints

If you are unhappy about the service you have received from your solicitor, you should first try to resolve the matter with the firm through its complaints-handling partner. If you still feel aggrieved you can approach the Solicitors Regulation Authority: **www.sra.org.uk**.

For practical assistance if you are having problems with your solicitor, you can approach the Legal Services Ombudsman. This must be done within three months or your complaint will risk being out of time and the ombudsman will not be able to help you. See the Legal Services Ombudsman website: **www.legalombudsman.org.uk**.

General queries

For queries of a more general nature, you should approach the Law Society; see website: **www.lawsociety.org.uk**. For those living in Scotland or Northern Ireland, see The Law Society of Scotland; website: **www.lawscot.org.uk** or The Law Society of Northern Ireland; website: **www.lawsoc-ni.org**, respectively.

Stockbrokers

A stockbroker is a regulated professional broker who buys and sells shares and other securities through market makers or agency-only firms on behalf of investors. A broker may be employed by a brokerage firm. A transaction on the stock exchange must be made between two members of the exchange.

There are three types of stockbroking service:

- *Execution only*: which means the broker will carry out only the client's instructions to buy or sell.

- *Advisory dealing*: where the broker advises the client on which shares to buy and sell, but leaves the financial decision to the investor.

- *Discretionary dealing*: where the stockbroker ascertains the client's investment objectives and then makes all the dealing decisions on the client's behalf.

Roles similar to that of stockbroker include investment adviser and financial adviser. A stockbroker may or may not be an investment adviser. While some stockbrokers now charge fees in the same way as a solicitor, generally stockbrokers make their living by charging commission on every transaction. You will need to establish what the terms and conditions are before committing yourself, as these can vary quite considerably between one firm and another. Nearly all major stockbrokers now run unit trusts.

To find a stockbroker: you can approach an individual through a recommendation or visit the London Stock Exchange website: **www.londonstockexchange.com**, or the Association of Private Client Investment Managers and Stockbrokers (APCIMS) website: **www.apcims.co.uk**.

Complaints

If you need to make a complaint about a financial product or service we have included some hints and tips about how to frame a complaint and further sources of help in Chapter 7 and, in summary, these tips are worth noting here:

- What are you unhappy about?
- Try to stay calm. This can help you get your points across more clearly and effectively.
- Contact the business you think is responsible and explain what has gone wrong. Try to have any relevant information to hand, such as statements or policy documents.
- Put your complaint in writing – and keep a copy of your letter.
- Professional advisers will have a complaints procedure and, if the business doesn't settle the matter to your satisfaction, the Financial Ombudsman Service or the adviser's authorizing body may be able to help.

Financial Ombudsman Service (FOS)

This is a free service, set up by law with the power to sort out problems between consumers and financial businesses. Follow the steps outlined above, then contact the FOS, which will investigate your complaint. If the ombudsman considers the complaint justified, it can award compensation. See Financial Ombudsman Service website: **www.financial-ombudsman.org.uk**.

The FOS is the single contact point for dissatisfied customers, as it covers complaints across almost the entire range of financial services, including consumer credit activities (such as store cards, credit cards and hire-purchase transactions). The service is free; however, before contacting the FOS you must first try to resolve your complaint with the organization concerned (see above). Also, the ombudsman is powerless to act if legal proceedings have been started. See the Financial Ombudsman Service website: **www.financial-ombudsman.org.uk**; and also their hints and tips as outlined in Chapter 3.

Other useful websites are:

www.ukinvestmentadvice.co.uk;

www.thisismoney.co.uk;

www.moneyweek.com;

www.wwfp.net;

www.best-advice.co.uk;

www.investment-advice.org.uk.

Chapter Seven
Scams and complaints

ALLAN ESLER SMITH, FCA

Allan is a Fellow of the Institute of Chartered Accountants and now specializes in helping people start up in business (as you will read in Chapter 10). Previously Allan managed the investigations and recoveries team at Investors Compensation Scheme (the predecessor of our current Financial Services Compensation Scheme). Allan's work paved the way for millions of pounds of compensation to be paid to victims of financial mis-selling scandals. He therefore knows a thing or two about scams pulled in the past, through this and other senior investigation roles, and shares advice here on how to safeguard your wealth.

Intelligent, honest people don't fall victim to scammers, do they? Read on and save yourself money, time and effort.

I first came across the scammers as a student returning from a back-packing holiday around the Greek Islands. The bus stopped somewhere in the mountains of Yugoslavia for a lunch break. Within minutes the local lads were out with three shells and a pea and launched into their game. All you had to do was watch them place the pea under the shell and spot it after they shuffled the three shells. Winners doubled their stake. My friend and I had no money at this stage of our holiday but we watched the locals take apart our fellow students, which included future doctors, lawyers and accountants. It enlightened me to a whole new world. Accomplices pretend to play the game to entice new entrants; slick talking and lightning-fast sleight of hand then ensure novice players lose as the stakes get higher. Muscle then trails any unlikely big winner to retrieve the money through intimidation or theft. The concept has been alive and well for thousands of years. I really need *you* to pause and take this in. Scammers employ sleight of hand, fast talk and a few back-up techniques such as vanity and knowing that people never want to admit to being stupid. You will never spot what they have done in the same way as a good magician really will leave you believing that they made someone 'float' on stage. Smoke, mirrors, sleight of hand and anything can be made to look possible.

So how can we protect ourselves? First of all forget the 'it could never happen to me' line. I've lost count of how many times I've read a story and thought the victim should have known better. The old saying that 'a fool and their money are easily parted' comes to mind when people who receive a cold call go on to invest in some wholly useless investment. We have all read the 'case studies' in the finance sections of the Sunday newspapers. However, many of the victims are just like you and me but have encountered very professional scammers who have employed all their tricks and, before you know it, a payment has been made. If it was a few pounds you might write it off to bad luck and experience, but what if it was a few hundred pounds, a few thousand, or even more?

The main solution is all about knowledge and awareness and looking after each other. My five 'tests' will help some readers, as will the excellent hints and tips from our well-placed contributors.

Finally, and almost inevitably, things do sometimes go wrong in life. If you do lose out and have encountered a genuine business that is at fault, there is also a section in this chapter on complaints. Sometimes it is the way in which an organization responds to a complaint that makes you feel scammed. My 'how to and how not to' complain section may help you if things go wrong.

The five tests for staying safe from the scammers

The duck test

A respected detective superintendent summed up the duck test for me. The test flows from cutting short a debate over the identification of a crook (duck) and, out of pure frustration, is drawn to a close by 'It looks like a duck, it walks like a duck, it quacks like a duck – it is a (expletive deleted) duck!' It's a simple common-sense approach – ignore the smoke and mirrors and sleight of hand – anything that is used to distract you from the real issue. Does it look, feel, and 'smell' like a scam? If so walk away, put the letter in the bin or put down the phone.

The granny test

Trust your instincts, especially after you ask yourself the rather telling question about whether you would let the character you are dealing with anywhere near an elderly relative on the subject of money or financial advice. Instincts have been honed in the human species over thousands of years – if they have served you well in the past, learn to trust them.

Actions speak louder than words

Scammers, generally, are all talk (unsurprisingly, they are very good at it) and no action. Delivering against what is said for any reasonable person should be easy to achieve. If the actions don't happen, then just walk away and don't give them a second chance to take advantage of you.

Too good to be true?

Scammers know that greed can get the better of many people and employ it to their purposes. If it sounds too good to be true, it is probably a scam.

Thank you but I'll just check with...

We have great financial institutions in the UK and this goes to the very heart of the UK economy. Our regulatory system is sound. You should therefore check precisely who you are dealing with. If it is a company and it is not a high-street name check out the company at Companies House (**www.companieshouse.gov.uk**) to see how long it has been in existence and whether it has filed its accounts on time. This will never be definitive but it is something you can check for yourself – and it can be very telling if the company involved has only been around for a year. For more definitive assurance and for investments you really must check that the firm is regulated by the Financial Conduct Authority (**www.fca.org.uk**). After all, the FCA says: 'Our aim is to help firms put the interests of their customers and the integrity of the market at the core of what they do.' If it is an investment and it is not regulated by the FCA then, again, this tells its own story and, if things go wrong, you are more likely to be on your own.

Also linked to the 'I'll just check with...' tip is the simple fact that crooks have one other objective in addition to taking your hard-earned cash – and that is not getting caught out. This is where nosy neighbours are brilliant – and a stroll over and a few questions can be of great assistance. The scammers quickly move on. This chapter unfolds with some examples of current scams and, to help you, we have also harnessed some further hints and tips from those at the forefront of fighting the scammers.

Some common scams

Advance fee fraud

This is one of the scammer's favourites and has been dressed up in a hundred different guises. The spine is remarkably simple. A payment is made by you with the promise of a bigger payout in return. Perhaps it is cloaked in terms of funds left to you by a mystery relative, where you pay a processing fee of £50, then maybe you are asked to pay another release fee of £150 and on it goes with a promise of £10,000 sucking you in (which, of course, you will never actually receive).

The surprise prize-ballot win

There is usually a premium-rate telephone number to call in order to claim the prize and the ultimate actual prize is probably worthless or trivial. File anything like this under 'B' for bin. It is, however, sometimes fun to read the small print in such 'prizes' in order to spot the scam or the impossibility of winning the surprise big win. This is how it works: there will be a token nominal prize for which there may be 10,000 or more winners and it will probably take you more than £15 in phone or other charges to 'win' and the prize will be pretty useless. As a final deterrent if you do reply, you are likely to be put on a 'suckers list' and will be bombarded by even more junk ballots and scams. Remember... just file under 'B' for bin.

Romance scams

The new lover or someone showing you interest or attention who, and unremarkably, shows you the attention you crave just when you need it or are at a low point. Maybe then they need some money for a sick mother or child. Scammers can be very clever and know how to manipulate you to get the response they want. They usually want you to keep things 'secret' as they know that any friend you confide in will tell you to run a mile. Sadly, emotional involvement and shame prevent people from acting rationally – and the scammers know this. Smoke, mirrors, sleight of hand and, just like a magician, your money is gone before you know it.

Credit and bank card cloning or snatching

This can be the jackpot for the scammers, but how can they actually get your credit or bank card? The cloning devices that they attach to a bank's cash machine are not so far-fetched these days. But how about the scammer who calls you and pretends to be from the police, explaining that they have just arrested someone who 'apparently' was caught with a clone of your card. They arrange for a courier to call and collect your actual card as part of their investigations. Unfortunately it is all just another scam and the supposed police officer is just another scammer. These guys really do have balls, but the bottom line is never ever to be worried about feeling to be made to look silly. Follow our five tips – and then if you spot a scam or have been scammed, report it and get help. Contact the Police Action Fraud team on 0300 123 2040 or online at **www.actionfraud.police.uk**, or contact the police in your area – unless a crime is in progress or about to be, the suspect is known or can be easily identified, or the crime involves a vulnerable victim, in which case dial 999 if it is an emergency or 101 if it isn't.

But don't just take my word for it. The Metropolitan Police are at the forefront of fighting fraud with Operation Sterling in their Specialist, Organized and Economic Crime Command. They know their crooks and know why the crooks are interested in us. We asked them about current trends and 'hotspots'. Their spokesperson set the scene very neatly:

MP: The over-50s are a more trusting generation and therefore more likely to be taken in by fraudsters and they tend to have more money at their immediate disposal and more that can be readily accessed.

We are seeing individuals with form for burglary, robbery and drug dealing being arrested in connection with fraud. Criminals follow the money. Where some have had success, others will follow.

AES: So what are the current 'hotspots'?

MP: Courier fraud is a particular type of fraud that is sweeping the country. It originated in London – at the time of writing the Metropolitan Police Service has had over 4,000 offences – but there have been incidents in almost every force area. In London, the average age of the victim is 74 and the average loss over £3,000 but we have seen a number of incidents where victims have lost over £50,000.

AES: This is part of the credit or bank card cloning or snatching we highlighted above, isn't it?

MP: Basically, yes, that's right. It's a real hotspot in 2014 and in 2015 we want everyone to watch out for it, so I will give you some more detail on this one. The crime has evolved over the last year but typically a fraudster will phone you at home pretending to be a police officer or a bank employee. He or she will be reading from a well-rehearsed script – they may be making hundreds of telephone calls a day until they succeed. They may say that they have arrested an individual with a cloned copy of your bank card (or if pretending to be a bank, say that there has been some recent unusual spending on your card) and that they need to confirm your personal and banking details.

To engender trust they typically ask you to dial 999 (or the telephone number on the back of your bank card) and ask to be put back through to the police officer (or bank employee). However, the fraudster keeps the line open at their end so no matter who you call, you end up speaking to the fraudster or their 'colleague'.

They then proceed to ask for your personal and banking details and will often ask you for your PIN or ask you to type it using your phone keypad. The fraudster uses special technology to decipher the keypad number tones. As a result they have all your details, including your PIN.

They will then say that they need your card for evidence (or if from the bank they may say that they need it for their investigations and will send out a replacement) and will send someone (typically a taxi or courier) to collect your card, often asking you to place it in an envelope and write a fake reference number on it – again, to engender trust but in fact the reference number means nothing. The taxi driver will then take the card to the fraudster (typically on a street corner) and the fraudster will then go on a spending spree as he or she has your card and PIN.

AES: It seems strange that people are taken in by this, doesn't it?

MP: No, not at all. I think people are just scared of being made to look silly and your magician analogy is spot on. Quick hands, quick talk and a bit of distraction and anything can happen. Over the last six months there has been a common variation with fraudsters claiming to be a police officer and asking for your help to investigate a bank employee at a particular branch. You may be asked to go to your local branch and ask to withdraw a large amount of cash – sometimes thousands of pounds. You are told that the objective is to get the bank employee's fingerprints on the cash and you are told not to tell anyone else about what you are doing, as it may compromise the investigation. There have been variations where the fraudster, pretending to be the police, goes on to scam the victim into thinking that their house is being targeted by burglars and persuades you to hand over valuables such as jewellery and electronics.

AES: We have set out some tests and tips earlier but this emerging scam sounds very sinister. Do have you any further tips?

MP: Your bank or the police will never ask for your PIN, your bank card or ask you to withdraw cash.

Never share your PIN with anyone – the only time you should use your PIN is at a cash machine or when you use a shop's chip and PIN machine.

Never give your bank card or any goods you have purchased as a result of a phone call to anyone who comes to your front door.

The Metropolitan Police Service has highlighted to OFCOM (the phone company regulators) the ability of fraudsters (or anyone else) to hold telephone lines open and, as a result, changes to the telephone systems are being introduced. However, to ensure safety if you are asked to phone back via 999 or a bank to confirm a caller's identity, wait at least five minutes or use a phone that has a different line – eg mobile phone or neighbour's phone.

The Metropolitan Police spokesperson then returned to another of the common scams we featured earlier – the surprise prize-ballot win. Scam lotteries are becoming a real menace and people are losing out. If you reply to just one of these letters you risk being inundated by more and the police spokesperson agreed that your name will form part of a 'suckers list'. This list is then traded amongst scam-mail fraudsters. Genuine lotteries will not ask you to pay a fee to collect your winnings. For more information visit **www.thinkjessica.com**. Operation Sterling is also working with Royal Mail to prevent scam mail entering the UK and being delivered to UK residents; you can help by reporting it at **scam.mail@royalmail.com** or report concerns by calling 08456 113413.

Keeping safe from telephone cold calls, e-mail scammers and online fraud

The above examples are just some of the higher-profile and potentially higher-value scams, but there are many more. Some of them you may encounter over the phone and internet on a weekly basis.

Cold callers on the telephone can be irritating at best and sometimes downright scary. They may not take 'no' for an answer. The way these calls are intruding into our life is becoming a real problem.

In a recent experience I had, my phone rings again and there is a temporary silence then a click and then the buzz of chatter in the background. It's yet another cold call from some overseas country that I really don't want to receive.

'Good afternoon, it's John from UK Lifestyle Survey.' I ask where he is calling from. 'I'm calling from India,' John says and cheerfully explains that he is representing UK leading energy suppliers and wants to know who my energy supplier is. I say that I am not prepared to say and he puts down the phone. These calls are just seeking to gather marketing data from you. The data is then sold on and you will be bombarded with more calls and literature after you are put on a 'suckers list'.

'Good morning, we are opening a home improvement shop in the local area and we would like to send you a £1,000 voucher': calls like these are also just seeking to gather marketing data and replying will just cause you to get more and more calls. This call is from the UK and I use the magic words 'I am signed up for the Telephone Preference Service and you should not be calling this number,' which helps them 'go away'.

The Telephone Preference Service (TPS) is a free service. It is the official central opt-out register on which you can record your preference not to receive unsolicited sales or marketing calls. It is a legal requirement that all organizations (including charities, voluntary organizations and political parties) do not make such calls to numbers registered on the TPS unless they have your consent to do so. You can register your phone number with the telephone preference service by calling 0845 070 0707 or you can do this online at **www.tpsonline.org.uk**.

Another day and another nuisance call. 'Good morning, your computer has reported a fault to Microsoft,' and they went on to explain that they were calling to help me fix it. Apparently they had 'received an error report from Windows' and in a fanfare they championed, 'We are Microsoft certified.'

'Please turn on your computer and check...' I had to intervene at this point as a good friend who works in IT had warned me about this lot. 'They are after access to your computer and it is like walking up to a stranger in the street and handing them your wallet.' After a moment's reflection my friend added, 'No, it's actually worse than that.' Basically these people are scammers; they take you through a very basic procedure that reveals an error code and they use your non-knowledge of IT to make you feel vulnerable. At best, they then get you to sign up for a maintenance package, which they say will improve the performance of your computer. At worst, they will gain access to your computer and leave spyware/software on it to collect data such as bank and other passwords – and you can imagine where this story will lead.

If these calls bug you, then sign up today for the TPS. Its powers in dealing with overseas callers are limited to information sharing with overseas authorities. However, armed with feedback from you they may be able to bring some pressure to bear on the way these overseas firms are intruding on our privacy and then scamming us. The TPS can definitely assist if UK-based callers are making nuisance marketing calls. My advice on overseas callers is just to state: 'I am a member of the Telephone Preference Service and you should not be calling me. What is your name, where are you calling from and what is your telephone number?' But don't hope for much, as one told me he was calling from Buckingham Palace Road! Do not engage in any other conversation, and then consider passing on the three facts to the TPS. In addition, and best of all, new technology allows you to acquire telephones that display the inbound number and, even better, block certain numbers including overseas numbers (other than those you want to receive).

E-mail scammers

The ingenuity and creativity of the e-mail scammers are reaching new heights. Someone somewhere has gathered thousands of e-mail addresses, including yours, and mass-mails them with a piece of information – designed with only one purpose in mind. That purpose is to gain your attention and engagement. All scam e-mails end up the same way, which is you losing out. I see a few e-mails every week offering a refund from HMRC or a bank, indicating that the security of my account has been compromised. The e-mail asks me to click on a link and then follow the instructions. The quality of the websites you link to is usually convincing, with lots of branding and official-looking information. Unfortunately, the reality is that they have been built by scammers and they want to steal your money. Never click on any refund links and always check with the organization directly.

Generally try to protect yourself by restricting yourself to known organizations and deal directly with their websites. If it is a UK business they must clearly show the company or business operating the website (usually in the 'contact us' or 'about us' section), which you can then check out – if in doubt... leave them out.

The other trigger that may help you to spot a fraudster e-mail is that they usually want you to act immediately. Recently I began to think that I had a pretty unlucky bunch of clients as a few had been mugged while abroad. Apparently their mobile phone had been stolen but they had access to e-mail and needed me to urgently wire £500 until their credit cards had been cancelled and reissued. Recognizing a potential scam I telephoned my clients to ask 'How are you?' and everything was, of course, fine. To cut to the end of the story, e-mail accounts were hacked and the scammers had sent out £500 requests to every person on the client's e-mail address book. Coming from real e-mail addresses it had all seemed plausible but, as already mentioned, the ingenuity and creativity of the e-mail scammers are reaching new heights. On this point you should think about changing your e-mail account password to a long, weird password with a mix of characters and numbers. Passwords like 'Password123' or 'Letmein', or your name spelt backwards, are ripe for picking off by the hackers.

Online fraud

One of the most common frauds at the moment is around the online sale of concert and event tickets, residential and holiday lettings, dating and romance scams and vehicles for sale.

There have been thousands of victims of online advert fraud. In 2014 the Metropolitan Police was investigating a case involving 3,500 victims across the country with a total loss of over £10.5 million. Victims have often transferred thousands of pounds into other bank accounts in the belief that they are buying a vehicle or some other product that they have successfully purchased through online sale/auction platforms and websites. However, the item they have paid for never actually turns up.

Again I turned to the Metropolitan Police's Operation Sterling team to understand a little more about this – as knowledge is king in the fight against the scammers. Their spokesperson explained:

> MP: Often, there are a series of e-mails going between the suspect and the victim during which the victim believes they are building a relationship with the suspect and levels of trust are increased. Sometimes the victim is persuaded that any money will go into an escrow/holding account and therefore the money is safe in the event that anything goes wrong. This is false and, in essence, the victim pays money to someone they have never met for something they have never seen. What chance is there of recovering their money, bearing in mind that e-mail addresses often cannot be traced, telephone numbers routinely have no subscribers and addresses given are false, and it is relatively easy to open a UK bank account with either stolen or false identity documents?

> AES: So what can we do to protect ourselves?

> MP: Read and follow the fraud prevention advice given on the auction websites themselves. Do not be tempted to stray from that advice. Consider the risks. Does the price of the item you are proposing to buy sound too good to be true? Do not let the excitement of a bargain get in the way of applying good common sense and caution. Consider viewing the item before purchase, especially if it is a significant sum of money. Also be aware that fraudsters copy genuine adverts and then change the contact details.
>
> In addition, there is some important general advice that should be followed; never open up attachments contained in e-mails that

you have received from someone you do not know. There are thousands of types of 'spam' e-mails that will ask you for personal and banking details whilst offering tax or other financial refunds, lottery prizes, etc. Others are threatening: for example, if you do not fill out certain details you will not be able to access your bank account, etc. Simply delete them.

Finally, ensure you have antivirus software on your computer and keep it up to date. Consider your personal safety before meeting with someone you have had contact with over the internet – take a friend along.

The Metropolitan Police Service's Operation Sterling has written *The Little Book of Big Scams*. This is now in its second edition and can be viewed online and printed. It has also been given to other forces who are printing their own copies. The booklet can be seen and printed by visiting **http://www.met.police.uk/fraudalert/**. The booklet provides further information on a variety of common frauds and advice on how to prevent yourself from falling victim.

Reporting fraud can be done online at **www.actionfraud.police.uk** or over the telephone on 0300 123 2040. In an emergency, dial 999. At Operation Sterling we know the crooks and scammers inside out. Be assured that the most effective method to combat fraud is to prevent it in the first place. Awareness of common frauds and taking simple action to prevent yourself from falling victim is the most vital thing you can do... so spread the word.

Complaints and 'how to complain'

Things in life inevitably go wrong and sometimes you lose out when it was not your fault. It is always satisfying when you explain your complaint and an organization says: 'We are terribly sorry for the inconvenience we have caused you. Thank you for taking the time to set out your concerns. We have now fixed the issue and it will not happen again and we would like you to accept a bunch of flowers as our way of saying sorry.'

This sort of response is rare and I find it irritating the way more and more companies hide behind websites and it is almost impossible to find someone to speak to directly. Perhaps some businesses will see the benefit of reverting to two-way communications. Many consumers are willing to pay that little bit more for decent service and the assurance that when something goes wrong there will be someone there to do something about it. Perhaps that is one of the reasons for the success of companies such as the John Lewis Partnership.

While *The Good Retirement Guide*'s campaign for better customer service continues, my hints and tips on complaints might just help you to get a better outcome:

- When something goes wrong contact the firm or organization responsible straight away and give them a chance to sort out the problem. It is only fair that they have a chance to look into your complaint as there are usually two sides to any story and perhaps you have simply misunderstood the situation. Clearly state your complaint. Spend time thinking about this beforehand so that you can be clear and concise about what has happened and what you expect. If you are vague and unclear when you complain then you can expect a vague and unclear reply. If you want compensation, state how much and why.

- When you complain, keep a note of who you spoke to, the date and time, and what they said will happen next and by when. Ask whether it would help if you put your complaint in writing.

- If the issue is not resolved, take steps to make it a formal complaint. Ask the organization for the name, address, telephone number and e-mail of the person or department that deals with complaints. Write a letter and head it up 'FORMAL COMPLAINT' in capitals. Spend time getting it factually correct and attach supporting evidence. If it goes beyond two pages it sounds like you could be rambling. Don't worry – we all do this when we feel aggrieved – but it probably means you need to set it aside and come back to it. Reread it and relegate some information to an attachment if it goes beyond two pages. Send it by recorded delivery and keep a copy, together with the post office tracking receipt.

- Take the case further if the organization rejects your complaint and you believe they have not addressed your concerns. Unfortunately some customer relations teams really don't seem to care what you say or how unfairly you have been treated and will just go through a formula approach. At best they may say 'Here are some discount vouchers to use against your next booking...' or words to that effect.

- If you remain dissatisfied, say so, and ask how you can escalate your complaint. Some organizations will try to get rid of you by sending you a 'go away' letter. This needs some explanation. They will say that they have 'fully considered' your complaint and have now exhausted all opportunities to reach a conclusion. The punchline is that they will no longer respond to any further letters or communications from you and they will close their file. At this stage it is up to you to decide whether to give up (that is what they want) or take them to court (but this could be expensive and is it really worth it?).

- But there may be another route. Some organizations have independent assessors and their service is completely free (for instance, Companies House and other quasi government agencies). Some have a free ombudsman service (banks, financial advisers, mobile phones). Others have regulating bodies (solicitors, surveyors and chartered accountants) that may be able to intervene on your behalf. Help could also be at hand from Citizens Advice, who also have very useful template letters and advice for complainants at **www.adviceguide.org.uk**.

- If there is no external organization, you could choose to use a complaints management service. These, however, charge a fee, so make sure you understand the costs you will have to pay. You could also consider legal proceedings, but again consider the costs you will pay including, perhaps, the other side's costs if the court decides you are wrong.

- Another useful route is to consider if mediation or arbitration is possible. The ABTA arbitration scheme, for example, deals with alleged breaches of contract and/or negligence between consumers and members of ABTA, the travel organization, and has been in operation for over 40 years. I have used it myself and was awarded £600 after initially being offered £200 in holiday vouchers after a 'full consideration' of my complaint by one of the leading holiday firms in the UK. The scheme is provided so that consumers can have disputes resolved without having to go to court and without having to go to the expense of instructing solicitors. It is important to understand that arbitration is a legal process; this means that if you do go through arbitration, but are not happy with the outcome, you cannot then go to court. You have to choose one or the other when pursuing your complaint.

- The final and perhaps most important tip is to consider whether or not your complaint is really worth the effort of pursuing. Perhaps an organization has been wrong and you have been dealt with unfairly. You should, of course, think about taking the first step as outlined above. But then do you just vote with your feet and go elsewhere – and tell your friends about it? Sadly I have to report that I have seen complainants who just went on and on (and on) making the same points that had been dealt with by the organization they are complaining against. The complainants then availed themselves of all appeal mechanisms, including involving their MPs. Perhaps they just didn't fully understand the issues or maybe they had too much time on their hands but they just managed to dig themselves into a rut. Obviously, this is to be avoided.

I hope this section tunes up your ability to complain more effectively or helps you just to drop the matter and move on. In addition to the Citizens Advice help, mentioned above, there is some further free help available (including letter templates) at the government-funded The Money Advice Service at **www.moneyadviceservice.org.uk** or on the Money Advice Line at 0300 500 5000.

Further reading

Our top four recommendations for further help, guidance and support on scams and complaints are:

- *The Little Book of Big Scams*, published by the Metropolitan Police Service, PSNI and other forces. You can download the booklet at **www.met.police.uk/docs/little_book_scam.pdf**.
- BBC's 'Rip Off Britain' via **www.bbc.co.uk**, then 'Rip Off Britain' and then their section on consumer advice.
- The Money Advice Service offering free, unbiased and independent help via **www.moneyadviceservice.org.uk**.
- Citizens Advice: **www.adviceguide.org.uk**.

Chapter Eight
Your home

"Don't own so much clutter that you will be relieved to see your house catch fire. WENDELL BERRY (AUTHOR)

According to the Office for National Statistics (ONS), nearly 60 per cent of the country's £7.3 trillion net worth is tied up in housing. It's no mystery as to why the well-off down the ages have invested so heavily in property: desirable land and buildings are a particularly durable form of wealth. Housing ownership lies at the very heart of middle-class aspiration. As house prices rise, people feel wealthier and they spend more. For most people in their 50s and 60s, their home becomes increasingly precious. There are around 10 million over-65s in Britain and the ONS says that figure will increase to more than 16 million by 2033. Retired homeowners currently have a total property wealth owned outright of more than £752 billion. The Office for Budget Responsibility recently revised its forecast suggesting that house prices in Britain could soar by 30 per cent by 2019. That means a house worth £250,000 today could cost £325,000 in four years' time.

Reaching retirement provides an ideal opportunity to consider whether your current home is the place in which you want to remain. This is a personal decision, dictated by many things. 'Future proofing' your home is something that a lot of people should do as they get older. Some things to consider include:

- can you get around your current home safely and manage its upkeep?
- do you have good support networks in the area – family, friends and neighbours?

- can you get to the places you need and want to go easily – by car, on foot, or by public transport?
- are you reasonably confident that this will still be the case in 5 or 10 years, or if your health and other circumstances change?

If the answer is 'no' to some of these questions, it might be the right time to investigate possible alternatives – in your local area or in another area, perhaps closer to family. Many retirees regard locality as highly important, and prefer to live within a familiar, safe community. Transport links need to be good quality and suitable. Many people put emotional considerations, such as the 'feel' of a home, as a priority. Even if you don't want to move now, thinking about the possibility will give you more choice in future, should your circumstances change. Make your decisions carefully, don't be rushed or persuaded by others: it is far better than making a costly mistake.

Staying put

Moving house is one of the most stressful things in life, so on reaching retirement you may prefer to sit tight. There are things to consider in terms of adapting your home to suit your needs once you've retired. Are you likely to need to convert a room for use as a study, or find extra space somewhere to pursue a favourite hobby? But beware, currently large numbers of 20–35-year-olds are moving back in with their parents (dubbed the 'Magpie Generation' because they come home to roost) in an attempt to cut down their overheads. This can put pressure on parents financially. But if you have a family-sized home free of magpies, you could consider letting one or two rooms. As well as solving the problem of empty space, it would also bring in some extra income.

Ways of increasing the size of and adding value to your property

There are many ways to improve your property and maximize its potential. If you're considering doing building works, be sure to get three quotes for each job, and references from previous clients. Make sure you apply for planning permission if you are adding an extension, and make it as big as permitted. Even a few more square metres can make a huge difference to space. Smaller extensions to the rear or side of a property can often be built without having to make a planning application, provided that the design complies with the rules for permitted development (see **www.planningportal.gov.uk**). Digging out a basement is very expensive, so it's only worth doing on valuable properties. You are much more likely to see a return on your investment from a loft conversion. Keep things in proportion – extra bedrooms are no good if there aren't enough bathrooms. Remember, any new work must comply with building regulations. Most important, under the Party Wall Act, where appropriate you must notify your neighbours. It is wise always to check with your local authority first before committing to any work.

If your budget allows, becoming your own neighbour by purchasing the next-door property is a great way to increase your property's value. Knocking through allows more space than an extension, without incurring moving costs or leaving the neighbourhood. But this option is neither cheap nor simple. Professional advice from an architect is essential, so that the finished conjoined house looks right. This also makes selling the property much easier in the future.

Even if you live in a flat you might be able to buy the adjoining unit or the one above or below, then knock through or install a staircase to achieve double living space. Any construction work being undertaken must, of course, adhere strictly to planning and building regulations and you must ensure the project is completed properly. With regard to any home extension or 'knock-through' option, if you can remain living in the property while the building work is being carried out then the disruption is less dramatic. Owners living on-site often make for a smoother and swifter conclusion to the project.

If there is no scope to go outwards or upwards, extending below ground level is proving increasingly popular, particularly in higher-value areas such as central London. Planning permission is normally required but is not usually an obstacle, because the new space has no visual impact on the streetscape. Converting an existing cellar is less expensive and does not usually require planning permission (however, do check first with your local authority). For further information, consult The Basement Information Centre; see **www.basements.org.uk**.

Another popular way to increase space in your home is to build above a garage. A conversion of this kind is reasonably simple and increases the size of your home easily and quickly. Any scheme would be subject to appropriate planning permission being granted. This is needed because of the extra height and alteration to the roof line. Whether your garage is single size or double, attached or detached, this type of extension is one of the quickest 'wins' because you are working with what you've got and you are spared the necessity of digging new foundations. You could extend into the garage itself as well as building above, if it's not being used to house a car. Rooms above a detached garage make an ideal guest suite, office, study, granny or nanny flat (or somewhere to carry on a noisy hobby). Should this idea appeal, search the internet for specialist companies dealing solely with garage conversions

Moving to a new home

Should moving to a new home be right for you, start looking at the various options and avoid rushing into anything. Moving to a new neighbourhood will require careful consideration: such as access to shops and social activities, proximity to friends and relatives, availability of public transport, health and social support services; and access to high-speed broadband is becoming another desirable asset for many. Living in the countryside is not always problem-free for older people. Lack of public transport is one of the main causes of rural deprivation, with the loss of village shops, pub and post offices being another. Moving from a city to a rural location in retirement is a major lifestyle change, and anyone contemplating this should review all the pros and cons before coming to a decision.

Points to consider when downsizing

- Saving money. The costs of running a smaller property will be substantially lower, reducing outgoings at the point when your income reduces in retirement.

- A family home will require more maintenance and have higher council tax. Don't hold on to more space than you need.

- If you have a large garden this could prove burdensome as you get older and are less agile.

- Releasing equity from your old property and the sale of your primary residence is free from capital gains tax (CGT).

- Moving to a purpose-built property with the needs of older people in mind is popular. You could gain a ready-made community and it will be a safe environment.

- If you are considering moving to a smaller property, discarding treasured possessions that are surplus to requirements is not easy. Check with family members to see if there are any items they want. Don't keep things you don't or can't use: pass on unwanted items to someone who could use them. For further help and advice, APDO UK is the Association of Professional De-clutterers and Organisers UK; see: **www.apdo-uk.co.uk**.

If you decide that a move is for you, even if you think you know an area well, check it out properly before coming to a final decision. If possible, take a self-catering let for a couple of months, preferably out of season when rents are low and the weather is bad. Do your research and look at the Office for National Statistics neighbourhood statistics website: **www.neighbourhoodstatistics.gov.uk**.

A good website to study for potential properties is: Rightmove: **www.rightmove.co.uk**.

If you are thinking of moving abroad, this requires careful consideration. Points to research: the political climate of that country; being far away from friends and family; not having the same health care arrangements and having to learn a new language – to name a few. For more information on the financial implications of living overseas, see the section 'Retiring abroad' in Chapter 4.

Counting the cost

Moving house can be expensive: it is estimated that the cost is between 5 and 10 per cent of the value of a new home, once you have added in search fees, removal charges, insurance, stamp duty, VAT, legal fees and estate agents' commission. There is a good guide to stamp duty land tax (SDLT) on HM Revenue & Customs website: **www.hmrc.gov.uk**.

When buying a new home, especially an older property, a full building (structural) survey is essential before committing yourself. This costs upwards of £500 depending on the type and size of property, but it will provide you with a comeback in law should things go wrong. A valuation report is cheaper but more superficial and may fail to detect flaws that could give you trouble and expense in the future.

If you are buying a newly built house, most mortgagees will lend on new homes only if they have a National House Building Council (NHBC) warranty or its equivalent. This is a 10-year 'Buildmark' residential warranty and insurance scheme under which the builder is responsible for putting right defects during the first two years. It is designed to protect owners of newly built or newly converted residential housing if a problem does occur in a new home registered with NHBC. See website: **www.nhbc.co.uk**. Also helpful to homebuyers, the Land Registry allows members of the public to seek information directly about the 23 million or so properties held on its register via the Land Registry website: **www.landregistry.gov.uk**.

If you are selling your home, you no longer require a Home Information Pack (HIP), but the requirement for the Energy Performance Certificate (EPC) has been retained, whether you are selling or renting out.

Energy Performance Certificates (EPCs)

An EPC rates the property's energy use and suggests ways to make energy-saving improvements. The EPC rating is on an A–G scale (like the EU energy label used on fridges and other white goods); the higher the rating, the more energy efficient the home is. The average UK home has a 'D' rating. Newer homes generally use less energy, so a recently built home should have an EPC rating of 'B' or above. EPCs are produced by accredited domestic energy assessors and cost from £30 to £80, depending on the size of the property. Vendors are required to commission (but won't need to have received) an EPC before marketing their property.

Information

For details about local domestic energy assessors see EPC Register; website: **www.epcregister.com**.

For a free and impartial home energy check visit Energy Saving Trust; website: **www.energysavingtrust.org.uk**.

For advice on leasehold legislation and policy, search: **www.gov.uk**.

For your protection

There is a Property Ombudsman scheme to provide an independent review service for buyers or sellers of UK residential property in the event of a complaint, also covering lettings agents and residential leasehold management. As with most ombudsman schemes, action can be taken only against firms that are actually members of the scheme. See The Property Ombudsman website: **www.tpos.co.uk**.

Living in leasehold

An ever-increasing number of people move into a flat as a retirement home. If acquiring a leasehold flat, there are one or two things to bear in mind before you buy. The freeholder of the building may be an investment company, a private investor, or ideally the leaseholders themselves in the form of a management company. With the advent of 'right to manage', leaseholders do not need to own the freehold but will be able to manage the building as if they were the freeholder. While it is important that leaseholders are aware of their rights, it is fundamental they are aware of their responsibilities. Principally this will be to keep the inside of their flat in good order, to pay their share of the cost of maintaining and running the building, to behave in a neighbourly manner and not to do certain things as set out in the lease, such as sublet their flat without the freeholder's prior consent, or keep a pet when the lease clearly states this is not permitted.

As for rights, first and foremost is the peaceful occupation of the flat, often referred to as 'quiet enjoyment'. In addition, the leaseholder has the right to expect the freeholder to maintain the building and common parts for which the leaseholder will be required to pay a 'service charge'. This is a payment made by a leaseholder to the freeholder or their managing agent to maintain, repair and insure the building as well as to provide other services, such as lifts, central heating or cleaners. These charges are liable to change from one year to the next, but must at all times be 'reasonable'. Leaseholders have a right to challenge the service charge if they feel it is 'unreasonable' via the Leasehold Valuation Tribunal (LVT). It is important to find out what the current charges are and the likely charges for future years and what, if any, reserves are held to cover the cost of major works such as external decoration of the building. For further information, see:

Leasehold Advisory Service (LAS): **www.lease-advice.org**.

Association of Retirement Housing Managers (ARHM):
www.arhm.org.

Retiring abroad

A number of people contemplating an adventurous retirement raise funds on their family home in the UK and purchase a small property abroad, becoming what is known as 'residential tourists'. This means they travel to and from their other house without much luggage and spend several months of each year in their overseas home. Such a property abroad tends to fall into the category of 'lock up and leave' and it bridges the gap between selling up and moving completely from the country you've lived in for years. It allows a certain amount of thinking time before you make a decision on whether or not the foreign property will at some point become your 'forever' home.

But for some, life as an expatriate isn't all roses. Since the credit crunch it has not been possible to get a UK mortgage on a property abroad, or even remortgage an existing property. Banks are not particularly helpful: some expats have seen their offshore bank accounts closed down or with a reduction of services offered to non-residents. Others who already live abroad have difficulties because they have no UK address. Another problem is people choosing to live in a certain place because a low-cost airline flies into a nearby airport, only to find a few years later that the airline no longer flies to that airport, making it difficult and expensive for them to visit friends and family back home.

Should you be considering retiring abroad, life may get more expensive. There are a number of additional costs, besides purchasing the property: legal expenses, notary fees, stamp duty, registration fees and local taxes, costs of a solicitor and surveyor and the cost of making a new will. Removal costs from the UK to the new country can be quite heavy too. So if you decide to retire overseas, be careful. Some ways of protecting yourself when buying property abroad include:

- Get all documents translated.
- If you are given something to sign, make sure you have a 14-day cooling-off period.
- Take the documents home to the UK and speak to a lawyer and financial adviser over here rather than in the country overseas.
- Make sure the lawyer you use is independent and not involved in the sale in any way.
- Do not use a lawyer recommended by the seller.
- If you are buying a repossessed property, find out what happened.

- If you are borrowing money, go to a reputable bank. The bank manager will want to be sure that the deal is sound – this adds another layer of checks and protection.

There are many websites offering advice and information on retiring abroad. Have a browse through the following:

www.gov.uk – Britons preparing to move or retire abroad.

www.propertyinretirement.co.uk – section on retiring abroad.

www.buyassociation.co.uk – section on advice on retiring abroad and homes abroad.

www.retirementexpert.co.uk – section on retiring abroad and popular locations.

www.shelteroffshore.com – information on living abroad.

www.expatfocus.com – provides essential information and advice for a successful move abroad.

Removals

Professional help is essential for anyone contemplating a house move. A reputable firm of removers and shippers will eliminate many of the headaches. A full packing service can save much anxiety and a lot of your time. Costs vary depending on the type and size of furniture, the distance over which it is being moved and other factors, including insurance and seasonal troughs and peaks. Get at least three quotes from different removal firms. Remember, the cheapest may not necessarily be the best. Find out exactly what you are paying for and whether the price includes packing and insurance. The British Association of Removers (BAR) promotes excellence in the removals industry; for approved member firms all of whom work to a rigorous code of practice, see their website: **www.bar.co.uk**.

Retirement housing and sheltered accommodation

Property that caters for older buyers is on the increase, whether that is specially developed villages – that provide independence, a like-minded community and, also, help and assistance where needed – or town-centre developments aimed at 'empty nesters', or developments that have varying levels of care attached to them. The terms 'retirement housing' and 'sheltered accommodation' cover a wide variety of housing but are designed primarily to bridge the gap between the family home and residential care. There are many well-designed, high-quality private developments of 'retirement homes' now on the market, for sale or rent, at prices to suit most pockets. As a general rule, you have to be over 55 when you buy property of this kind. While you may not wish to move into this type of accommodation just now, it is worth planning ahead, as there are often very long waiting lists. For full details see Chapter 15 (Caring for elderly parents).

Other options

Caravan or mobile home

Many retired people consider living in a caravan or mobile home. You may already own one as a holiday home that you are thinking of turning into more permanent accommodation. If you want to live in a caravan on land you own, or other private land, you should contact your local authority for information about any planning permission or site licensing requirements that may apply. If you want to keep it on an established site, there is a varied choice. Check carefully, whichever you choose, that the site owner has all the necessary permissions. All disputes, since 30 April 2011 are, under the Mobile Homes Act 1983, being dealt with by residential property tribunals in place of the county court.

Park mobile homes are modern, bungalow-style residential properties, usually sited on private estates. Impartial advice can be obtained from the NCC, the trade body that represents the UK tourer, motor home, holiday home and park home industries (**www.thencc.org.uk**). Before entering into a commitment to purchase a park home, it's well worth visiting an exhibition dedicated to park homes to gain useful information, of which there are several held annually.

Park Home & Holiday Caravan magazine is the UK's biggest and best-selling park home magazine and is full of information for those interested in park homes. See website: **www.parkhomemagazine.co.uk**.

For companies that specialize in new homes for sale on residential parks, ready for immediate occupation, see **www.parkhome-living.co.uk**.

Self-build

Since the March 2014 budget, self-build homes have become more popular, in the main due to the axing of the community infrastructure levy. This change saves self-builders thousands of pounds and should encourage more people to build their own home. With typical cost savings estimated at between 25 and 40 per cent, self-build is very popular with the over-50s. No prior building experience is necessary; however, obtaining planning permission from local councils is essential, though this can often be a protracted business. Individuals who wish to build on their own can make arrangements with an architect or company that sells standard plans and building kits. Be sure to do your research and seek professional advice first.

If this sort of project is of interest to you, a day spent at one of the UK's major exhibitions will provide all the information and advice you need:

The National Self-Build and Renovation Show: **www.nsbrc.co.uk**.

The National Homebuilding and Renovation Show:
   www.homebuildingshow.co.uk.

The following websites are worth browsing for information:

www.homebuilding.co.uk: inspiration and advice for your building
   project.

www.buildstore.co.uk: comprehensive website for self-build,
   renovation, plots of land for sale, buying building materials.

www.selfbuildland.co.uk: will help you find your ideal building
   plot.

How green is your house?

The best way to make properties more sustainable is to adopt an holistic approach. Saving energy needs to benefit consumers, not impose heavy additional costs. Don't think in terms of eco-designed new builds, with hi-tech modern features. All homes should be eco-friendly – in terms of fuel bills, you can save much energy and money from things as simple as roof insulation and double glazing.

Practical suggestions for reducing your energy bills

Here are some suggestions provided by the *Telegraph* (**www.telegraph. co.uk/property/greenproperty/7939220**):

- *Install underfloor heating*: this tends to be associated with new-build homes, but can be installed to good effect in older properties. It is particularly suited to bathrooms.

- *Insulate your loft*: many people still do not have their lofts insulated. Homeowners should recoup the cost of loft insulation (about £200–£300 in a standard house) within two to three years. If possible, use natural or recycled materials.

- *Use locally sourced or supplied building materials*: if possible also use local tradespeople. This is part of the holistic approach and helps the local economy.

- *Use water-based paints with natural pigments*: most paints used in homes are oil-based and therefore less energy-efficient. Water-based paints using natural pigments can also be much more aesthetically attractive.

- *If renovating or building, make sure your builder reduces waste and recycles rather than sending material to landfill*: we are becoming far more used to recycling domestic waste, so why throw all discarded building materials into a skip?

- *Fill cavity walls with insulation*: masses of energy gets wasted in homes that were built before energy saving became a priority. Uninsulated cavity walls can be almost as wasteful as uninsulated lofts.

- *Consider investing in solar panels*: these can be expensive to install, but make long-term savings. You can also use the energy generated in your home or, under a 'tariff' system, sell it on to the National Grid.

- *Replace single-glazed windows with double-glazed ones*: in terms of potential energy savings, every house in the country ought to be double-glazed. This applies to old houses as much as new ones. With so many styles to choose from, double-glazed windows can be attractive.

- *Choose wood-framed windows rather than UPVC or metal*: they are easier to repair, more insulating, last a lifetime and are less polluting than the cheaper UPVC (unplasticized polyvinyl chloride), which emits toxic compounds.

- *Keep your boiler serviced and upgrade to a more efficient model when possible*: older boilers are incredibly inefficient when compared to the latest models. Ideally boilers should be renewed every 10 years.

- *Replace old-style bulbs with energy-saving ones*: the newer-style energy-saving bulbs are many times more efficient than filament bulbs.

- *Add thick curtains at windows or doors*: if you are serious about conserving energy, ditch the blinds and buy something more substantial.

- *Monitor your electricity consumption*: it is possible to buy digital displays that monitor your electricity consumption – as easily as watching the meter in a taxi. An educational experience.

- *Lower your thermostat and check the temperature of your hot water*: many people have their water temperature set too high. Just reducing the thermostat setting by a few degrees can lead to significant savings.

- *When buying or renting a new house, check its Energy Performance Certificate*: an EPC will give you information on the house's energy use and CO_2 emissions. EPCs grade properties from A (most efficient) to G (least efficient). The average score is currently D.

- *Block draughts around doors, chimneys and windows*: if there is a howling draught then energy is being wasted. Draught-excluders may not look attractive, but they work.

- *Buy an eco-kettle*: kettles use a huge amount of electricity. Why boil enough water for six cups of tea when you only need one? Eco-kettles are more energy efficient and can beneficially impact on your electricity bills.

- *Fit a water-saving shower head*: taking a shower instead of a bath can be considered ecologically helpful, but if you use a power shower you might undo all the good work. An aerated or low-flow shower head saves energy, as does cutting down the amount of time you spend in the shower.

- *Switch suppliers*: most households have never switched energy provider and as a result are paying around £180 a year more than they need. Switching takes about 10 minutes.

- *Switch tariff*: changes have taken place regarding the number of tariffs a consumer can choose from: it is now just four, and it's getting simpler to switch. Contact your energy supplier for advice: switching could save up to £250.

- *Watch your water usage*: if you have more bedrooms than people in your home you could save over £200 by switching to a water meter, so you only pay for the water you actually use.

- *Insure your boiler*: for peace of mind take out boiler insurance, such as British Gas's Home Care (**www.britishgas.co.uk**).

For further research on saving energy, see the following websites:

Energy Saving Trust: **www.energysavingtrust.org.uk**.

National Insulation Association: **www.nia-uk.org.uk**.

Glass and Glazing Federation: **www.ggf.org.uk**.

Draught Proofing Advisory Association: **www.dpaa-association.org.uk**.

British Standards Institution: **www.bsigroup.co.uk**.

Cavity Insulation Guarantee Agency (CIGA): **www.ciga.co.uk**.

Getting advice

It's easy to get independent advice about your energy supply, how to get a better deal, how to make a complaint or ask for help if you are struggling to pay your bills. The big six electricity companies give a £135 annual rebate to certain customers, especially anyone on a small pension. Those receiving the guaranteed credit element of Pension Credit automatically get the money. At their discretion, energy companies can also give the refund to other vulnerable customers, including people with a disability or long-term illness. You could qualify for the Social Tariff from your energy suppliers. You can ask also your gas or electricity supplier to put you on the Priority Service Register.

Visit **www.adviceguide.org.uk**.

To find out about Green Deal and other government schemes visit:

www.gov.uk/energy-grants-calculator.

NEST (Wales only): **www.nestwales.org.uk**.

Home Energy Scotland: **www.energysavingtrust.org.uk/scotland**.

Energy Saving Trust has information on grants and money-saving ideas wherever you live in the UK – England, Scotland, Wales and N Ireland: **www.energysavingtrust.org.uk**.

National Energy Action (NEA) is a national charity that aims to eradicate fuel poverty and helps people with low incomes to heat and insulate their homes: **www.nea.org.uk**.

Improvement and repair

If your house needs structural repairs, a wise first step would be to contact the Royal Institution of Chartered Surveyors to help you find a reputable chartered surveyor. See website: **www.rics.org**.

Disabled facilities grant (DFG)

This is obtainable from your local council and helps towards the costs of adapting your home to enable you to live there, should you become disabled. It can cover a wide range of improvements, including the provision of suitable bathroom or kitchen facilities. Provided the applicant is eligible, a mandatory grant of up to £30,000 may be available in England, £25,000 in Northern Ireland and up to £36,000 in Wales.

As with most other grants, there is a means test. The local authority will want to check that the proposed work is reasonable and practicable according to the age and condition of the property, and the local social services department will need to be satisfied that the work is necessary and appropriate to meet the individual's needs. The grant can be applied for either by the disabled person or by a joint owner or joint tenant or landlord on his or her behalf. For further information, contact the environmental health or housing department of your local authority. See website: **www.gov.uk** – Disabled people.

NB. Do not start work until approval has been given to your grant application, as you will not be eligible for a grant once work has started.

Community care grant

People on low incomes or the disabled may be eligible for help from the Social Fund; see website: **www.gov.uk** – Benefits.

Other help for disabled people

Your local authority may be able to help with the provision of certain special facilities such as a stairlift, telephone installations or a ramp to replace steps. Other useful contacts:

APHC Ltd (Association of Plumbing and Heating Contractors Ltd) holds a national register of licensed members. See website: **www.aphc.co.uk**.

Chartered Association of Building Engineers can supply names of qualified building engineers/surveyors. See website: **www.cbuilde.com**.

Association of Master Upholsterers & Soft Furnishers Ltd has a list of approved members. See website: **www.upholsterers.co.uk**.

Building Centre can give guidance on building problems. See website: **www.buildingcentre.co.uk**.

Federation of Master Builders (FMB): lists of members are available from regional offices. See website: **www.fmb.org.uk**.

Guild of Master Craftsmen supplies names of all types of specialist craftspeople. See website: **www.guildmc.com**.

Chartered Institute of Plumbing and Heating Engineering lists professional plumbers. See website: **www.ciphe.org.uk**.

Royal Institute of British Architects (RIBA) has a free 'clients service' that will recommend up to three suitable architects. See website: **www.architecture.com**.

Scottish and Northern Ireland Plumbing Employers' Federation (SNIPEF) is the national trade association for plumbing and domestic heating contractors in Scotland and Northern Ireland. See website: **www.snipef.org**.

Home improvement agencies (HIAs)

Home improvement agencies (sometimes known as 'staying put' or 'care and repair' agencies) work with older or disabled people to help them remain in their own homes by providing advice and assistance on repairs, improvements and adaptations. They also advise on the availability of funding and welfare benefits, obtain prices, recommend reliable builders and inspect the completed job.

The British Legion and Age UK offer a handyman service to carry out small household repairs, and keep a list of home improvement agencies:

Age UK website: **www.ageuk.org.uk**.

British Legion website: **www.britishlegion.org.uk**.

Foundations is the national body for home improvement agencies in England. See website: **www.foundations.uk.com**.

Elderly Accommodation Counsel provides information on home improvement agencies. See website: **www.housingcare.org**.

Safety in the home

Accidents in the home account for 40 per cent of all fatal accidents, resulting in nearly 5,000 deaths per year. Of these victims 70 per cent are over retirement age, and nearly 80 per cent of deaths are caused by falls; a further 3 million people per year need medical treatment. Tragically, it is all too often the little things that we keep meaning to attend to but never quite get round to that prove fatal. To make your home safer:

- *Steps and stairs*: these should be well lit, with light switches at both the top and the bottom. All stairs should have a handrail to provide extra support – preferably on both sides. To do high jobs in the house, invest in a proper safety stepladder, preferably with a handrail.

- *Floors*: rugs and mats that can slip should be laid on some form of non-slip backing material. Stockinged feet are slippery on all but carpeted floors, and new leather-soled shoes should always have the soles scratched before you wear them.

- *Bathroom*: this is a hazardous area for falls. Sensible precautionary measures include a suction-type bath mat; handrails on the bath or alongside the shower. For older people who have difficulty getting in and out of the bath, a bath seat can be helpful.

- *Kitchen*: any spills should be wiped up immediately to avoid slips. Any items you use regularly should be kept easily within reach. If you are having trouble preparing meals or doing the cleaning, your local social services can assist you with advice on helpful equipment. The Disability Living Foundation can provide equipment such as handrails, automatic lights and kettle tippers.

- *Falls*: these are a great risk for older people. For every two people who fracture a hip in later life, one never regains the same level of mobility. So it pays to try to prevent such accidents. If you have a fall:

  - Stay calm. If you're unhurt, look for something firm to hold on to and get slowly to your feet again. Then sit down and rest.

  - If you are injured, try to get comfortable, stay warm, and shift position every half hour or so until help arrives.

  - Should you have had several falls or fear falling, ask your GP to refer you to an NHS Falls Clinic. A falls prevention nurse can test your balance, recommend foot care and make sure you stay as fit as possible.

- *Fires*: if you have an open fire, you should always use a fireguard and sparkguard at night. The chimney should be regularly swept at least once a year, maybe more if you have a wood-burning stove. New upholstered furniture should carry a red triangle label, indicating that it is resistant to smouldering cigarettes. Furniture that also passes the match ignition test carries a green label.

- *Portable heaters*: these should be kept away from furniture and curtains and positioned where you cannot trip over them. Paraffin heaters should be handled particularly carefully and should never be filled while alight. Paraffin should be kept in a metal container outside the house. Never dry clothes near a portable heater or open fire.

- *Gas appliances*: these should be serviced regularly by British Gas or other Gas Safe Register registered installers. You should also ensure that there is adequate ventilation when using heaters. Never block air vents: carbon monoxide fumes can kill.

  If you smell gas or suspect a carbon monoxide leak – call free on the National Grid 24-hour emergency line free: 0800 111 999.
  Practical steps: What to do if you smell gas:

  - *Do* turn off the gas at the meter unless the meter is in the cellar or basement.

  - *Don't* smoke or strike matches.

- – *Don't* turn electrical switches off or on.
- – *Do* put out naked flames.
- – *Do* open doors and windows.
- – *Do* keep people away from the affected area.

- *Cookers*: cooking appliances cause more than one in three fires in the home. Chip pans are a particular hazard. Pan handles should be turned away from the heat and positioned so you cannot knock them off the stove. Always take the pan off the ring and turn off the heat before you leave the kitchen.

- *Cigarettes*: if left smouldering in an ashtray this could be dangerous if the ashtray is full. Smoking in bed is a potential killer.

- *Faulty electric wiring*: this frequently causes fires, as do overloaded power points. Check wiring every five years and avoid using too many appliances off a single plug. Where possible, have electric sockets moved to waist height to avoid unnecessary bending whenever you want to turn on the switch.

- *Electric blankets*: these should be routinely overhauled and checked in accordance with the manufacturer's instructions. It is dangerous to use both a hot water bottle and electric blanket – and never use an under blanket as an over blanket.

- *Gardening*: using electrical appliances in the garden can be dangerous. They should never be used when it is raining. Always wear rubber-soled shoes or boots, and avoid floppy clothing that could get caught in the equipment.

- *Fire extinguishers*: these should be readily accessible. They should be regularly maintained and in good working order. Portable extinguishers should conform to BS EN standards. Smoke alarms should be fitted as they are an effective and cheap early-warning device.

Here are some other useful websites:

www.ageuk.org.uk;

www.dlf.org.uk;

www.independentliving.co.uk;

www.saferhouses.co.uk.

Home security

According to the Home Office, the elderly are not more at risk from crime than any other section of society. Should you feel nervous or vulnerable, the crime prevention officer at your local police station will advise you on how to improve your security arrangements. He or she will also tell you whether there is a neighbourhood watch scheme and how you join it. This is a free service that the police are happy to provide.

If you are going away, the Royal Mail's 'Keepsafe' service will store your mail so as to avoid it piling up and alerting potential burglars to your absence. There is a charge for the service. See: **www.royalmail.com**.

If your home will be unoccupied for any length of time, it is sensible to ask the local police to put it on their unattended premises register. Finally, time switches (cost around £15) turn lights on and off when you are away and can be used to switch on the heating before your return.

If you want to know of a reputable locksmith, you should contact the Master Locksmiths Association; website: **www.locksmiths.co.uk**.

The BBC Crimewatch Roadshow (**www.bbc.co.uk/crimewatchroadshow**) offers the following tips to stay safe:

- Keep your possessions safe by securing your home. You may be entitled to help towards paying for security improvements from your local council. Check with the housing department about these payments.

- Don't keep large amounts of money in your home. Keep it in a bank or building society where it is much safer.

- Get to know your neighbours, as it will be helpful to both of you if you are aware of each other's routines.

- Make sure you have good exterior lighting on your home. Call the council and let them know if street lights have burned out on your road.

- It is especially important not to let strangers into your home. Fit a door chain and viewer.

- Never give out personal details, such as credit card information, to strangers who call to see you.

- Never let a maintenance or service operative who has just turned up at your door into your home.

- Always check the ID of maintenance personnel that you are expecting. You can check these details with their employer before you let them in. If in doubt, ask them to come back when someone else is with you.

- If you're out after dark, leave a light and radio on in the sitting room.

- Get advice from the crime prevention officer at your local police station. Some areas have schemes to help older people.

Further useful information is supplied by:

Victim Support, a support and witness service for those affected by crime. See website: **www.victimsupport.com**.

Trustmark Scheme, which finds reliable, trustworthy tradespeople. See website: **www.trustmark.org.uk**.

Trading Standards, where you can search for trusted traders in your area. See website: **www.tradingstandards.gov.uk**.

Age UK Advice provide a booklet *Staying Safe*. See website: **www.ageuk.org.uk**.

Safe Partnership runs local schemes providing free home security to vulnerable people: **www.safepartnership.org**.

Burglar alarms and safes

More elaborate precautions such as a burglar alarm are among the best ways of protecting your home. Although alarms are expensive they could be worth every penny. In the event of a break-in, you can summon help or ask the police to do what they can if you are away. Many insurance companies will recommend suitable contractors to install burglar alarm equipment. The National Security Inspectorate website lists approved contractors and also investigates technical complaints. See website: **www.nsi.org.uk**.

If you keep valuables or money in the house, you should think about buying a concealed wall or floor safe. If you are going away, it is a good idea to inform your neighbours. It is advisable to give them a key so that they can turn off and reset the alarm should the need arise.

Insurance discounts

According to recent research, 7 out of 10 householders are under-insured, some of them unknowingly but some intentionally in order to keep premiums lower. Reassessing your policy makes sense for two reasons: first, because the number of burglaries has risen, so the risks are greater; second, you may be able to obtain better value than you are getting at present. A number of insurance companies now give discounts on house contents premiums if proper security precautions have been installed.

Some insurance companies approach the problem differently and arrange discounts for their policyholders with manufacturers of security devices. The British Insurance Brokers Association and the Institute of Insurance Brokers offer independent advice. See website: **www.biba.org.uk**.

Personal safety

Older people who live on their own can be particularly at risk. A number of personal alarms are now available that are highly effective and can generally give you peace of mind. A sensible precaution is to carry a 'screamer alarm', sometimes known as a 'personal attack button'. A mobile telephone can also increase your sense of security. Older people feel particularly vulnerable to mugging so it is sensible to take precautions when out and about. Many councils run community alarm schemes for those who are housebound. For a small fee you get a panic button, usually on a pendant or wristband, so you can contact an emergency operator if you have a fall, are taken ill, or suspect a break-in. The operator phones a friend, relative or the emergency services. Age UK has been running its alarm scheme for 30 years, but try your local council first.

Insurance

If your buildings and contents insurance was originally arranged through your building society, it may cease when your mortgage is paid off. If you buy a house with cash – for instance when moving to a smaller home – it is advisable to get a qualified assessor to work out the rebuilding costs and insurance value of your new home. The cost of replacing the fabric of your house, were it to burn down, could possibly be significantly greater than the amount for which it is currently insured. Remember, you must insure for the full rebuilding cost: the market value may be inappropriate. Your policy should also provide money to meet architects' or surveyors' fees, as well as alternative accommodation for you and your family if your home were completely destroyed by fire.

If you are planning to move into accommodation that has been converted from one large house into several flats or maisonettes, check with the landlord or managing agent that the insurance on the structure of the total building is adequate. When buying a new property you are under no obligation to insure your home with the particular company suggested by your building society. With all insurance, policies vary and it pays to shop around.

Owners of properties in flood-prone areas in the UK have difficulty getting insurance. Even if they manage to find a policy that will cover them for flood damage, the premiums are high and have huge excesses. It is advisable to check whether you live in a high-risk area and, if so, take steps to protect your property. Information on flood-risk areas and how to get help in obtaining insurance can be found on the Environment Agency website: **www.environment-agency.gov.uk**. The British Insurance Brokers' Association can also provide information on registered insurance brokers in your area; website: **www.biba.org.uk**.

Another important extra feature of home insurance is 'public liability cover'. This is designed to meet claims against you as a homeowner, tenant or landlord – for example if a visitor tripped and was injured in your home (contents insurance) or if a tile fell from your roof and damaged a neighbour's car (buildings insurance) – and you are found liable for the damage or injury.

Buildings insurance

If you rent your home, it is up to your landlord to arrange buildings insurance. If you own your own home, it is up to you. Even if you no longer have a mortgage, make sure your home is insured. The Royal Institution of Chartered Surveyors' (RICS) Building Cost Information Service (BCIS), provides cost information on all aspects of construction. It has an online calculator at **www.rics.co.uk** to estimate how much cover you need.

Contents insurance

It is important to have the right level of cover. Once you stop work, you may need to review the value of your home contents. With older possessions, you should assess the replacement cost and make sure you have a 'new for old' or 'replacement as new' policy. Cancel items on your contents policy that you no longer possess and add new valuables that have been bought or received as presents. In particular, do check that you are adequately covered for any home improvements you may have added.

Where antiques and jewellery are concerned, values can rise and fall disproportionately to inflation and depending on current market trends. For a professional valuation, contact the British Antique Dealers' Association (BADA) website: **www.bada.org**; or Association of Art & Antiques Dealers (LAPADA), website: **www.lapada.org**. Photographs of particularly valuable items can help in the assessment of premiums and settlement of claims. Property marking, for example with an ultraviolet marker, is another useful ploy, as it will help the police trace your possessions should any be stolen.

The Association of British Insurers has information on various aspects of household insurance and loss prevention; see website: **www.abi.org.uk**.

The British Insurance Brokers' Association can provide information on registered insurance brokers in your area; see website: **www.biba.org.uk**.

Some insurance companies offer home and contents policies for older people at substantially reduced rates. See the following websites:

www.rias.co.uk;

www.castlecover.co.uk;

www.ageuk.org.uk;

www.staysure.co.uk;

www.50plusinsurance.co.uk;

www.saga.co.uk.

An increasing number of insurance companies offer generous no-claims discounts. Another type of discount-linked policy is one that carries an excess. If you automatically renew your policy every year with the same company, you may find that your premiums have increased each year. Financial institutions are keen on 'loyalty marketing' but loyalty should work both ways. Don't stay with a provider out of loyalty. Nowadays *disloyalty* pays because the winners are those customers who constantly switch from one provider to another.

Raising money on your home – equity release

An increasing number of homeowners find they have wealth tied up in their home but fewer savings or less income than they would like. If you don't want to move, or can't move, another option is equity release.

Taking money out of your home through an equity release scheme is a monumental – and one-way – decision. *Which?* magazine has a lot of advice on equity release; see their website: **www.which.co.uk**.

With equity release, homeowners take out a lifetime mortgage on their property and either pay interest every month, or more commonly allow the interest to roll up until they die or go into a care home. These products are not for those who are desperate for money, but more typically are for those who have always enjoyed a good standard of living and are making a lifestyle choice. Homeowners are restricted in the amount of equity they can release – up to one-third of the value of the property – at the age of 65. This rises with age. The important equation to bear in mind is that after 11 years your debt roughly doubles, and it doubles again after another 11 years.

There are two main types of plan: a *lifetime mortgage* is where you raise money by taking out a mortgage against your property. The loan is repaid when the home is eventually sold. With a *home reversion plan* you sell part, or all, of your home now in return for a cash sum. You have the right to stay in your home as a tenant, paying little or no rent. Equity release plans are designed to run until you die or move out, for example if you move permanently into a care home. You can have a plan just for yourself, or for you and your partner. In the latter case, the plan runs until you both no longer need the home.

Tips for choosing the right equity release scheme

- Explore all other options first to make sure you find out how equity release would affect you and your entitlement to state benefits.

- Borrow the minimum amount you need to or choose a drawdown scheme that will give you the option to borrow money as and when you need it.

- Consider taking out a scheme that lets you make interest payments each month if you can afford to.

- Choose a scheme with no early-repayment charges, or ones that apply only for a limited period.

- 'Sale and rent back' schemes are not the same as, nor similar to, equity release. This is a sector to steer clear of. Companies typically offer to buy your home at a discounted price and there are serious pitfalls.

How much equity release might cost

You will need to account for the following:

- *Arrangement and administration fees*: the plan provider will normally charge an arrangement fee. With a drawdown mortgage or instalment reversion plan, there may be a separate administration fee for each withdrawal.

- *Valuation and legal fees*: you will have to pay for a surveyor to value your property and a solicitor to handle the paperwork and check the legal aspects of the agreement. You must pay the valuation fee in advance but the provider might reimburse this if the plan goes ahead. Some deals refund your legal costs too.

- *Insurance and maintenance*: in addition to the direct costs of the scheme, the provider will require you to have buildings insurance and to maintain the property to a reasonable standard.

Remember, equity release plans are complex. You are strongly recommended to get advice from an independent financial adviser specializing in equity release and a solicitor who is familiar with this type of plan. When getting legal advice use your own solicitor (not one appointed by the equity release firm). You should also ensure that the property is independently valued by a qualified surveyor. The adviser may charge a fee, be paid by commission, or a combination of both.

For further information, see the Money Advice Service website: **www.moneyadviceservice.org.uk**. You should also check with the Equity Release Council: this is the industry body for the equity release sector and represents the providers, qualified financial advisers, lawyers, intermediaries and surveyors who work in the equity release sector. For further information see website: **www.equityreleasecouncil.com**. Alternatively, the Equity Release Information Centre publishes a free 32-page guide to equity release. Visit: **www.askeric.tv**.

The following websites offer further information:

www.homereversionschemes.co.uk;

www.sixtyplusonline.co.uk;

www.societyoflaterlifeadvisers.co.uk;

www.learnmoney.co.uk.

Using your home to earn money

Some people whose home has become too large are tempted by the idea of taking in tenants. There are three broad choices: taking in paying guests or lodgers, letting part of your home as self-contained accommodation, or renting the whole house for a specified period of time. In all cases, for your own protection it is essential to have a written agreement and to take up bank references, unless the let is a strictly temporary one where the money is paid in advance. Otherwise, rent should be collected quarterly and you should arrange a hefty deposit to cover any damage. An important point to be aware of is that there is now a set of strict rules concerning the treatment of deposits, with the risk of large fines for landlords and agents who fail to abide by them.

Paying guests or lodgers

In a move to encourage more people to let out rooms in their home, the government allows you to earn up to £4,250 (£2,150 if letting jointly) per year free of tax. Any excess rental income you receive over £4,250 will be assessed for tax in the normal way. For further information, see HMRC website: **www.hmrc.gov.uk**; and the government website: **www.gov.uk**. If you have a mortgage, or are a tenant yourself (even with a very long lease), check with your building society or landlord that you are entitled to sublet.

This is the most informal arrangement, and will normally be either a casual holiday-type bed-and-breakfast let or a lodger who might be with you for a couple of years. In either case, the visitor will be sharing part of your home, the accommodation will be fully furnished, and you will be providing at least one full meal per day and possibly also basic cleaning services. You do not have to commit to having a lodger around the house full-time; some employees need a room only between Monday and Friday. Foreign students are around all term time but not in the holidays. Foreign language students might need a room only for a six-week term. You can stipulate whether to take younger or older people.

There are few legal formalities involved in these types of lettings, and rent is entirely a matter for friendly agreement. As a resident owner you are also in a very strong position if you want your lodger to leave. Lodging arrangements can easily be ended, as your lodger has no legal rights to stay after the agreed period. A wise precaution is to check with your insurance company that your home contents policy will not be affected, since some insurers restrict cover to households with lodgers. Also, unless you make arrangements to the contrary, you should inform your lodger that his or her possessions are not covered by your policy.

If, as opposed to a lodger or the occasional summer paying guest, you offer regular B&B accommodation, you could be liable to pay business rates. Although this is not new, it appears that in recent years the Valuation Office Agency has been enforcing the regulation more strictly against people running B&B establishments. It is a good idea to register with your tourist information centre and to contact the environmental health office at your local council for any help and advice.

Letting rooms in your home

You could convert a basement or part of your house into a self-contained flat and let this either furnished or unfurnished. Alternatively, you could let a single room or rooms. As a general rule, provided you continue to live in the house your tenant(s) have little security of tenure and equally do not have the right to appeal against the rent. You would be advised to check your home contents policy with your insurance company. As a resident landlord, you have a guaranteed right to repossession of your property. If the letting is for a fixed term (eg six months or a year), the let will automatically cease at the end of that fixed period. If the arrangement is on a more ad hoc basis with no specified leaving date, it may be legally necessary to give at least four weeks' notice in writing. The position over notices to quit will vary according to circumstances. Should you encounter any difficulties, it is possible that you may need to apply to the courts for an eviction order.

Tax note

If you subsequently sell your home, you may not be able to claim exemption from capital gains tax on the increase in value of a flat if it is entirely self-contained: it is therefore a good idea to retain some means of access to the main house or flat – but take legal advice as to what will qualify.

Renting out your home on a temporary basis

If you are thinking of spending the winter in the sun or are considering buying a retirement home that you will not occupy for a year or two, you need to understand the assured shorthold tenancy rules. Your tenant – unless notified in advance that you need the property back sooner (there are very few grounds on which you can make this notification) or unless earlier possession is sought because of the tenant's behaviour – has the right to stay for at least six months and must be given two months' notice before you want the tenancy to end. It is strongly advisable to ask a solicitor or letting agent to help you draw up the agreement.

The safest solution if possible is to let your property to a company rather than to private individuals, since company tenants do not have the same security of tenure. However, it is important that the contract should make clear that your let is for residential, not business, purposes. Before entering into any agreement, you should seek professional advice.

And some other ideas...

If you think a little extra cash might be useful, depending on where you live you could turn your garden into a 'micro campsite' and earn up to £40 per night: **www.campinmygarden.com** gives information. Or you could hire out your garden for a number of uses – vegetable plots, storage, or even wedding receptions: **www.rentmygarden.co.uk**.

Should you have extra space in your house and don't mind renting out a room, by signing up to certain websites you can reach potential guests from all round the world. Try: **www.gumtree.com**; **www.airbnb.co.uk**; **www.wimdu.co.uk**; **www.spareroom.co.uk**; **www.hosts-international.com**.

If you'd rather not have people, you can make extra money out of the empty space in your house by renting out your garage, loft, store room or shed to people who have too much stuff: **www.storemates.co.uk**. If parking is difficult or expensive in your area, drivers will pay to use your parking space or garage: **www.yourparkingspace.co.uk**; **www.parkonmydrive.com**.

You can offer your home for film and advertisement locations if you can cope with a lot of disruption. But it pays good money and film producers need other types of homes besides stately ones. Look at **www.filmlocations.co.uk** or **www.amazingspace.co.uk**.

Holiday lets

Buying a future retirement home in the country and renting it out as a holiday home in the summer months is another option worth considering. This can prove a useful and profitable investment. As long as certain conditions are met, income from furnished holiday lettings enjoys most of the benefits that there would be if it were taxed as trading income rather than as investment income. This means you can claim 10 per cent writing-down capital allowances on such items as carpets, curtains and furniture as well as fixtures and fittings. Alternatively, you can claim an annual 10 per cent wear-and-tear allowance. The running expenses of a holiday home, including maintenance, advertising, insurance cover and council tax (or business rates – see below) are all largely allowable for tax, excluding that element that relates to your own occupation of the property. Married couples should consider whether the property is to be held in the husband's or the wife's name, or owned jointly. A solicitor or accountant will be able to advise you.

To qualify as furnished holiday accommodation, the property must be situated in the UK, be let on a commercial basis, be available for holiday letting for at least 140 days during the tax year and be actually let for at least 70 days. Moreover, for at least seven months per year, not necessarily continuous, the property must not normally be occupied by the same tenant for more than 31 consecutive days. There is always the danger that you might create an assured tenancy, so do take professional advice on drawing up the letting agreement. Similarly, if you decide to use one of the holiday rental agents to market your property, get a solicitor to check any contract you enter into with the company.

For more information see the RICS (Royal Institution of Chartered Surveyors) website: **www.rics.org**.

A further point to note is that tax inspectors are taking a tougher line as to what is 'commercial' renting (ie for 140 days or more per year). To safeguard yourself, it is important to draw up a broad business plan before you start and to make a real effort to satisfy the minimum letting requirements.

Tenants' deposits

The Tenancy Deposit Scheme that came into force in April 2007 was created to ensure tenants get back the amount owing to them, to make any disputes about the deposit easier to resolve, and to encourage tenants to look after the property during the agreed term of their let. Landlords or agents must now protect deposits under an approved scheme. Failure to do so within 14 days of receiving the money could result in the landlord being forced to pay the tenant three times the deposit amount.

The two types of tenancy deposit protection schemes available for landlords and letting agents are insurance-based schemes and custodial schemes. All schemes provide a free dispute resolution service. The schemes allow tenants to get all or part of their deposit back when they are entitled to it and encourage tenants and landlords to make a clear agreement from the start on the condition of the property. The schemes make any disputes easier to resolve. For further information see the following:

www.gov.uk – Tenancy Deposit Protection;

www.rla.org.uk – Residential Landlords Association;

www.thedisputeservice.co.uk – Dispute Service.

Finally, property that is rented 'commercially' (ie for 140 days or more per year) is normally liable for business rates, instead of the council tax you would otherwise pay. This could be more expensive, even though partially allowable against tax.

Useful reading

The Complete Guide to Letting Property, by Liz Hodgkinson, published by Kogan Page (website: **www.koganpage.com**).

Benefits and taxes

Housing Benefit

Provided you have no more than £16,000 in savings, you may be able to get help with your rent from your local council. You may qualify for Housing Benefit whether you are a council or private tenant or live in a hotel or hostel. For advice about your own particular circumstances, contact your local authority or the Citizens Advice Bureau.

The amount of benefit you get depends on five factors: the number of people in your household; your eligible rent (up to a prescribed maximum); your capital or savings; your income; and your 'applicable amount', which is the amount of money the government considers you need for basic living expenses. There have been cuts to Housing Benefit, sometimes dubbed 'the bedroom tax', so apply to your local authority to check if you are eligible for help.

If your income is less than your applicable amount you will receive maximum Housing Benefit towards your eligible rent (less any non-dependant deduction). You may be eligible for Income Support if your capital is less than £8,000, or less than £16,000 if you are aged 60 or over. If your income is equal to your applicable amount, you will also receive maximum Housing Benefit.

How to claim

If you think you are eligible for benefit you can apply online or ask your council for an application form. It should let you know within 14 days of receiving your completed application whether you are entitled to benefit, and will inform you of the amount. See website: **www.gov.uk** – Benefits.

Special accommodation

If you live in a mobile home or houseboat, you may be able to claim benefit for site fees or mooring charges. If you live in a private nursing or residential care home you will not normally be able to get Housing Benefit to help with the cost. However, you may be able to get help towards both the accommodation part of your fees and your living expenses through Income Support or possibly under the Community Care arrangements. If you make a claim for Income Support you can claim Housing Benefit and Council Tax Benefit at the same time.

Council tax

Council tax is based on the value of the dwelling in which you live (the property element) and also consists of a personal element – with discounts and exemptions applying to certain groups of people.

The property element

Most domestic properties are liable for council tax, including rented property, mobile homes and houseboats. The value of the property is assessed according to a banding system, with eight different bands (A to H). The banding of each property is determined by the government's Valuation Office Agency. Small extensions or other improvements made after this date do not affect the valuation until the property changes hands. Notification of the band is shown on the bill when it is sent out in April. If you think there has been a misunderstanding about the valuation (or your liability to pay the full amount) you may have the right of appeal.

Liability

Not everyone pays council tax. The bill is normally sent to the resident owner or joint owners of the property or, in the case of rented accommodation, to the tenant or joint tenants. Married couples and people with a shared legal interest in the property are jointly liable for the bill, unless they are students or severely mentally impaired. In some cases, for example in hostels or multi-occupied property, a non-resident landlord or owner will be liable but may pass on a share of the bill to the tenants or residents, which would probably be included as part of the rental charge.

The personal element

The valuation of each dwelling assumes that two adults will be resident. The charge does not increase if there are more adults. However, if as in many homes there is a single adult, your council tax bill will be reduced by 25 per cent. Certain people are disregarded when determining the number of residents in a household: for full details see **www.gov.uk** – Council Tax.

Discounts and exemptions applying to property

Certain property is exempt from council tax, including:

- Property that has been unoccupied and unfurnished for less than six months.

- The home of a deceased person; the exemption lasts until six months after the grant of probate.

- A home that is empty because the occupier is absent in order to care for someone else.

- The home of a person who is or would be exempted from council tax because of moving to a residential home, hospital care or similar.

- Empty properties in need of major repairs or undergoing structural alteration can be exempt from council tax for an initial period of six months, but this can be extended for a further six months. After 12 months, the standard 50 (or possibly full 100) per cent charge for empty properties will apply.

- Granny flats that are part of another private domestic dwelling may be exempt, but this depends on access and other conditions. To check, contact your local Valuation Office.

Business-cum-domestic property

Business-cum-domestic property is rated according to usage, with the business section assessed for business rates and the domestic section for council tax.

Appeals

If you become the new person responsible for paying the council tax on a property that you feel has been wrongly banded, you have six months to appeal and can request that the valuation be reconsidered. Otherwise, there are only three other circumstances in which you can appeal:

- if there has been a material increase or reduction in the property's value;

- if you start, or stop, using part of the property for business or the balance between domestic and business use changes;

- if either of the latter two apply and the listing officer has altered the council tax list without giving you a chance to put your side.

If you have grounds for appeal, you should take up the matter with the Valuation Office. If the matter is not resolved, you can then appeal to an independent valuation tribunal. For advice and further information, contact your local Citizens Advice Bureau.

Council Tax Benefit

If you cannot afford your council tax because you have a low income, you may be able to obtain Council Tax Benefit. People on Pension Credit (Guarantee Credit) are entitled to rebates of up to 100 per cent. Even if you are not receiving any other social security benefit, you may still qualify for some Council Tax Benefit. The amount you get depends on your income, savings, personal circumstances, who else lives in your home (in particular whether they would be counted as 'non-dependants') and your net council tax bill (ie after any deductions that apply to your home). If you are not sure whether your income is low enough to entitle you to Council Tax Benefit, it is worth enquiring. If you disagree with your council's decision, you can appeal. For further information see:

Citizens Advice Bureau, website: **www.citizensadvice.org.uk**.

Federation of Private Residents' Associations Ltd (FPRA) website: **www.fpra.org.uk**.

Chapter Nine
Leisure activities

What most persons consider as virtue, after the age of 40, is simply a loss of energy. VOLTAIRE

Question: What is the biggest complaint amongst retirees?
Answer: There's never enough time to get everything done.

The over-60s are some of the busiest people because many of them are catching up on doing things they haven't had time to do during their working lives. According to research from the former government 'Happiness Czar', Richard Layard, psychological wellbeing can be derived from 10 key steps:

1 *Giving.* If you want to feel good, do good. Helping other people makes us happier and healthier.

2 *Relating.* Close relationships with family and friends provide love, meaning, support and increase our feelings of self-worth.

3 *Exercising.* Being active instantly improves mood and can even lift depression.

4 *Appreciating.* Notice the world about you. Be mindful of your feelings and don't dwell on the past or worry about the future.

5 *Trying out.* Learning new things gives you a sense of accomplishment.

6 *Direction.* Goals motivate but they need to be challenging and achievable.

7 *Resilience.* You often can't choose what happens to you but you can choose your attitude to what happens. Resilience can be learned.

8 *Emotion.* Regularly experiencing joy, gratitude and pride creates 'an upward spiral'. Focus on the glass half full.

9 *Acceptance.* Dwelling on flaws makes it much harder to be happy. Accept yourself and be kind to yourself when things go wrong.

10 *Meaning.* People who have purpose in their lives feel more in control and gain more from what they do.

Source: **actionforhappiness.org**

If you are able to embrace all the above points you are likely to have a well-balanced life in retirement. One of the most important things is to be able to enjoy good-quality leisure time: the freedom to indulge in recreational activities without any pricking of conscience that you should perhaps be doing something else. Whatever your views on how to spend your retirement years, doing nothing, it seems, is rarely an option people take. If, as we are led to believe, many of us will live to be around 100 years old, there are almost 40 years of retirement to fill with leisure activities – and no shortage of advice on what's available. Doing something – being active and involved – is without doubt beneficial to mental and physical health.

Looking for inspiration?

If you're feeling enthused so far, how about emulating intrepid 93-year-old Tom Lackey from the West Midlands? He took up aerobatic stunts and wing walking over 14 years ago and has to date achieved nine Guinness World Records and, in memory of his wife, has raised over £1.25 million for breast cancer research. At the time of writing, he is attempting his tenth Guinness World Record – a wing walk from Lands Ends to the Scilly Isles, at the age of 94.

SOURCE: www.motability.co.uk/lifestyle, May 2014.

For more information on how to get the most from your leisure, this chapter is best read in conjunction with Chapter 14 (Holidays), as many of the organizations listed there would be equally relevant here. However, those that appear in Chapter 14 would probably involve most people spending a few days away from home. The latest information is always available on the relevant websites, so do check there for further details.

Adult education

What about some new challenges? It's never too late to learn. From the occasional local evening class to a part-time degree course, or online distance learning, opportunities for education abound. There are scores of subjects easily available to everyone, regardless of age or previous qualifications. Not all educational courses are free; however, there are a number of different funding options available for those over 50. Those who have never taken any form of educational course through a university or college may also be able to obtain financial assistance. Where to find help? Agencies such as Saga, Age UK and LaterLife will supply information on free and subsidized educational courses. Local libraries are another place to find information on educational matters.

One of the biggest advantages of going back to school in retirement is that if you miss a class, no one calls your parents. Learning new skills is always beneficial and can lead to new opportunities. Many retired people have actually found new careers in later life. To find courses available throughout the UK, here are a few suggestions:

Adult Education Finder: **www.adulteducationfinder.co.uk**.

BBC Learning: **www.bbc.co.uk/learning/adults**.

Home Learning College: **www.homelearningcollege.com**.

National Extension College (NEC): **www.nec.ac.uk**.

National Institute of Adult Continuing Education (NIACE):
   www.niace.org.uk.

Open and Distance Learning Quality Council (ODLQC):
   www.odlqc.org.uk.

Open University (OU): **www.open.ac.uk**.

University extra-mural departments – non-degree and short courses

Many universities have a department of extra-mural studies that arranges courses for adults, sometimes in the evening or during holiday periods. If you live near a university, ask there, but here are three websites to check:

Birkbeck, University of London: **www.bbk.ac.uk**.

U3A (The University of the Third Age): **www.u3a.org.uk**.

Workers' Educational Association (WEA): **www.wea.org.uk**.

Animals

Whether you enjoy wildlife or have a much loved pet, there is plenty of choice if you are an animal lover. You may already have connections with charities and organizations that relate to your favourite animals, some of which will be listed in Chapter 12 (Volunteering), but here are some suggestions, which include online publications:

Birdlife International: **www.birdlife.org**.

British Beekeepers Association: **www.bbka.org.uk**.

Your Cat: **www.yourcat.co.uk**.

Dogs Monthly: **www.dogsmonthly.co.uk**.

Horse and Hound: **www.horseandhound.co.uk**.

RSPCA: **www.rspca.org.uk**.

Wildfowl & Wetlands Trust (WWT): **www.wwt.org.uk**.

Arts and culture

Wherever you live you can enjoy the arts. Arts and culture illuminate our inner lives and enrich our emotional world. Whether you are interested in active participation or just appreciating the performance of others, there is an exhilarating choice of events. Many entertainments offer concessionary prices to retired people. The Arts Council England works to get great art to everyone by championing, developing and investing in artistic experiences that enrich everyone's lives. For information and details of each regional office, see website: **www.artscouncil.org.uk**.

If you're passionate about the creative arts, you can study with the specialists. For courses ranging through art history, creative writing, fine art, illustration, graphic design, music, painting, photography, textiles and visual communications, see the Open College of Arts website: **www.oca-uk.com**.

For those who wish to join in with amateur arts activities, most public libraries keep lists of choirs, amateur theatre groups, painting clubs and similar pursuits in their locality.

Films

Cinema is a hugely popular art form and should you enjoy film you could join your community cinema, local film society or visit the National Film Theatre. Here are some other websites to look at:

British Federation of Film Societies (BFFS): **www.bffs.org.uk**.

British Film Institute (BFI): **www.bfi.org.uk**.

Music making

Whatever style of music you enjoy, there are associations to suit your taste. For example:

Handbell Ringers of Great Britain: **www.hrgb.org.uk**.

Making Music: **www.makingmusic.org.uk**.

National Association of Choirs:
www.nationalassociationofchoirs.org.uk.

Society of Recorder Players: **www.srp.org.uk**.

Opera, ballet and concerts

Classical music, ballet or opera can be enjoyed by anyone at any age. Here are some of the obvious places to experience such treats, but you will find venues throughout the country:

Covent Garden: **www.roh.org.uk**.

English National Opera (ENO): **www.eno.org**.

Royal Albert Hall: **www.royalalberthall.com**

Sadler's Wells: **www.sadlerswells.com**.

Scottish National Opera: **www.scottishopera.org.uk**.

Southbank Centre: **www.southbankcentre.co.uk**.

Welsh National Opera: **www.wno.org.uk**.

Poetry

There is an increasing enthusiasm for poetry and poetry readings in clubs, pubs and other places of entertainment. Special local events may be advertised in your neighbourhood. The Poetry Society is a charitable organization and aims to promote a more general recognition and appreciation of poetry, and publishes the leading poetry magazine: **www.poetrysociety.org.uk**.

Television and radio audiences

People of all ages, backgrounds and abilities enjoy participating as members of studio audiences and contributors to programmes. For those wishing to take part there are a couple of websites that can help:

Applause Store: **www.applausestore.com**.

BBC Shows: **www.bbc.co.uk/showsandtours/tickets**.

Theatre

For all keen theatregoers, details of current and forthcoming productions for national and regional theatres, as well as theatre reviews, are easily researched on the internet. See the following websites:

ATG Tickets: **www.atgtickets.com**.

Barbican: **www.barbican.org.uk**.

Donmar Warehouse: **www.donmarwarehouse.com**.

National Theatre: **www.nationaltheatre.org.uk**.

National Theatre Wales: **www.nationaltheatrewales.org**.

Official London Theatre: **www.officiallondontheatre.co.uk**.

Scottish Community Drama Association (SCDA):
   www.scda.org.uk.

Theatre Network: **www.uktheatre.net**.

The Old Vic: **www.oldvictheatre.com**.

TKTS: **www.tkts.co.uk**.

Visual arts

Attending exhibitions and lectures, if you enjoy art, is something you should be able to accomplish in retirement. Some of the following art societies offer a good choice of such activities:

Art Fund: **www.artfund.org**.

Contemporary Art Society: **www.contemporaryartsociety.org**.

National Association of Decorative & Fine Arts Societies (NADFAS): **www.nadfas.org.uk**.

Royal Academy of Arts: **www.royalacademy.org.uk**.

Tate: **www.tate.org.uk**.

Painting as a hobby

If you are interested in improving your own painting technique, art courses should be available at your local adult education institute. Similarly, your library may have details of local art groups and societies in your area. The Society for All Artists (SAA) is the largest art society and exists for everyone with a love of painting. It supplies inspiration, information, help and advice – all that you need to enjoy this leisure activity: **www.saa.co.uk**.

Computing and IT

Keeping up to date with the latest advances of technology is easier for some than others. Computing is one of the most popular courses for retired people, and you can learn online or in class. Local libraries have set times throughout the week for retired people either to learn computing skills or update those they already have. There is a huge range of free learning resources available on the internet, if you know where to look. Two websites to look at are:

www.ageuk.org.uk/work-and-learning/technology-and-internet;

www.homeandlearn.co.uk.

Crafts

The majority of suggestions are contained in Chapter 14 (Holidays), variously under 'Arts and crafts' and 'Special interest holidays', since many organizations offer residential courses and painting holidays. If you are interested in a particular form of crafting, many of the societies and others listed in Chapter 14 should be able to help you. Here are a couple more:

Crafts Council: **www.craftscouncil.org.uk**.

Open College of the Arts (OCA): **www.oca-uk.com**.

Creative writing

It is said that there is a book in everyone, and many retired people have a yen to write. As this is a solitary occupation you may find that joining a writing group is a worthwhile and pleasurable thing to do. The National Association of Writing Groups – **www.nawg.co.uk** – is one place to find a local one; though not all creative writing groups are linked to that site. Whatever the style, creative writing groups provide company, support and a degree of critique too. Some specialize – but many take fiction, non-fiction and poetry in their stride, so you can write anything from an essay to an article, from a rant to a novel – and, who knows, you might even get published and earn some money.

If any of this interests you, something else to check is *Writing Magazine* (see **www.writers-online.co.uk**). This is a monthly journal designed to help aspiring and actual writers. Patrick Forsyth (a many-times-published Kogan Page author) writes regularly for that magazine, and is a great fan of writing groups. 'They are,' he says, 'if not essential, a very great help to those who love to write, but lack confidence, want a bit of advice, support or motivation. I certainly recommend you give attendance a go. Getting published is not easy, and it is said that the single word that best describes a writer with no persistence is *unpublished*. But it *is* possible and seeing a book or article with your name on, and having it followed by a cheque, is very satisfying.' Patrick knows; one of his recently published books, a hilarious critique of inappropriate public writing, is called *Empty when Half Full*.

Dance/keep fit

Did you know that dancing is a key evolutionary strategy? And there are right and wrong ways of doing it. Men should concentrate on moving the top half of their bodies, whereas women should be working on their waist, legs and hips. Wild arm movements, however, are not advisable for either gender as they are considered off-putting. Dancing is immensely popular again, partly due to the television programmes that are devoted to it on a regular basis. Ballroom, line, Scottish, tap, jive, salsa and many other forms of dancing are being enjoyed by people of all ages and are a great way of keeping fit as well as meeting new people. Additionally, there are music and relaxation classes, aerobics and more gentle keep-fit sessions. To find out what is available in your area, ask at your library, or see the list below (there are further suggestions in Chapter 13 in the section 'Keep fit'):

British Dance Council: **www.bdconline.org**.

English Folk Dance and Song Society: **www.efdss.org**.

Imperial Society of Teachers of Dancing: **www.istd.org**.

Keep Fit Association (KFA): **www.keepfit.org.uk**.

Royal Scottish Country Dance Society: **www.rscds.org**.

Sport and Recreation Alliance: **www.sportandrecreation.org.uk**.

Games

Board and card games are fun: there are clubs in most local areas for backgammon, bridge, chess, cribbage, whist, dominos, Scrabble and others. Depending on your taste and level of obsession, you should be able to find groups that meet together regularly in a club, hall, pub or other social venue to enjoy friendly games and tournaments. If you prefer, it is also possible to join online clubs and play remotely. Here are some national organizations that can provide information:

Boardgame Players Association: **www.boardgamers.org**.

English Bridge Union: **www.ebu.co.uk**.

English Chess Federation: **www.englishchess.org.uk**.

Scrabble Clubs UK: **www.absp.org.uk**.

Gardens and gardening

Gardening has recently been knocked off pole position as the nation's favourite hobby and cookery has taken the number one spot. However, thousands of people are still enthusiastic about horticulture. Courses, gardens to visit, charitable and special help for people with disabilities, and how to run a gardening association; these and other interests are all catered for by the following organizations:

English Gardening School: **www.englishgardeningschool.co.uk**.

Garden Organic: **www.gardenorganic.org.uk**.

Gardening for Disabled Trust: **www.gardeningfordisabledtrust.org.uk**.

National Gardens Scheme: **www.ngs.org.uk**.

National Society of Allotment & Leisure Gardeners Ltd:
   www.nsalg.org.uk.

Perennial: **www.perennial.org.uk**.

Royal Horticultural Society: **www.rhs.org.uk**.

Scotland's Gardens: **www.scotlandsgardens.org**.

Thrive: **www.thrive.org.uk**.

Welsh Historic Gardens Trust (WHGT): **www.whgt.org.uk**.

History

There are many people who are history enthusiasts: you may read and research exhaustively; watch the excellent programmes on TV; explore historic monuments, including ancient castles and stately homes in all parts of the country; study genealogy or investigate the history of your local area. There are loads of organizations to consider, and you should find some to your taste. Here are a few websites to give you some ideas:

Age Exchange: **www.age-exchange.org.uk**.

Architectural Heritage Society of Scotland: **www.ahss.org.uk**.

British Association for Local History: **www.balh.co.uk**.

Churches Conservation Trust: **www.visitchurches.org.uk**

City of London Information Centre: **www.cityoflondon.gov.uk**.

English Heritage: **www.english-heritage.org.uk**.

Federation of Family History Societies: **www.ffhs.org.uk**.

Garden History Society: **www.gardenhistorysociety.org**.

Georgian Group: **www.georgiangroup.org.uk**.

Historic Houses Association (HHA): **www.hha.org.uk**.

Historical Association: **www.history.org.uk**.

Monumental Brass Society: **www.mbs-brasses.co.uk**.

National Trust: **www.nationaltrust.org.uk**.

National Trust for Scotland: **www.nts.org.uk**.

Northern Ireland Tourist Board: **www.discovernorthernireland.com**.

Oral History Society: **www.ohs.org.uk**.

Society of Genealogists: **www.sog.org.uk**.

Victorian Society: **www.victorian-society.org.uk**.

Magazines

There are a growing number of magazines dedicated to the over-50s with articles and features on topics that include health, travel, finances and lifestyle. Here are some of the most popular (with some of the magazines actually available online):

50 Plus Magazine: **www.50plusmagazine.co.uk**.

55 Life Scotland: **www.55life.co.uk**.

Giddy Limits: **www.giddylimits.co.uk**.

Laterlife: **www.laterlife.com**.

Mature Times: **www.maturetimes.co.uk**.

Over 65 Magazine: **www.over65magazine.co.uk**.

Retirement Today: **www.retirement-today.co.uk**.

Savista Magazine: **www.savistamagazine.com**.

The Oldie: **www.the.oldie.magazine.co.uk**.

The Positive: **www.thepositive.com**.

Third Age: **www.thirdage.co.uk**.

YOURS Magazine: **www.yours.co.uk**.

Museums

Most museums organize free lectures and guided tours on aspects of their collections or special exhibitions. If you join as a Friend, you can enjoy certain advantages, such as access to private views, visits to places of interest, receptions and other social activities. Apart from the famous national museums, there are many fascinating smaller ones to be found around the country, depending on your area of interest. Local museums should not be missed, so look for what is in your neighbourhood. Enjoy your research, but here are a few useful websites to start you off:

British Association of Friends of Museums (BAFM): **www.bafm.org.uk**.

Ashmolean Museum of Art and Archaeology: **www.ashmolean.org**.

British Museum: **www.britishmuseum.org**.

Fitzwilliam Museum: **www.fitzmuseum.cam.ac.uk**.

National Museums of Scotland: **www.nms.ac.uk**.

Natural History Museum: **www.nhm.ac.uk**.

Royal Museums Greenwich: **www.rmg.co.uk**.

Science Museum: **www.sciencemuseum.org.uk**.

V&A (Victoria and Albert Museum): **www.vam.ac.uk**.

Nature and conservation

Many conservation organizations are very keen to recruit volunteers; the majority are therefore listed in Chapter 12 (Volunteering). Also, many of those concerned with field studies arrange courses and other special activity interests. Where there is usually a residential content you should find these listed in Chapter 14 (Holidays). Here are a few that don't appear elsewhere in this book:

Field Studies Council: **www.field-studies-council.org**.

Forestry Commission: **www.forestry.gov.uk**.

Inland Waterways Association: **www.waterways.org.uk**.

The Wildlife Trusts: **www.wildlifetrusts.org**.

Public library service

The public library in the UK is an endangered species and needs your support. Library services that are run by local authorities provide free services that empower people to access resources. Libraries still fulfil their traditional role of lending books, but also improve people's lives through a whole range of activities and services. The UK library service is a huge resource, which not only lends millions of books free each year, but also CDs and DVDs. Most are now equipped with the internet, so visitors can browse websites and do research. One of their traditional main attractions is as a source of masses of information about both local and national activities. Additionally, there are reference sections containing newspapers and periodicals as well as a wide selection of reference books covering any subject.

The UK's public library service is excellent – please support and help to keep it going by using your local facilities.

Sciences and other related subjects

If astronomy, meteorology or geology fascinate you, there are several societies and associations that may be of interest:

British Astronomical Association: **www.britastro.org**.

Geologists' Association: **www.geologistsassociation.org.uk**.

Royal Meteorological Society: **www.rmets.org**.

Special interests

Whether your special enthusiasm is stamp collecting or model flying, most of the associations listed have magazines, organize events, answer queries and can put you in contact with kindred spirits:

Aviation Historian: **www.theaviationhistorian.com**.

British Association of Numismatic Societies (BANS):
    www.coinclubs.freeserve.co.uk.

British Model Flying Association (BMFA): **www.bmfa.org**.

Central Council of Church Bell Ringers (CCCBR): **www.cccbr.org.uk**.

Miniature Armoured Fighting Vehicle Association (MAFVA): **www.mafva.net**.

National Association of Flower Arrangement Societies (NAFAS): **www.nafas.org.uk**.

National Philatelic Society: **www.ukphilately.org.uk**.

Railway Correspondence and Travel Society: **www.rcts.org.uk**.

Sport and activities

Doing some exercise as we get older is important. You don't have to take up a sport to keep fit – housework, gardening and DIY will provide you with exercise. But retirement presents an ideal opportunity to take up (or spend more time enjoying) a sporting hobby. To find out what is available in your area, contact your local authority recreational department or your nearest sports or leisure centre. Here are some suggestions.

Angling

Whether you are an experienced angler, or are thinking of taking up fishing as a hobby, this sport offers a wide variety of opportunities (particularly good news for women whose pheromones apparently attract fish onto their rods...):

Angling Trust: **www.anglingtrust.net**.

UK Fishing: **www.uk-fishing.com**.

Badminton

Badminton is a popular sport for all ages. You can play badminton at any leisure centre. If you haven't played before, start with doubles as it is less demanding than singles. Most people play it for leisure but it can be competitive as well as keeping you fit. For more information see:

Badminton England: **www.badmintonengland.co.uk**.

Play Badminton: **www.playbadminton.co.uk**.

Bowling

Bowls clubs are very sociable and the sport provides some gentle exercise. The action of bowling helps maintain our sense of balance. The game comes in a variety of forms: crown green bowls, lawn bowls, short mat bowls and carpet bowls. For further information see:

Bowls England: **www.bowlsengland.com**.

British Crown Green Bowling Association: **www.crowngreenbowls.org**.

English Indoor Bowling Association: **www.eiba.co.uk**.

English Short Mat Bowling Association: **www.esmba.co.uk**.

Clay pigeon shooting

Clay pigeon shooting is enjoyed by people from 9 years to 90, of either sex. It is a hobby that can provide great personal fulfilment on an informal basis, or in a more organized and competitive fashion:

Clay Pigeon Shooting Association (CPSA): **www.cpsa.co.uk**.

Clay Shooting: **www.englishsportingclays.co.uk**.

The Big Shoot: **www.thebigshoot.co.uk**.

Cricket

There are many different playing opportunities for all ages and abilities, such as club cricket, indoor cricket and new shorter formats of the game. If playing is not for you, there are plenty of opportunities to watch matches:

England and Wales Cricket Board (ECB): **www.ecb.co.uk**.

Kia Oval – Surrey County Cricket Club: **www.kiaoval.com**.

Lord's Cricket Ground: **www.lords.org**.

Croquet

Croquet has been popular in England since it was first introduced in 1851 at The Great Exhibition. It can be played as a recreational pastime or competitive sport. See:

Croquet Association: **www.croquet.org.uk**.

Cycling

Cycling is a popular pastime for people of all ages. For the older person it is beneficial as it is a non-impact sport: it doesn't put strain on the joints. Whatever your level of experience, whether you wish to cycle in a group, meet new friends, or get into cycling for leisure or as a competitor, there are plenty of ways into the sport:

British Cycling: **www.britishcycling.org.uk**.

CTC (Cyclists' Touring Club): **www.ctc.org.uk**.

Road Cycling UK (RCUK): **www.roadcyclinguk.com**.

UK Cycling Events: **www.ukcyclingevents.co.uk**.

Darts

As well as being a professional competitive sport, darts is also a traditional pub game. Today it is played by over 6 million people regularly, and watched by millions on television:

British Darts Organisation (BDO): **www.bdodarts.com**.

Golf

Golf is another sport that provides some gentle exercise with a good social scene and plenty of fresh air. National golf unions can provide information about municipal courses and private clubs, of which there are some 1,700 in England alone. Additionally, many adult education institutes and sports centres run classes for beginners. Take a look at:

England Golf: **www.englandgolf.org**.

Golf Union of Wales: **www.golfunionwales.org**.

Golfing Union of Ireland: **www.gui.ie**.

Scottish Golf Union: **www.scottishgolf.org**.

Running

Regardless of age, fitness level, aspiration, background or location, running is fun and good for you. According to recent research, older people can defy the ageing process by undertaking the kind of strength and endurance training usually reserved for elite athletes. Age has proved no barrier to some elderly Britons: in the 2013 London marathon there were 237 runners over age 70 and a dozen more in their 80s. If that is something you aspire to, start by becoming one of the UK's running community. To help get you going, here are a few websites:

ARC (Association of Running Clubs): **www.runningclubs.org.uk**.

Good Run Guide: **www.goodrunguide.co.uk**.

Run England: **www.runengland.org**.

Runners Forum: **www.runnersforum.co.uk**.

Swimming

Did you know that over 450 people in the UK die from drowning each year? Swimming is the only sport that can save your life. It can be fairly gentle if you are not used to exercise. Whether you are a beginner, a seasoned swimmer, or planning to make a return to the pool after years (or decades) away, the following website will give you lots of information:

British Swimming: **www.swimming.org**.

Table tennis

Table tennis is a cheap and accessible sport, played by 2.4 million people in the UK. For people of all ages and abilities, table tennis clubs provide the best place to learn and play the sport:

English Table Tennis: **www.englishtabletennis.org.uk**.

English Table Tennis Association: **www.etta.co.uk**.

Veterans English Table Tennis Society: **www.vetts.org.uk**.

Tennis

Tennis is enjoyed by millions of recreational players, including seniors, and is also a hugely popular worldwide spectator sport:

International Tennis Federation: **www.ifttennis.com**.

Lawn Tennis Association: **www.lta.org.uk**.

Seniors' Lawn Tennis Club of Great Britain: **www.sltcofgb.org.uk**.

Rowing

Rowing has enthusiasts of all ages, from youngsters to those who are well past 80. Since 2010 'veteran' rowers have been known as 'Masters'. There has also been a change in the lower age so that rowers from 27 to over 80 can now compete in Masters events. See:

British Rowing: **www.britishrowing.org**.

Walking

Walking is an excellent form of exercise that is truly accessible. Almost everyone can do it, anywhere and at any time. It won't cost you anything and you don't need any fancy equipment. You don't need to find time for it, you can build it into your daily routine by walking to the shops. You can take things at your own pace, starting slowly and building up. Your legs were made for walking: it's a wonderful form of natural exercise that can keep you healthy, living longer and improve your mental health. Walking can also help you recover from illness, as well as prevent it. If you still need convincing, here are some positive things that walking can do for your health:

- help your heart and lungs work better;
- lower your blood pressure;
- keep your weight down;
- lighten your mood;
- keep your joints, muscles and bones strong;
- increase 'good' cholesterol.

Walking as part of a small group is a good way to start and keep going. If you walk with a group, you will maintain or increase your social contacts:

Ramblers' Charity: **www.ramblers.org.uk**.

Walking for Health: **www.walkingforhealth.org.uk**.

Windsurfing

Windsurfing as an activity in middle age can lead to a more active, healthier and happier old age. If you need a bit of encouragement to enjoy the challenge of windsurfing, see:

Seavets (Senior and Veteran Windsurfers Association): **www.seavets.co.uk**.

Yachting

If you want to try sailing to see if you like it, there are ways to take part without any major financial commitment. Your nearest sailing club may be able to arrange a trial sail, or you could try a water sports holiday:

New To Sailing: **www.newtosailing.com**.

Royal Yachting: **www.rya.org.uk**.

For people with disabilities

Facilities for the disabled have improved dramatically recently. Here are some sporting organizations that cater specifically for the disabled:

British Blind Sport: **www.britishblindsport.org.uk**.

British Disabled Fencing Association (BDFA): **www.bdfa.org.uk**.

British Wheelchair Sport: **www.wheelpower.org.uk**.

Disability Snowsport UK: **www.disabilitysnowpsort.org.uk**.

English Federation of Disability Sport: **www.efds.co.uk**.

UK Deaf Sport: **www.ukdeafsport.org.uk**.

Women's organizations

Here are some women's clubs and organizations that are enormously popular:

Association of Inner Wheel Clubs UK: **www.associationofinnerwheelclubs**.

Federation of Women's Institutes of Northern Ireland: **www.wini.org.uk**.

Mothers' Union (MU): **www.themothersunion.org**.

National Association of Women's Clubs: **www.nawc.org.uk**.

National Women's Register (NWR): **www.nwr.org.uk**.

Scottish Women's Rural Institutes (SWRI): **www.swri.org.uk**.

Women's Institute (WI): **www.thewi.org.uk**.

Chapter Ten
Starting your own business

ALLAN ESLER SMITH, FCA

Allan is a Fellow of the Institute of Chartered Accountants and specializes in helping people start up in business. He has helped thousands of mature people do this, and shares his hints and tips in this chapter.

You can find Allan at **www.allaneslersmith.com**.

> *Perfect freedom is reserved for the man who lives by his own work and in that work does what he wants to do.*
>
> R G COLLINGWOOD (1889–1943) *SPECULUM MENTIS*

In the 10 years from December 2003 to December 2013 the number of self-employed in the United Kingdom increased from 3.5 million to 4.5 million and they now account for over 15 per cent of occupations. More and more people are setting up their own business and becoming their own boss – and we even tell you how you can do it in just one page. There is lots more information to help if you want to delve deeper. So whether it is earning £2,000 to supplement a pension, or building a business that can keep you earning and occupied for years to come, this is the chapter for you. While financially rewarding, this is not the only reason people want to start a business, as social and emotional benefits also feature. Importantly you will not be alone and this chapter will signpost you to plenty of help and support – and most of it is free (it is just a matter of knowing where to look!). You are also in good company as 91 per cent of businesses in the UK have fewer than four staff, and the enterprise culture in the UK is gathering momentum again.

This chapter will give you the confidence to get started and has plenty of straightforward advice. The key issues covered are:

- Starting a small business in just one page.
- Understanding the differences between starting a small business and employment, especially if both options are still open to you.
- Do I need to bother with a business plan?
- Getting off to a good start – practical and emotional tips and buying your first equipment.
- Administration, finance and tax – keep on top of the paperwork or it will keep on top of you!
- Filling the diary with work, and some clever tips for marketing that will make a difference.
- The trading format – should you set up your own limited liability company, work as a sole trader or maybe go into partnership?
- Other ways of getting started and operational issues.
- Where you can go for further help – remember you are not alone and these are enterprising times in the UK.

Additionally, in the three real-life case studies featured at the end of this chapter, you will see how Karin, Phil and Paul are coping after starting up in business. This includes what did or did not work for them as they grew their businesses and even coped with going bust. Finally, we have included a summary checklist to help you tick off the key issues once you decide to get started in business.

Start a small business – in one page

This one page will get you on the way to starting a small business and earning vital pounds to help with living costs – or just to treat yourself. Maybe it is from writing, selling crafts, doing odd jobs, gardening, dog walking/kennelling or making household items. Follow this step-by-step guide:

1 Find something you enjoy doing and that you can sell.
2 Register as self-employed with Her Majesty's Revenue and Customs (HMRC) on 0300 200 3504, or for customers who are deaf or hard of hearing on 0845 915 3296 (textphone).

3 You will then have to complete a tax return each year and declare your taxable income from your business every year. Check out HMRC's website (**www.hmrc.gov.uk**) for guidance on the basics of income tax – and keep a list of your income and costs.

4 Acquire some files and keep all your business records to prove your business and its transactions – sales invoices, purchases receipts, bank statements, cash books. If it 'proves' your business transactions you must keep it for seven years after the end of the tax year.

5 The big lesson: HMRC don't like people evading tax (it is illegal!) and have taken on lots of new investigators in the last few years. If you have acted honestly, kept your records and help HMRC with their questions you will have little to worry about. But if you can't prove your transactions then you will be charged the tax that HMRC believe they were due, plus a penalty of up to an extra 100 per cent plus interest. They can go back six years without much fuss and even longer if they believe your errors were deliberate.

6 If you are self-employed you don't actually need an accountant to prepare the year-end accounts and self-assessment tax return – many people can do this themselves. In time your business may generate enough to pay an accountant or a bookkeeper for some assistance.

7 To help your business grow (the vital bit!), jump to the marketing section and case studies of this chapter. The tips should take you to the next level and, in time, you may benefit from delving into even more of this chapter and our hints and tips.

Yes, you can!

Broadcaster Liz Barclay and Maree Atkinson of the Federation of Small Businesses share their insights into starting a business and offer some tips, which reveal that 'Yes, you can!'

Liz Barclay is one of the most recognized voices on British radio today with her common-sense approach to money and finance on BBC London. She presented *You and Yours* for more than 10 years, presents *Pick of the Week* on Radio 4 and writes for the *Independent on Sunday* as well as personal finance and small business magazines. She shares her experience and tips below:

First, forget about the salary spiral where you will only consider taking a job that offers you as much as or more than you have earned in the past. Do your calculations carefully and work out how much you need to make to pay your bills and enjoy life. That shift in thinking alone opens up all sorts of possibilities. You can do work that pays less but that you enjoy more, choose your own working hours and when to take breaks, and mix work with rest, play, retraining, learning and even unpaid voluntary work. The world is your oyster.

Many of the people I talk to who are moving out of full-time employment are thinking of retraining or brushing up long-disused skills at a further education college, or about how they can turn a hobby into an income-generating venture. Self-employment or starting a small business after a lifetime of being an employee can be daunting, but it can be done and this chapter will help you on the way. The people I know who are most successful are those who are doing something they love. Judith is writing verses for greetings cards and taking photos for postcards – using her creative side after retiring from social work. Dawn is similarly going back to her artistic roots and Diane is teaching older people Pilates and complementary therapies. They're passionate about their businesses and willing to give them the time and TLC they need to make them flourish. Hard work doesn't seem like a chore so they're less likely to give up when the going gets tough, as it will.

The section within this chapter on 'Marketing tips to fill your diary' will assist you with your marketing and research. The case studies at the end of this chapter show how new start-up businesses have secured their very first few clients. On generating business ideas Liz adds:

There are ideas everywhere. You don't have to come up with something new. You might do what you did before as an employee but on a consultancy basis with new customers. The more important thing is research. Be sure there are enough people who will pay you for what you do and that they have easy access to your products or services. Just because two tanning salons on the high street are buzzing doesn't mean there are enough customers to support a third. Many businesses that I saw fail had not done enough market research before spending money. Ask your customers what they like about your business and what they don't. Listen, act and add value – like the butcher in Glasgow who has long queues because he gives his customers recipes for the meat they buy. Talk to your employees who often know the business and customers better than you do. Keep building those relationships so that you spot the trends and stay ahead of the competition.

Liz's concluding advice is:

> Success comes with having a positive and optimistic attitude to your business. This is a must – yes, you can. The glass is always half full! Be passionate about your business. Do not just turn up to work, but enjoy what you do. Put your life and soul into achieving a good day's work.

Maree Atkinson runs her own business and sees hundreds of small businesses start up in her role as an award-winning membership adviser for the Federation of Small Businesses (FSB). The FSB has around 200,000 members and promotes and protects the interests of the self-employed and owners of small firms. For Maree, the watchwords are 'Yes, you can', but she advises that you take special care over your marketing:

> Certainly starting a business later in life may be daunting – I can personally vouch for that. But one big advantage for mature entrepreneurs is the wealth of experience and contacts gathered in work and general life over many years. The more successful start-ups that I see have a real passion to succeed and normally a willingness to adapt. I would agree with Liz Barclay about the importance of market research and really getting to know your customers and the competition you face. This is also a key part of planning and I definitely agree with Allan that the first draft of your business plan does not need to run on for pages and pages. Indeed some business plan 'templates' that I have seen put people off the whole planning process.
>
> I would encourage you to start the planning process by getting something down in writing to show you have researched and understood your business idea and your target customers. Where are they? What is their profile and what might they need (could you change your proposition)? What price are they prepared to pay? How will you get your product or service to them? These are all good starting questions and you can then build things from there by investigating the competition. With further help from your advice network your plan will start to take shape. Remember that there is a lot of help out there and you are definitely not alone. I see lots of idea sharing, hints and tips and introductions at the various

members' networking and social events we run at the FSB: this is one of the vital needs in the first year of starting a business – knowing where to find the *right* answers.

Maree goes on to advise:

One challenge that I see is new business owners becoming overwhelmed by the many hats they have to wear. People underestimate the time it takes to do even the simplest of tasks. Perhaps this is because they came from larger organizations with in-house functions for marketing, legal, accounts and health and safety. Unless you bring in specialists to deal with these areas you are left with a choice: deal with the issues or they will simply get left behind. So manage your time and make lists to make sure all the 'must dos' are tackled first. If you find your precious family time is being spent on disliked jobs, think about hiring in help if you can afford it. Check out trade and professional associations (including the Federation of Small Businesses, which I represent) as these can provide contacts to assist you.

Maree's concluding advice is:

I must have seen over 4,000 people start up in business over the past 10 years. Those who have taken time to research their product or service, sought input from others, understood the financial requirements and developed the plans needed to launch and continue have a much better prospect of success.

Some further marketing tips from Maree feature in the 'Marketing tips to fill your diary' section of this chapter.

Some of the differences between starting a small business and employment

In some cases where there is an opportunity to start a small business there could be a similar opportunity to take a full- or part-time employed position. Which route is right for you?

Here are some of the reasons for starting a small business:

- focus on what you are best at or enjoy;
- be your own boss;
- provide a legacy for your children;

- flexibility (around other interests/responsibilities);
- freedom to organize things your way;
- no commuting;
- less involvement in internal politics and no more useless meetings;
- enjoy working on your own;
- try something new/an experiment;
- getting paid for overtime.

On the other hand, here are some of the reasons for seeking a part- or full-time employed position:

- a local employer with known travel requirements;
- security of income;
- benefits of holiday pay, pension, paid sick leave, and perhaps private health and life cover;
- bonuses and perhaps a car;
- team aspect and friendship of colleagues;
- no personal liability if things go badly wrong;
- staff discounts or other perks.

Why bother with a plan?

There are thousands of success stories about those who took the plunge nearing or post retirement to build a business that provided involvement, fun and income, plus a legacy for their children. However, for every three success stories there is a business that does not work out and your money could disappear fast if you set up in the wrong way or over-stretch yourself. Worst of all you could lose your home if things go really badly wrong, so the reasons below and tips throughout this chapter should help you understand and deal with the risks.

Why businesses fail – learning the lessons

Businesses can fail for many reasons. Learn from the mistakes of others and you will be doing yourself a favour. The number one reason why businesses fail is that *the market moves on and you are left behind*. Take time out to think and keep abreast of what your customers really want (have you tried asking them recently?). Where are your competitors and what are they doing to keep on top of or ahead of the market and, overall, how is the market moving?

A second reason (and one that will increase in 2015) is the *failure to deal with tax affairs properly*. The implications of penalties and interest levied by HMRC (Her Majesty's Revenue & Customs) are often ignored and only hit home when it is too late. Keep your books properly and retain all records for seven years after the year end – in brief, if you can't prove it, you may lose the tax benefit and pay additional tax, penalties and interest. If there is a problem, HMRC can go back and inspect previous years' accounts (for up to six years or even longer). If you fail to pay your tax fully when it is due, HMRC will pursue you vigorously and you are giving them a reason to have a closer look at you and your business. On the other hand, if you have genuine cash flow difficulties and cannot pay your tax on the due date, talk to HMRC and you may find their attitude refreshing if it is the first time you have stumbled.

A third reason is a *failure to manage your cash flow and this includes a lack of access to funding*. Vee Bharakda is a director of business recovery specialists Wilkins Kennedy and advises: 'access to funding is becoming a real issue! If you go to a bank they will want to know exactly why the business requires funding and will be vigilant in their lending criteria. They will require, in most cases, security over the business assets or the owners' residential homes.' Vee adds: 'in certain cases businesses have found alternative funding through invoice discounting and factoring, which can be an effective way to fund an expanding business'. So, for someone setting up in business in later life, the scale of the anticipated business will be a key issue. On the one hand you may not need external finance if you fund the business from your own resources, or if you start small and grow organically. On the other hand, if external finance is needed you may have to 'get real' and recognize that banks and others are not in the habit of lending money to unviable propositions. It is often the case that the bank will be the largest stakeholder in a business. For this reason security is normally required, which may well include a charge on your home.

A *failure to plan and poor management* are a fourth reason for businesses failing. Vee Bharakda comments that the failure to plan and basic management deficiencies are often interlinked: 'Over the years we have seen various examples of inadequate management skills. The day-to-day running of the business sadly seems to take priority rather than planning for the future. Unfortunately the owners are so busy in immediate and minor issues that they fail to recognize the need to spend time on longer-term planning and strategic decisions and the business spirals downwards to failure.'

A fifth reason for business failure is *bad debts* (where the customer goes bust and cannot pay your invoices), as this will come off your bottom-line profit and can really hurt. There are a few simple steps that you can take to reduce the potential of taking such a hit. What are your credit terms and have you encouraged all customers to pay electronically? Do you contact them as soon as your invoices become overdue? Do you require cash on delivery or prepayment? (PayPal and mobile credit card machines are transforming the payment services.) In some cases it is worth remembering that a bad customer is sometimes worse than no customer at all.

Vee Bharakda comments: 'Businesses tend to fail for the reasons Allan has mentioned and one additional reason that we have seen recently – trying to expand too quickly.' Vee goes on to explain: 'Some businesses start on the right track, but tend to expand far too quickly either by overtrading, selling more than their cash flow will allow, overproduction of stock or not researching the marketplace or competitors adequately. The most common mistake that we see in this area is businesses employing the wrong staff and additional staff rather than first looking to motivate and incentivize the existing workforce. Extra staff increase overheads and decrease profit. Beware!'

So 'why bother' when it comes to planning? The answer should now be evident from the above – you are improving your chances of succeeding and may even do rather better than you first thought. On that positive note Vee remembers many positive turnaround stories from her career in business recovery and believes that 'success comes from having a positive and optimistic attitude to your business. Business owners need to be open-minded and realize that they do not need to know everything and must always be willing to learn and adapt with the business in mind. And with that in mind, if a business owner is experiencing financial difficulties and is worried about the risk they could be facing it is always best to talk to a business recovery specialist sooner rather than later.'

What goes into a plan?

'I have always found that plans are useless but planning is indispensable': this is a quote from General Eisenhower and is about planning for battle. We can draw a couple of lessons from this but the starting point is to make a promise that you will put your plan in writing. Too many people run a mile when the subject of a plan comes up, especially the notion of a grand-sounding business plan. Some new businesses – perhaps armed with confidence gained from a book on setting up a business, business banking literature, or even after attending a setting-up-in-business course – start a plan but never get it finished.

The reason for this is twofold: first, fear of the planning process and, second, intimidation by daunting plan templates and spreadsheets seen in books or banking literature. The prescription is a three-stage plan that will get you started and then, with experience, you can tweak it and make it that bit slicker.

Stage 1 of the plan: objectives

What, financially, do you need to set as objectives to bring you in that £2,000 or £20,000 or £60,000? This takes a bit of thinking through but you should be able to come up with two or three simple objectives based on income, gross profit (if you sell stock) and overheads.

For a contractor or freelancer who does not sell stock there could be just two objectives. *Objective 1*: I aim to invoice £30,000 in my first year of trading based on working at least 100 days at an average billing rate of £300 per day. I will review my billing rates quarterly and my performance monthly. *Objective 2*: I will aim to keep my overheads (after expenses recharged to clients) in my first year to £5,000. For businesses that sell stock, *Objective 3* will be something like: I will aim to achieve the following gross profit percentages:

Product line A: 30 per cent;

Product line B: 40 per cent;

Product line C: 50 per cent.

Gross profit percentages are calculated using:

(Sales price less cost of materials/product sold ÷ sales price) × 100

The key point with objectives is that less gives more: you don't want a long list of objectives.

Stage 2 of the plan: your market research

The next page of your plan should be all about your marketing effort: this is a topic that is often misunderstood and mistaken for advertising. Think about approaching this section under the following three headings: products, customers and competitors.

Products

Start with your main product or service and think about the features and benefits of what you are selling. Understanding these and discussing them with your trusted advisers will allow you to start thinking about other related services or goods that you could offer.

Customers

For each main product area ask lots of questions to tease out your research. Who are my customers? Where are they based? When do they tend to buy? How and where do they tend to buy and at what price? How should I contact them? Keep asking those important questions of who, what, why, where, when and how – as they tease out all sorts of gems.

Competitors

Again, ask yourself who, what, why, where, when and how? This should lead to a series of activities that you can do to help secure new quality work and customers (note that the marketing section later on in this chapter has further tips). If you end up with a jumble of unfocused ideas try ranking each idea on the basis of priority, impact and cost (free is good!).

Stage 3 of the plan: your income and expenditure forecast

This is your income and expenditure forecast for the year and this third page is the tricky one. It is your map for the year ahead financially and will allow you to monitor your actual performance against the plan. You can then do something about it when you are off target. You should be able to do this yourself but if it becomes a struggle, ask your accountant to help.

Is there more?

Once you have completed your first plan keep it alive and keep reviewing how you are doing against it; even if the plan is useless you will find, as Eisenhower did, that the planning process itself teases out things that will make things that little bit better – guaranteed!

Practical and emotional tips

Your partner's attitude is crucial. Even if not directly involved, he or she will have to accept (at least initially) the loss of some space in the house to give you an office. Do you have space available to work from home initially or would you need/prefer to rent accommodation? There will be the added distractions of out-of-hours phone calls and, perhaps, suddenly cancelled social engagements. Can your family/partner cope with having you and your business in the house? Can you cope without the resources/back-up provided by an employer (IT/ HR/training/administrative support) – as you will have to do it yourself or buy it in.

Keep on top of the paperwork

Generally, this one topic causes the most groans! But simple bookkeeping, if done properly, is just a by-product of your business and flows naturally from raising sales invoices and paying for purchases. As a bonus, you will never miss an unpaid invoice if you are on top of your bookkeeping.

An even more compelling reason for doing your own bookkeeping is that HMRC has a 'prove it or lose it' view if enquiring into an aspect of your tax return. Under the system of self-assessment, HMRC relies on you completing your tax returns. In the case of an enquiry, HMRC tells you precisely what part of your tax return is under investigation and you are expected to be able to validate sample payments. If you are unable to prove the expenditure, you lose it as far as HMRC is concerned, resulting in fewer purchases being accepted as a deduction from your profits and more tax to pay. There will be penalties and interest to pay and the scope of HMRC's enquiries will be widened.

Basic bookkeeping

All incoming and outgoing payments need to be recorded throughout the year. When recording income, you will need to differentiate between your fees and your expenses (or other 'recharged' items). You will also need to keep a record of income from other sources, such as bank/building society interest. Records of outgoings need to be categorized according to type; examples of some categories you might need to consider are: stock, subscriptions/meeting fees, office equipment, office supplies, post and courier costs; travel fares, parking and subsistence; telephone and internet; sundry; accountancy and professional fees; and insurance.

Many small business owners opt to do their own bookkeeping, with or without the help of a computer software package. If you opt for a software package choose one that your accountant understands as their fees should then be less. For many small businesses your accountant should be able to provide some Excel spreadsheets that will do the job, together with a bookkeeping guide to help get you started.

If you are really averse to bookkeeping yourself, consider hiring a bookkeeper. Bookkeepers currently charge between about £16 and £23 per hour, depending on geographical location and experience, and can be found by recommendation from your accountant or business network contacts.

Accountants

Depending on qualifications and experience, accountants assisting new small start-up businesses could charge from £35 to about £120 per hour to assist you in setting up in business and to prepare your accounts and tax. Anyone can call themselves an accountant so it can be a bit of a free-for-all, with very variable quality when things go wrong at the lower end of the spectrum (and sometimes even with seemingly respectable firms claiming to have thousands of clients). Unreturned calls and not dealing factually with enquiries and questions, vague verbal assurances and not dealing with formal complaints are all part of the 'deal' when you end up with a 'nightmare accountant'. Even worse, when you realize the short-falls in their service and knowledge they could try to withhold fees that were paid up front. If there are mistakes in your accounts and tax you will also find that you are very much on your own when it comes to dealing with HMRC enquiries.

Some accountancy firms offer a combination of bookkeeping, accountancy and tax services and, if so, you can expect to pay a premium on the bookkeeping hourly rates quoted above.

Ask your trusted family members or friends if they can recommend an accountant. Then ensure you get clarity on three things: 1) confirmation of the accountant's qualifications (the type of qualification); 2) the professional body you would complain to if there is ever a problem; and 3) check that they hold professional indemnity insurance. These three points would usually be clarified by an accountant; if you have to actually ask for them it probably tells you a lot. It is advisable to meet at least two accountants and see how you feel about rapport and the availability of proactive hints and tips. Will the person you meet be the person who does your accounts and tax and provides proactive advice? Get written confirmation of hourly rates plus an estimate of fees for the year, and get clarity on what happens if you decide to change accountants halfway through the year if fees are paid up front or monthly. Most accountants would be used to providing clients with a 'retainer', clarifying the above and what you and the accountant will do and by when. A good accountant who knows your industry area will be able to help with general guidance and offer input to your plan on marketing and pricing, drawing on experience beyond accounting and tax.

Finally, there is sometimes some confusion over the term 'audit of accounts'. Many years ago, smallish companies in the UK had to have an audit of their accounts. The turnover threshold (one of three thresholds) for being required to have an audit has been increased and currently stands at £6.5 million, so the vast majority of start-ups need not concern themselves with audited accounts.

Paying tax and National Insurance

Sole traders

Self-employed individuals running their own businesses are usually called 'sole traders'. All new businesses that trade as sole traders need to register as self-employed with HMRC on 0300 200 3504, or for customers who are deaf or hard of hearing on 0845 915 3296 (textphone), or via the website: **www.hmrc.gov.uk/selfemployed/**.

While tax can be daunting, some sole traders with relatively straight-forward billing and overheads do their own tax returns and pay income tax on their profits. With income tax, you first have a personal allowance, which gives you a tax-free amount, and then any excess income (including your profits) is taxed at 20 per cent, then over a certain limit at 40 per cent and then 45 per cent. The precise yearly limits are available from the HMRC website or your accountant. In very broad terms, if you are under 65, you currently (summer 2014) have a tax-free allowance of £10,000. You are then taxed on the next £31,865 at 20 per cent and then 40 per cent tax applies to further taxable income up to £150,000. Anything above £150,000 gets taxed at 45 per cent. Many sole traders choose to run their bookkeeping for the year to 5 April to coincide with the tax year end (or 31 March, which HMRC effectively accepts as equivalent to 5 April).

If you are past the state retirement age there will be no National Insurance contributions (NICs) to pay. Subject to this, sole traders are liable for Class 2 NICs (currently a nominal amount of £2.75 per week), which are collected by direct debit either monthly or quarterly. The mandate is set up automatically when you register as self-employed. After starting, you have three months to register and if you forget there is an automatic £100 fine. You are also liable for the much more significant Class 4 NICs that are assessed and collected by HMRC at the same time as assessing your income tax on profits. Currently these are at 9 per cent on profits between £7,956 and £41,865 and this reduces to just 2 per cent on profits over £41,865.

The payment of sole-trader income tax is reasonably straightforward but there is a twist in your first year of trading. Assuming that you have a year end of 5 April 2016, the first payment will be due by 31 January 2017 so you have a long period of (effectively) interest-free credit, as some of the profits on which the tax is due may have been earned as long ago as May 2015. With the first payment, however, you get a 'double whammy' as you also have to pay on 31 January 2017 a payment on account of your second year's trading. Then on 31 July 2017 you have to make a second on-account payment of the second year's trading. Both on-account payments are set by default on the basis of your year 1 profits. You can 'claim' a reduction if year 2 is proving to have lower profits than year 1; your accountant will help you with this if it is appropriate.

After this initial tax famine, followed by double payment of tax, you will thereafter receive a tax demand twice a year. Payments need to be made by 31 January (during the tax year) and then by 31 July after the end of that tax year, with any overpayment or underpayment sorted out by the following 31 January. Many sole-trader businesses set up a reserve bank account in addition to their current account, and place a percentage of their income aside, which is earning interest each month (albeit not amounting to much in the current climate). This tactic should help you resist the temptation to raid money that is not for spending – and ensure you can pay your tax on time.

Additionally, as a self-employed person you are allowed certain other reliefs. Ask your accountant, but the following expenses and allowances are usually tax deductible:

- *Business expenses.* These must be incurred 'wholly and exclusively' for the purposes of the trade. Office supplies that you buy will probably qualify; however, any business entertaining will not.

- *Partially allowable expenses.* These mainly apply if you are working from home. They include such items as the part of your rent, heating, lighting and telephone usage that you devote to business purposes, and also possibly some of the running expenses on your car, if you use your car for your business.

- *Spouse's wages.* If you employ your partner in the business, his or her pay (provided this is reasonable) qualifies as a legitimate expense, in the same way as any other employee's, but must be accounted for through a PAYE system.

- *Pension contributions.* Tax relief is generally available for pension contributions at the higher of £3,600 (gross) or 100 per cent of relevant earnings up to a maximum of £40,000 for 2014/15.

- *Capital allowances.* This is a tax break for expenditure on equipment.

Partnerships

Partnership tax is broadly similar to the process described above for a sole trader, with the exception of some more paperwork. In addition to submitting each partner's individual personal self-assessment tax return a composite partnership tax return must also be submitted.

Limited company

Companies pay corporation tax on their profits (currently 20 per cent). There is a slightly higher rate of corporation tax of 21 per cent on profits above £300,000. This higher rate has been cut aggressively in recent years and will reduce to 20 per cent from 1 April 2015. The logic of cutting the higher rate is to provide the UK with a very competitive business tax regime to encourage international business to stay in or relocate to the UK. The logic continues that if big business does well, the hundreds of small businesses that feed off every big business will follow in their wake and the economy grows.

Your company accounts need to be finalized and any corporation tax paid nine months after your year end.

The key point with a company is that the money coming in is not your money – it is the company's money – so how do you extract your money? The first option is salary and this means running a 'pay as you earn' (PAYE) system: another form of tax with a rigorous calculation regime and payments that have to be made to HMRC. PAYE carries the income tax rates as featured for the sole trader, but NICs (National Insurance contributions) can be much higher as these are a composite of employee *and* employer NICs (as the company is an employer). Currently these are 12 per cent employee NICs on £7,956 to £41,860, reducing to 2 per cent for amounts above £41,860, and then an additional 13.8 per cent employer NICs on everything above £7,956. Salary and employer's NICs are deductible when calculating corporation tax.

The second option for extracting funds is dividends, but these are not deductible when calculating your corporation tax. The big selling point for dividends is that, at face value, they are not subject to NICs. This leads us neatly into a possible 'tax trap' for the unwary. As a director, you can decide whether or not to pay yourself a salary, dividends or both. The appeal of dividends is the lack of NICs. However, this is before we have outlined HMRC regulation number 35 (IR35) that came into force in April 2000.

HMRC is particularly interested in ex-employees setting up service companies that work exclusively for their former employer or for just a few clients (sometimes called 'personal service companies' to use an HMRC term). This is an extremely wide-ranging and difficult subject but, in very simplified terms, IR35 is to be avoided if at all possible and it only applies to companies (not sole traders).

There are many hints and tips and some urban myths about IR35; the bottom line as we go into 2015 is that HMRC is strengthening its specialist compliance teams that investigate IR35. HMRC has also sought to provide more information to assist businesses in understanding whether or not IR35 affects them. For instance, in 2012 HMRC introduced tests and depending on your answers you obtain a risk rating – the higher the score the lower your risk to IR35. You can quickly build up your score with some big-hitting points, for instance operating from your own premises (not a residential home) and substituting another person in the delivery of your services. There are also some modest point earners (such as maintaining professional indemnity insurance and having a written business plan). On the other hand, you can almost wipe out your points by going back to work for an employer that you were on PAYE with 'within the 12 months which ended on the last 31 March'. For some, these tests will provide a quick fix to IR35 (own premises and a substitution 'arrangement') but for most personal-service-type companies (freelancers, consultants and contractors mainly) it is now even more complex and seems to be a step backwards.

Tips and hints on IR35 are outside the scope of this guide. It is a big issue and one that you have first got to recognize and then do something about. One of the key players in helping freelancers guide themselves through the minefield of IR35 is the Professional Contractors Group (PCG) at **www.pcg.org.uk**. This organization, working in conjunction with a chartered accountant who understands IR35, is probably your next step if you are concerned. Briefly, if you fall foul of IR35, the tax inspector will seek to set aside the dividends you have paid and treat the dividend payment as if it were subject to PAYE and NICs (including employer NICs) and the tax advantage you thought you may have had will disappear.

Registering for VAT

Value added tax (VAT) was introduced in 1973 and it seems that many people have lost sight of the name of this tax and especially the word 'added'. You are, in effect, adding a tax and are an unpaid tax collector.

If your taxable turnover is likely to be more than £81,000 in a 12-month period or less, you must register for VAT unless your supplies/services are outside the scope of VAT. Any expenses that you recharge to clients need to be included in the calculation of taxable turnover.

UK business clients are invariably registered for VAT so are not concerned about having it added to your invoice, and for that reason some businesses register for VAT before reaching the £81,000 compulsory registration limit so that they can claim VAT on their purchases. Before voluntarily applying consider whether registration will really be of benefit to you, that is, whether reclaiming the VAT paid on items needed for your business (such as office equipment) is worth the trouble of sending in mandatory, quarterly VAT returns and keeping separate VAT records for possible inspection by visiting VAT officers.

You can claim back VAT on pre-start/pre-registration expenditure involved in setting up the business. If you elect for 'Cash Accounting' status, this means that VAT only becomes payable or reclaimable when invoices are actually paid. It avoids having to pay the VAT on your own invoices before slow-paying clients pay you, which can create cash-flow problems. One final positive if you do register for VAT is that it seems to give you added credibility with clients.

VAT flat-rate scheme

HMRC introduced the flat-rate scheme in 2004, with the aim of simplifying record keeping for small businesses. This allows you to charge VAT to your clients at the standard rate of 20 per cent and to pay VAT as a percentage of your VAT-inclusive turnover (instead of having to work out the VAT payable on your sales less purchases). You can apply to join the scheme if your taxable turnover (excluding VAT) will not be more than £150,000 in the next 12 months.

HMRC publishes a list of business categories from which you need to decide which best describes your business. A further bonus is that you can deduct 1 per cent from the flat rate that you use for your first year of VAT registration. As a tip, do not do anything without checking it out with your accountant as there are a few twists and turns that could make the VAT flat-rate scheme unsuitable. But, at face value, it seems to have been beneficial to many small businesses.

Marketing tips to fill your diary

It is a sad fact that many new business owners believe that marketing simply means placing an advert in some well-known directory. This will achieve only a fraction of the sales of any comparable business with a decent grasp of marketing. So how can you generate sales for a new business? The following nine tips should start to help you along.

Your own website and/or social media

Business and the public now rely so heavily on the internet that a presence seems almost vital either through a website and/or harnessing social media. Is there a vital domain name (website unique address) that you need to secure and register? If this one question alone fills you with fear the solutions are nearer than you think – just try asking friends and don't ignore help that is right in front of your nose: young friends or relatives may know more than you.

It is also worth checking out websites run by trade or professional associations that may allow you to register and set up a profile. You can set up profiles on various social media 'networking websites' such as LinkedIn. Depending on your business, Facebook and Twitter can provide the benefits of building your online contacts and allow you to showcase your expertise in a certain area. Social media (very like networking, below) is not about sell, sell, sell. It is more about building relationships and trust with an ever-increasing contact list.

Personal contacts and networking

Once you decide to set up your own business, your personal contacts, ex-colleagues or other small business owners are a potential source of work. Too many small businesses forget that behind every contact there is another layer of potential contacts, who are just one introduction away; so ignore this multiplier effect at your peril. In your first year you should be re-educating your contacts to think of you not as 'Jane who used to work at IBM' but 'Jane who now runs her own business advising small businesses on their IT needs'. Do not be afraid to pick up the phone or send business cards explaining your new business and what you can offer. Joining the best trade or professional association you can find will be a great way of networking, with the added bonus of research facilities, information and other fringe benefits.

Discounts and offers

These can be used to great effect during seasonal dips, introducing a new service or clearing old stock. Whether it is 20 per cent off, a buy-one-get-one-free offer or the numerous variations of this basic approach, there are three golden rules:

- Always state the original or usual price (to show the value in the offer).
- Always specify an expiry date.
- Always explain that the offer is subject to availability.

Flyers and business cards

Generally speaking, a response rate of 1 per cent to a flyer is considered fairly good. With some clever thinking you can increase the response rate. Have you targeted the flyer? A good example would be a wedding gown designer who neatly persuades a sought-after wedding location hotel to keep a flyer dispenser in their foyer. Are you able to include your professional or trade association logo on your flyer and business cards? Have you asked if this is possible? There are two sides to a flyer and business card – have you thought about putting information on the blank reverse side? Could this contain some useful tips or, perhaps, a special offer or discount? Anything that ensures the card or flyer is kept rather than dumped will help your business to edge ahead.

Testimonials

People generally buy on trust, and testimonials show prospective customers that you have done a good job and can be relied upon. Positive testimonials can be powerful and should never be underestimated.

Agencies

Agencies will be especially important for prospective consultants or contractors as many recruitment agencies also place full and part-time contracts (as opposed to employed positions). The contract market is growing and offers dynamic and fast-moving industries the opportunity to hire (and fire) swiftly. When marketing yourself through an agency the same rules apply as when marketing yourself to a potential employer. Good personal and written presentation will help the agency to sell you on to its clients – and it is in their interest to find you work, given the fee they receive for placing you.

Advertising

There are many options for advertising yourself and your business such as website banners, free and paid-for directory listings. Another approach could be 'free' advertising through a press release that you forward to local or trade press with an interesting story. A clever variant is advertising yourself and your skills by writing articles in professional or trade journals – what do you have that is news or novel or leading edge?

Another subset of advertising is sponsorship. The driving instructor who sponsored the playing shirts on the local under-17s football team is a great example of cost-effective and rather clever sponsorship.

Awards

Business awards can offer new businesses an opportunity to make a splash in the local area, introduce you to other vibrant businesses, and there may even be a category for mature business owners newly starting up. These are often sponsored by local press and the Federation of Small Businesses (**www.fsb.org.uk/**) where more information can be found.

Learn when to say 'no'

This is one of the hardest lessons to learn and comes with experience. The fear of losing a sale to a competitor, or the uncertainty of where the next piece of work or sale will come from if you reject this one, may induce you to overstretch or undercut yourself. If you continually face this dilemma the resulting stress means you may not survive in business for long. So learning how to say 'no' in a way that does not burn bridges is important.

Maree Atkinson of the Federation of Small Businesses (see 'Yes, you can!' above) has some tips to help you say 'no' and advises:

> *Be wary of the promises of business.* You will want to help customers and will want to secure those early sales. You may even find yourself bending over backwards to help. But have you given away your ideas and spent hours of your time with no prospect of the work? A very talented garden designer was asked to redesign a large garden. Excited by the project he prepared some initial plans and the client made a number of changes, which he incorporated. The client did go ahead with the work but used the plans with another contractor. I guess it is a balance between 'marketing time'

and showing your wares but not going too far – all of which you will learn in time!

Marketing to the wrong people. In the early days of starting a small business you will receive invitations for a meeting from possible business partners or joint ventures, who want to 'see if there's a way we could do some work together'. Networking is vital to many businesses, but don't network with random people just because you think you're supposed to network. Do some research about the offer and listen to your 'gut feeling' before you say 'yes'. In time, work out what sort of networking is best for you and what offers to explore further.

Maree's advice reminds me of Lord Alan Sugar's words on what makes an entrepreneur, in his latest book *The Way I See It*: 'If you have partners, they have to bring something to the party.'

Trading formats

Sole trader

A self-employed person is someone who works for him/herself, instead of an employer, and draws an income from their personally run business. If the profits from the work are accounted for on one person's tax return, that person is known as a sole trader. If the profits are shared between two or more people, it is a partnership (see below).

There is no clear definition of self-employment. Defining an employee, on the other hand, is slightly easier as it can generally be assumed that if income tax and NICs are deducted from an individual's salary before they are paid, then that individual is an employee.

Importantly, the business has no separate existence from the owner and, therefore, all debts of the business are debts of the owner who is personally liable for all amounts owed by the business. This strikes fear into the hearts of many business owners. You only need to think of the number of business owners who go bust every time a recession comes around and lose their house. Should this be a worry?

First and foremost, you must consider the risk to you in any work that you do. Could it go wrong and could you be sued? Is that a realistic prospect or so remote that it does not even warrant thinking about? Or is it somewhere in the middle? Can insurance help? (On this, see the relevant section later in this chapter.) Remember that such insurance is only as good as the disclosures you make and the levels of cover provided. At the end of the day you know your business, your customers and the work that you do, so the risk assessment can only be done by you.

How to start up as a sole trader

You can start trading immediately.

You can trade under virtually any name, subject to some restrictions that are mostly common sense, such as not suggesting something you are not (connection to government, royalty or international pre-eminence). A B Jones trading as Super Lawns is fine.

The full name and address of the owner and any trading name must be disclosed on letters, orders and invoices.

A phone call to HMRC's helpline for the newly self-employed (0300 200 3504) must be made within three months of starting up, or visit the website: **www.hmrc.gov.uk/selfemployed/**.

Partnership

Two or more self-employed people who work together on a business and share the profits are trading in partnership. The profits from the work are accounted for on a partnership tax return and extracts from that partnership tax return are then copied into the partners' individual tax returns.

The business has no separate existence from the partners and, therefore, all debts of the business are debts of the partners, so they are personally liable for all amounts owed by the business. In addition, partners are jointly and severally liable for the debts of the business or, put more simply, the last person standing pays the lot. There is a saying that you need to trust your business partner better than your husband/wife/civil partner.

As with sole traders, the first consideration is the potential for business risk, since your personal wealth is backing the debts of the business. First and foremost you must consider the risk to you in any work that you do and, given the 'joint and several liability' point explained above, the trust and faith you have in your business partner. As mentioned above, could it go wrong and could you be sued? Is that a realistic prospect or so remote that it does not even warrant thinking about? Or is it somewhere in the middle? Can insurance help? Again, remember that such insurance is only as good as the disclosures you make and the levels of cover provided.

At the end of the day you know your business, your business partner, your customers and the work that you do, so the risk assessment can only be done by you.

How to start up as a partnership

You can start trading immediately.

You can trade under virtually any name, subject to some restrictions that are mostly common sense, such as not suggesting something you are not (connection to government, royalty or international pre-eminence). A B Jones and A B Smith trading as J & S Super Lawns is fine.

You will need to consult a solicitor to assist with the preparation and signing of a partnership deed. The partnership deed is for your protection and is essential because it sets out the rules of the partnership including, for example, the profit or loss split between partners, what happens if one partner wishes to leave or you wish to admit a new partner.

The full name and address of the partners and any trading name must be disclosed on letters, orders and invoices.

A phone call to HMRC's helpline for the newly self-employed (0300 200 3504) explaining that you are starting a partnership must be made within three months of starting up, or visit the website: **www.hmrc.gov.uk/partnerships/**.

Limited company

A limited liability company (often the shorthand of 'limited company' is used to describe this trading format) is a company whose liability is limited by shares and is the most common form of trading format. The company is owned by its shareholders. The company is run by directors who are appointed by the shareholders.

The shareholders are liable to contribute the amount remaining unpaid on the shares – usually zero as most shares are issued fully paid up. The shareholders therefore achieve limited liability.

How to start up a limited company

A company needs to be registered with Companies House and cannot trade until it is granted a Certificate of Incorporation. The registration process is a quick and inexpensive process using Companies House's web incorporation service (it currently costs £15 and is completed within 24 hours). Some people use a company formation agent (Google this term to find such an agent – there are plenty of them) and the process should cost less than £100.

The company name needs to be approved by Companies House and no two companies can have the same name. Names that suggest, for instance, an international aspect will require evidence to support the claim and certain names are prohibited unless there is a dispensation. An example of this latter category would be the word 'Royal'.

You must appoint a director and this 'officer' of the company carries responsibilities that can incur penalties and/or a fine. The appointment of directors should therefore not be done lightly. The full range of re-sponsibilities is set out in The Companies Act; further guidance is available from the Companies House website (**www.companieshouse.co.uk**). Some examples of the responsibilities include the duty to maintain the financial records of the company, to prepare accounts, to retain the paperwork and to avoid conflicts of interest. Small businesses no longer have to have a separate company secretary but it can be useful to have another office-holder signatory and the risks associated with this position are relatively light. In addition you will need to appoint a registered office, which is a designated address at which official notices and communica-tions can be received. The company's main place of business is usually used as the registered office but you could also use the address of your accountant or solicitor (there may be a charge for this).

Alternative ways of getting started

Rather than start a new business, you could buy into one that is already established, or consider franchising.

Buying a business

Buying an established business can be an attractive route to becoming your own boss, as it eliminates many of the problems of start-up. The enterprise is likely to come equipped with stock, suppliers, an order book, premises and possibly employees. It is also likely to have debtors and creditors. Take professional advice before buying any business, even one from friends. In particular, you should consider why the business is being sold. It may be for perfectly respectable reasons – for instance, a change of circumstances such as retirement. But equally, it may be that the market is saturated, that the rent is about to go sky-high or that major competition has opened up nearby.

Before parting with your money, verify that the assets are owned by the business and get the stock professionally valued. You should also ensure that the debts are collectable and that the same credit terms will apply from existing suppliers. Get an accountant to look at the figures for the last three years and have a chartered surveyor check the premises. A solicitor should be engaged to vet any legal documents, including staff and other ongoing contracts.

The value of the company's assets will be reflected in its purchase price, as will the 'goodwill' (or reputation) that it has established. For more information, agents specializing in small business sales have useful guides (for instance see **www.christie.com**).

Franchising

Franchising continues to be a popular form of business entry route with attractions for both franchisor and franchisee. The franchisor gains, as their 'brand' is able to expand quickly. The advantage to the franchisee is that there are normally fewer risks than starting a business from scratch.

A franchisee buys into an established business and builds up his or her own enterprise under its wing. In return for the investment, plus regular royalty payments, he or she acquires the right to sell the franchisor's products or services within a specified geographic area and enjoys the benefits of its reputation, buying power and marketing expertise. As a franchisee you are effectively your own boss. You finance the business, employ the staff and retain the profits after the franchisor has had its cut. You are usually expected to maintain certain standards and conform to the broad corporate approach of the organization. In return, the franchisor should train you in the business, provide management support and give you access to a wide range of backup services.

The amount of capital needed to buy a franchise varies enormously according to the type of business, and can be anywhere between a few hundred pounds and £500,000 or more. The franchisee is normally liable to pay an initial fee, covering both the entry cost and the initial support services provided by the franchisor, such as advice about location and market research.

The length of the agreement will depend both on the type of business involved and on the front-end fee. Agreements can run from 3 to 20 years and many franchisors include an option to renew the agreement, which should be treated as a valuable asset.

Many franchises have built up a good track record and raising money to invest in good franchises may not be too difficult. Most of the leading high-street banks operate specialist franchise loan sections. Franchisors may also be able to help in raising the money and can sometimes arrange more advantageous terms through their connections with financial institutions.

The British Franchise Association (BFA) represents 'the responsible face' of franchising, and its members have to conform to a code of practice. The BFA publishes a *Franchisee Guide*, which provides comprehensive advice on buying a franchise, together with a list of BFA member franchisors and affiliated advisers. It is well worth attending a franchise seminar to find out more and compare the various franchise options on offer.

A good franchisor will provide a great deal of invaluable help. However, some franchisors are very casual in their approach and can be lacking in competence, or even downright unethical. Make careful enquiries before committing any money: as basic information, you should ask for a bank reference together with a copy of the previous year's accounts. Also check with the BFA whether the franchisor in question is a member, and visit some of the other franchisees to find out what their experience has been. Before signing, seek advice from an accountant or solicitor. For more information, see the British Franchise Association website: **www.thebfa.org**.

Operational and other issues

Inventions and intellectual property

If you have a clever idea that you would like to market, you should ensure that your intellectual property is protected. For information about patenting an invention, and much more, look at the UK Intellectual Property Office website: **www.ipo.gov.uk**.

Licences

Certain types of business require a licence or permit to trade; these include pubs, off-licences, nursing agencies, pet shops, kennels, minicabs or buses, driving instructors, betting shops, auction sale rooms, cinemas, street traders and, in some cases, travel agents and tour operators. You will also require a licence to import certain goods. Your local authority planning office will advise you whether you require a licence, and in many cases your council will be the licensing authority.

Permissions

Depending on the nature of your business, other permissions may need to be obtained, including those of the police, the environmental health department, licensing authorities and the fire prevention officer. In particular, there are special requirements concerning the sale of food, and safety measures for hotels and guest houses. Your local authority will advise you on what is necessary.

Employing staff

Should you consider employing staff, you will immediately increase the complexity of your business. As well as paying salaries, you will have to account for PAYE, keep National Insurance records and conform to the multiple requirements of employment legislation. If you are worried or don't want the bother of doing the paperwork yourself, your accountant is likely to be able to introduce you to a payroll service, which will cost you money but will take some of the burden off your shoulders. Keeping personnel records will bring you into the scope of data protection; see **www.ico.gov.uk**.

Employment legislation

As an employer, you have certain legal obligations in respect of your staff. The most important of these cover such issues as health and safety at work, terms and conditions of employment, and the provision of employee rights including, for example, parental leave, trade union activity and protection against unfair dismissal. Very small firms are exempt from some of the more onerous requirements, and the government is taking steps to reduce more of the red tape. However, it is important that you understand in general terms what legislation could affect you. You will usually find free support on this subject via membership of a trade association or organization such as the Federation of Small Businesses (**www.fsb.org.uk/**). The Health and Safety Executive has a useful website: **www.hse.gov.uk**.

An employer, however small the business, may not discriminate against someone on the grounds of sex, race, disability, religion, marital status, sexual orientation or age. This applies to all aspects of employment, including training, promotion, recruitment, company benefits and facilities. More information at: **www.equalityhumanrights.com**.

Disputes

If you find yourself with a potential dispute on your hands, it is sensible to approach ACAS, which operates an effective information and advisory service for employers and employees on a variety of workplace problems, including employment legislation and employment relations. It also has a wide range of useful publications, giving practical guidance on employment matters. See website: **www.acas.org.uk**.

Insurance

Insurance is more than just a wise precaution. It is essential if you employ staff, have business premises or use your car regularly for commercial purposes. Many insurance companies now offer 'package insurance' for small businesses, which covers most of the main contingencies in a single policy. This usually works out cheaper than buying a collection of individual policies. An insurance broker should be able to guide you through the risks and insurance products available:

- *Employers' liability*: this is compulsory if you employ staff. It provides indemnity against liability for death or bodily injury to employees and subcontractors arising in connection with the business.

- *Product and public liability*: this insures the business and its products against claims by customers or the public.

- *Professional indemnity*: this is essential if a client could suffer a mishap, loss or other damage in consequence of advice or services received.

- *House insurance*: if you operate your business from home, check that you have notified your house insurer of this fact.

- *Motor risks*: check that you have notified your insurer if you use your motor vehicle for your business.

- *Life assurance*: this ensures that funds are available to pay off any debts or to enable the business to continue in the event of your death.

- *Permanent health insurance*: otherwise known as 'income protection', it provides insurance against long-term loss of income as a result of severe illness or disability.

- *Key person insurance*: this applies to the loss of a key person through prolonged illness as well as death. In small companies where the success or failure of the business is dependent upon the skills of one or two key executives, key person insurance may be demanded by lenders.

You should discuss these points with your insurance company or a broker. To find an insurance broker, see the British Insurance Brokers' Association website: **www.biba.org.uk**, or the Association of British Insurers website: **www.abi.org.uk**.

Property investment

A frequent avenue that some people explore when nearing retirement is property investment, either in the UK or abroad. Since they may be armed with spare funds and perhaps have the advantage of more time available and perhaps even some maintenance skills, you can understand why this happens. Up until 2007 people thought they had it made in property investment with the magic mix of good capital growth and decent returns on their investment through rental income. The capital growth bubble burst in the summer of 2007 and some people have been nervous about this sector ever since. It is beyond the scope of this section to comment on whether or not the tide is turning but it can alert you to some of the key issues and potential sources of further help. Some of the issues are around minimizing your property tax bill, deciding whether to use a letting agent or not, complying with all the red tape and avoiding 'tenants from hell'.

Remember that there are many players in this market – including mortgage lenders, mortgage brokers, developers, property syndicates and letting agents – and that most will know more than you and all will want some of your money. Some even pay for your flights and travel expenses to visit property abroad and then play on this in a subsequent high-pressure sales environment. You are strongly advised to consider carefully before signing up – there will always, of course, be another day, another deal. For anyone thinking about property investment you would be wise to invest in David Lawrenson's bestselling property book *Successful Property Letting* and review his website, **www.lettingfocus.com**. This will open your eyes to some of the issues touched upon here and will give you straightforward and clear advice and information on this market. For instance, one of David's candid tips is: 'You must like property. So, if houses bore you stiff, you're probably better off doing something else.'

Armed with this and advice from friends and relatives who have invested in property, you might then be ready to put your toe in the water and start to explore this area.

Further help, advice and training

Small businesses are well served when it comes to general help and training. Some of the best available feature below.

Organizations providing free or subsidized help

Government resources

The government website (**www.gov.uk**) contains the government's online resource for businesses.

Regional or country-specific support is also available at:

Regional help – **www.nationalenterprisenetwork.org**.

Funding and start-up help – **www.enterprisenation.com**.

Northern Ireland – **www.nibusinessinfo.co.uk**.

Scotland – **www.business.scotland.gov.uk**.

Wales – **www.business.wales.gov.uk**.

Start-up Britain

Start-up Britain has been set up by the government to help you find information about starting a business and contains offers and discounts available to new business start-ups. Further information is available from: **www.startupbritain.org**.

HMRC

HMRC provides free training aimed at start-up businesses and on how to run a payroll. Further information is available at: **www.hmrc.gov.uk/ startingup/help-support.htm**.

Adult education centres

Short courses in specific business skills are run by business schools and colleges of higher and further education. Further information is available from **www.learndirect.co.uk** and the Workers Education Association, website: **www.wea.org.uk**.

PRIME

PRIME (The Prince's Initiative for Mature Enterprise) helps people over the age of 50 to set up in business and offers free information and business-networking events. See website: **www.prime.org.uk**.

Other useful organizations

- Many solicitors offers a free initial consultation and advice can be sought on a range of issues. To find solicitors in your local area use the 'find a solicitor' section at the website: **www.lawsociety.org**.
- The Federation of Small Businesses (**www.fsb.org.uk**). The networking opportunities and benefits of FSB make it a 'must have' for most new small businesses.
- Professional Contractors Group (PCG). The PCG's 'Guide to Freelancing' is free and can be downloaded from its website, **www.pcg.org.uk**. PCG's knowledge of and guidance on IR35 for consultants and contractors are second to none.
- Business start-up websites. These are packed with free hints and tips and a useful one is **www.bstartup.com**; their exhibitions are free, well attended and have some excellent free workshops and guest speakers.

Useful reading

An extensive list of books for small and start-up businesses is published by Kogan Page, website: **www.koganpage.com**, including *Start Up and Run Your Own Business* and *Working for Yourself: An entrepreneur's guide*, both by Jonathan Reuvid; *Soul Trader: Putting the heart back into* *your business*, by Rasheed Ogunlaru; *The Rebel Entrepreneur: Rewriting the business rulebook*, by Jonathan Moules.

CASE STUDY   Karin Whittaker, sole trader, designer jewellery

Karin originally comes from Germany and lives in the Forest of Dean. In 2005, after working in the arts in both therapeutic teaching and designing/making, Karin decided to start her own silver-jewellery design business. This was at first a bit of a hobby, but she soon realized she had a passion and aptitude for turning sterling silver sheet and wire into intricate shapes, making pendants, earrings and bracelets.

Karin has been selling her uniquely handcrafted products for over five years since the launch of her website in 2011 (**www.karosajewellery.co.uk**). Her business profile has increased with two awards in 2012 – the Rising Star and Business of the Year in the Forest Business Womens' Network Awards. Following this success, she also won Business of the Year and Innovation in Business in 2013, also for the Forest Business Women's Network. Business never stands still and Karin's new range of faith-inspired jewellery is also now available in the abbeys of Bath and Glastonbury, and at Wells Cathedral.

How have you found making and selling jewellery as a career?

It takes a few years to build up a name in this trade. There is a huge amount of competition, a lot of cheap imports, and in an age where people are being more careful with money it is a simple fact that jewellery is not the easiest business to be in. It is a 'luxury', therefore I found it very important to find a niche to develop into a unique business.

Selling doesn't come naturally to artists, and it's often at this point, when struggling to sell their wares, that giving up is their 'out'. I found that craft fairs can be very disappointing when they take place in areas where the footfall isn't great or you find mass manufactured goods being sold a couple of tables away. My first tip is to always check out unknown craft fairs beforehand and maybe return 'next year'. On the flip side, shop outlets can take high commissions (usually between 30 per cent and 50 per cent) but a shop in a good location with regular clients that meet your 'client profile' can be a rewarding place to sell – but do try to secure a prominent location, include an 'artist profile' and 'take-away' cards (reference Facebook, your website and other profile links as people buy into the vision of the artist). And keep up strong communication lines with the shop and remember to replenish your stock.

Why did you set up as a sole trader?

For myself there was never actually a specific question of setting up a company or going as a sole trader. I was just going to work on my own and start off in a very small way and I wanted to keep things simple and personal. The complications of a limited company, with its further tax implications, just sounded too complicated whereas the risk of sole trader that Allan describes did not pose a fear, given my business model.

I can also bolt on new trades quite easily and the joy of being your own boss is still there, especially when new avenues open such as running workshops or starting the writing of an e-book. These are projects that are ongoing, and I am implementing them to have a second and third income stream, which seems to be a must for most businesses nowadays. You can't rely on just selling your product – diversification is a much used word now but it has become very important to also give me new and inspiring challenges – yes, I can!

What was the best tip you were given when you set up?

This tip came from the second meeting I attended as a member of the Forest of Dean Business Women's Network; and it is that 60 per cent of your business success comes from exposure. I have been doing this by increasing my networking over the last two years, and it has paid off, by getting a high number of contacts, and quite a good percentage resulted in sales. And it is the problem of working on your own as an artist: you can do the work on your own and absolutely love it but it's not practical to go on creating unless people know about you.

If you were starting again, what would you do differently?

Social media is a very important part of most businesses now. It has grown exponentially over the last few years and it's certainly a big part of my business. It would have been good to have implemented it a lot sooner as visual businesses with 'luxury' have products that 'speak for themselves'; Facebook pages and images shared on Twitter and Pinterest can boost sales. My final tip – gosh... I would be much more careful about spending money on advertising; even if it is with a glamorous magazine – it does not guarantee sales and I found through experience that there are better ways!

CASE STUDY Phil Champ, FIMMM, MSLL, MFSB – product, industrial, mechanical designer; sole trader initially and then a limited company

Phil set up his own business in 2011 having worked as an employee in and around the design industry for over 30 years. In early 2011 Phil's then employer decided to restructure and ceased to offer product design as an activity. This left Phil wondering 'What now?' During the time spent creating a new CV and updating his portfolio, and wondering if any of his interview suits would still fit, his phone started to ring. Past clients wondered whether he could carry out design projects for them as his former employer no longer offered this service. After some initial meetings and a consultation with his wife, who is an AAT qualified bookkeeper, Phil decided to bite a big bullet and set up on his own in business – and Champ Industrial Design was born.

Why did you decide to set up as a sole trader and then change to a limited company?

At the time, it seemed like the quickest way to get up and running, but after two and a half years of trading I decided to make the move to become a limited company – and what a lot of paperwork that was. New bank account, transferring VAT number, etc. I did wonder if it was all worth it during the six weeks it took just to get the bank account set up. All very distracting!

How have you found your first years of trading?

A vertical line of learning – there has been no 'curve'! Business has been great but the new skills that you need to develop quickly can be very distracting and time-consuming. These include: writing non-disclosure agreements, terms and conditions, checking that you have the right insurance policies in place. Also, making sure that your terms and conditions are legal and binding brings you into contact with the legal profession, which gets quite expensive very quickly.

How did you obtain your first few clients?

I was actually very lucky in that several of the clients from my previous job liked my work and approached me directly to see if I would like to work on certain projects for them. Articles in trade journals helped my services – who says you have to pay for advertising? I see this done by more and more businesses now that I know what to look for. Articles seem to be a good win–win for all concerned.

What were the best tips you were given when you set up?

Get a good accountant who understands your industry, which I did. His first bit of advice was to join the Federation of Small Businesses, which again I did. This proved to be very useful in the first few months as the advice available was invaluable. They also help you to realize that you are not alone and that there are other people out there in exactly the same boat as you are. Another good tip came from an unusual source. I had taken up the offer to meet with a 'business mentor' and had spent a whole morning with him. It was useful but I came away asking myself more questions than I had gone to see him with. On my way home, I popped into my local off-licence for a couple of bottles of wine for the weekend and there was an assistant there who I hadn't seen for a couple of years. He explained that he had now come back as manager. I asked him how it felt to be responsible, to which he replied, 'I have always been responsible; the difference is that I am now accountable.' I found this one small statement to be more useful than the whole three or so hours with the business mentor, as it had totally highlighted my inner feeling of disquiet that I had felt since setting up. Once I realized that this was what the disquiet was about, I could set about dealing with it. I started to sleep a little better after this.

If you were starting again, what would you do differently?

I do constantly make an effort to be more organized but as a designer, your natural thought process is quite chaotic, lateral and tangential. Thinking in logical straight lines sometimes takes a lot of a very different kind of concentration. If it weren't for having a wife who does do the straight-line thinking, is very thorough, methodical and logical, I would probably have given up and tried to find another 'normal' PAYE job. This makes me conclude that you do need a good bookkeeper to keep you on the straight and narrow if your business exists in any 'creative' industry.

I think self-discipline is important together with strict allocation of time, as there is a tendency to knee jerk every time a client asks something of you. This approach does not best serve their needs, or allow you to fully concentrate on whatever is the task at hand. I have also become something of a workaholic, so taking time out for other things is important. I guess that this is partly due to having my office at home. I need to learn how to shut the door and stay out sometimes!

Website: **www.champ-id.co.uk**.

CASE STUDY   Paul Riley, fire safety business, company

Paul served in the Royal Navy and saw action in the Falklands, where he mastered a number of trades including serving as a fireman. He subsequently became a chief fire safety trainer for a major fire protection company and later set up his own business, which subsequently went bust. Undefeated, Paul has started up again.

Why did you set up as a company?

I set up a limited company because I asked my potential customers what they preferred and the majority said they would rather deal with a company than a sole trader. Companies have more credibility.

What services did you provide?

The core business was fire safety training and the style and method of delivery were well received. Bolt-on services including fire-extinguisher servicing, fireproofing and fire risk assessments. Basically if a client asked, 'Paul, can you...?' and it was about fire safety the answer was always 'yes'! In 2004 a major bank asked me to provide my 'off the wall' training style electronically by e-learning. To cut a long story very short, it was successful and we ended up with three of the largest banks in the world as clients.

Where did it all go wrong?

In autumn 2008 the banking crisis hit: soon banks cancelled orders and I tried refinancing, factoring and loans. The company became insolvent and I placed it into administration in September 2009.

What did you lose?

I lost my house and cars (oh, and a wife). After two years of licking my wounds I decided it's time to start afresh. However, this time I, and not my bank, would be in control! I got a £1,000 loan from my sister and in the summer of 2012 I started My Fire Safety Ltd, with the tag line 'Because fire safety is all about you'.

What have you learnt?

I think I have learnt three things and I hope these help new businesses. Number one: it's all about the customer (90 per cent of the time!). Network, network, network. Get on the phone or Skype and talk to your customers – what do they want and do they know all of your services? Send newsletters and tweet about your services, and try to trigger that request for a chat about how you can help. But a dose of reality now – you can't please all the people all of the time and sometimes you have to say no (I wish I had after I overexpanded first time around).

Number two: keep on top of your costs. I now count every single penny and look for quality at a good price. I use freelancers on small projects and zero-hours employment contracts help me expand and control risk. My IT support comes from Mexico, which reduced my time and cost to undertake projects by nearly 75 per cent.

Number three: finances. Keep on top of your numbers and especially credit control. My terms are 'payment on presentation of invoice', so a week after I send out my invoice I gently follow up (just to ensure they have my invoice and there are no queries – as those two are the usual snag points). On the other side of the finance equation, and having 'been there', I can assure you that when the going gets really tough the bank managers at 'head office' are tough. Do all you can to keep your borrowing low and your banking relationship at a local level where there is more discretion. My Fire Safety Ltd is a success, but this time it's on my terms and in my control – having learnt from the above three tips.

Starting and running a business – checklist

When starting or running a business you will encounter a vast range of information and this can lead to you feeling swamped. This checklist has been developed to help you on the journey. Try annotating each item – N: not applicable; W: work on now; A: review with accountant; C: complete:

- If you want to travel somewhere you use a map. In business it's just the same except you get yourself a *plan*. Commit it to writing and don't expect to get it right first time (no one does!). A few pages are fine to start with based on objectives, a profit-and-loss forecast and your marketing research and action plan. Review it with your accountant and a trusted friend, then build it up.

- Choose your *trading format*, ie company (usually signified by 'limited') or sole trader or partnership or limited liability partnership. This is an important step and one to talk through with your

accountant or a business adviser. You can set up a company for
£15 at Companies House (**www.companieshouse.gov.uk**) 'web
incorporation service'. Understand the personal liability risks of
sole trader/partnership and, indeed, joint and several liability if
trading in partnership ('last person standing pays the lot'!). If
things go badly wrong your personal wealth could be at risk – but
perhaps insurance could help (see below).

- Choose your *accountant* – there are many accountancy
  organizations; chartered accountants can be found at
  www.icaew.co.uk (England and Wales); **www.icas.org.uk** (Scotland)
  and **www.charteredaccountants.ie** (Ireland). Accountants are
  usually prepared to see you for an initial 'no obligation' meeting.
  Be clear about who your regular contact will be, and their
  qualifications and knowledge of your industry.

- Make sure you have a source of *legal help*. Could your local
  solicitor help? Alternatively, your trade association may offer a
  free legal helpline that may suffice initially. An early legal question
  that will usually arise is about your terms and conditions of trade
  or contracts.

- There is some *free government help* that you will find at
  www.gov.uk, which contains the government's online resource
  for businesses.
  You should also check out the government-backed initiative
  www.startupbritain.org for inspiration and ideas.
  Regional or country-specific support is also available at:

  - Regional help: **www.nationalenterprisenetwork.org**.

  - Northern Ireland: at **www.nibusinessinfo.co.uk**.

  - Scotland: at **www.business.scotland.gov.uk**.

  - Wales: at **www.business.wales.gov.uk**.

  - For the over-50s try: **www.prime.org.uk**.

- Join the best *trade or professional association* that you can
  identify and consider the extra benefits each provides in the areas
  of research information, networking events, helplines, tax
  investigation help and insurance offerings.

- Choose and, if appropriate, protect your *business name*. There is
  some useful free help available on intellectual property (patents,
  brands, etc) at the Intellectual Property Office at **www.ipo.gov.uk**.

- Choose a *business bank account*. Shop around for the best deal that suits your business (often a trade-off between the convenience of a local 'bricks and mortar' branch accompanied by internet banking versus free or reduced charges for internet-only accounts).

- Assess your *pension* needs. See **www.unbiased.co.uk** for finding an independent financial adviser (IFA).

- Sort out your *tax and record keeping* (documents need to be kept for seven years and you need to become a receipt/invoice hoarder with a logical 'system for filing'), as the taxman might say, 'Prove it or lose it.' Check with your accountant that your proposed bookkeeping and record-keeping systems are acceptable before you buy them.

- Understand the implications of failing to deal with your *tax* affairs properly. This can be penalties ranging from 30 per cent to 100 per cent plus interest. Some trade associations include 'free' tax investigation cover – a very useful benefit.

- Understand your key *tax obligations* and deadlines. For companies you are obliged to file your annual accounts at Companies House nine months after your year end and your *annual return* on the anniversary of setting up a company each year. There is good-quality free help at Companies House, **www.companieshouse.gov.uk**.

- Understand your obligations on *VAT*. The current registration threshold for compulsory registration is £81,000. Consider VAT schemes especially the VAT flat-rate scheme for small businesses.

- Set up your *premises* so that you can work effectively. If you work from home, manage your family's and neighbours' expectations – suddenly the phrase 'Time is money' takes on a new meaning.

- Set up your *suppliers* (set up contracts and bills in the company or business name) and, if appropriate, set up stock control and delivery systems.

- Consider *insurance* policies for identified business risks (professional indemnity, public liability, product liability, etc). An insurance broker can advise on this and you should also consider policies available via trade associations as these can provide increased cover at less cost.

- Consider protecting the income you take from your business (especially if you have dependants) in the event of long-term *illness* or of *death* (**www.unbiased.co.uk** for finding an independent financial adviser).

- If running your *business at home* you must tell your insurer that you run a business from home.

- *Marketing and selling* will be massively important to your success. If you are not from a selling/marketing background, talk to trusted friends who run their own business and your accountant/adviser or mentor about your market research and marketing plan. Understand your customers and what they need. Do not underestimate the importance of networking.

- Plan the *pricing* strategies for your product or service. A different package means a different price. How have you benchmarked your price and how have you differentiated your offering (features and benefits) to allow you to charge that little bit more? Conversely, what features and benefits have you stripped out to allow you to offer a headline price that comes in beneath the competition?

- Plan your *marketing promotion strategy*. Remember that 'folk are different' and that it is a bit like fishing – you use different hooks depending on what you are trying to catch.

- Get paid promptly for your sale. What are your *payment terms* (terms and conditions)? Follow up on outstanding debts. If you sell stock have you included a reservation of title clause to help you retrieve unpaid stock if your client goes bust?

- Set up your *IT system* and support and have a system to back up your data securely. Check whether you need to notify the Information Commissioner under the *data protection* laws (**www.ico.gov.uk**).

- Consider other *red tape*, especially if your area is a specialized sector (food, health and safety, etc). Investigate and apply for the licences and permits that your business may need.

Review and update your business plan in the light of experience and keep it a living document.

Chapter Eleven
Looking for paid work

> *Success is stumbling from failure to failure, with no loss of enthusiasm.* **WINSTON CHURCHILL, QUOTED IN *STYLIST MAGAZINE***

Believe it or not, it's now fashionable to be grey: there's nothing the over-60s cannot accomplish, if one reads the reports of 'Grey Power' in the media. There are successful films made with ageing actors, for example *The Best Exotic Marigold Hotel* and *Quartet*; TV programmes featuring the older generation, like *Last Tango in Halifax* and *Amazing Greys* to name but two. Mary Berry (79) is more popular than some of the younger chefs, drawing millions of viewers to her TV programmes, and there are others who regularly appear on our screens, or the radio, well past retirement age. Apparently most of the people who watch BBC1 are over 55, while BBC2's audience is even older. If you're really ancient it's Radio 4... Maybe at last the media have realised that mixed with youth and beauty a bit of maturity and experience is good.

Source: *Radio Times*, 12–18 April 2014

In the world of work it is revealing how many later-lifers have been successful long past retirement age. Lots of people begin to fulfil their dreams only as they get older. Mary Wesley wrote her first novel for adults when she was 70; Marina Lewycka was 58 when she wrote her first novel, *A Short History of Tractors in Ukrainian*. Look at the number of politicians and statespersons who rose to high office in their 60s and 70s: Winston Churchill, Golda Meir, Ronald Reagan and Nelson Mandela to name but a few. In history, musicians and artists are well known for producing some of their best work at an age when most people would have laid down their batons or brushes. Another fine example is

100-year-old Dorothy Saville, who is thought to be the world's oldest barmaid. She started working at The Red Lion Hotel in Wendover, Buckinghamshire in 1940 and this great-great-grandmother still works lunchtime shifts. At the time of writing she has no plans to throw in the towel (cited in *The Week*, 19 April 2014). So it's never too late...

If you want to excel in certain areas it does help to start practising when you are young, such as playing a sport or a musical instrument. But it is possible to learn new skills and do many new things after 50: you may not become rich or famous, but you can decide on something you want to do and set about achieving it. You only have one life: as you get older it becomes more important not to have any regrets; to make sure you have done the things you've always wanted to do. One of the things to bear in mind, if searching for paid work, is what job will give you satisfaction. A recent survey suggests that vicars and priests are the happiest workers, along with farmers and fitness instructors; while publicans, brickies and debt collectors are amongst the unhappiest. This doesn't mean you can't be a joyful publican or a miserable vicar, but it highlights the importance of choosing work that is likely to be fulfilling and right for you.

In 2013 the overall number of people in work in the UK had reached a record 30.1 million. The labour market is recovering, thanks to a rise in the creation of full-time jobs, along with part-time jobs and self-employment boosting the figures. However, employees over 50 can find themselves in a tricky position as many may find that they need to make plans to supplement their state pension by working beyond retirement; others may simply want to carry on working past the normal retirement age. Remember, employers who are keen to ease older employees out to make way for younger staff will find themselves up against age-discrimination laws, so you have this protection if you need it. In older workers' favour, perhaps, some employers find it hard to persuade younger employees to take foreign postings. For those whose families are grown up, becoming an ex-pat could be ideal timing, so give this option consideration if it is offered. One reason that some companies get rid of older staff is because they cost more. As an option to consider, if you offer to work four days a week this will save your employer 20 per cent of your salary – and possibly banish any immediate thought of their asking you to retire. If this course of action suits, you can use that free day to develop other activities and interests beyond your current job.

Should you wish to have a complete change and set up in business for yourself, Chapter 10 is where you will find all you need to know about doing this. When looking for paid employment you could contact previous employers if you have enjoyed working for them in the past. Many do welcome older workers: they are viewed as reliable and have good workplace experience. Over the course of your working life you will have picked up many skills, some of which are transferable and could be utilized in a whole host of jobs. Be ready to show potential employers how keen you are to learn. Be able to demonstrate that undergoing training and learning new skills and working methods are not a problem to you. One of the older worker's trump cards is reliability. This can be reinforced by references from previous employers. Provided you come across well at interview, potential employers are likely to value your stability. So if you want to keep at it – make your plans and enjoy your job hunting.

Financial considerations

Since the abolition of the earnings rule, no matter what age you are or how much you earn there is no longer any forfeit to your state pension, although of course you may have to pay tax on your additional income. If you are working close to a full-time week and/or have enough money to live on, there could be an advantage in asking the DWP to defer your pension, as this will entitle you to a bigger one in the future. Each year of deferral earns an increment of about 10.4 per cent of the pension. Another advantage is that, if you choose to defer your pension by at least a year, you will have the option of taking the money as a taxable lump sum instead of in higher weekly pension payments. For other information concerning your pension, tax and working for yourself, refer to Chapters 3, 4 and 10.

Age discrimination and equality

Age discrimination legislation came into force in October 2006, and the Equality Act was enshrined in 2010. These laws make it illegal for employers to discriminate against older candidates on account of age as regards recruitment, training and promotion. In particular, provided individuals are still physically and mentally capable of doing their job, an employer can no longer oblige them to retire at a 'default' retirement age. Employers also now have a duty to consider requests by employees who want to postpone their retirement, and will need to give those they want to retire at least six months' written notice of their decision. The government scrapped 65 as the UK's default retirement age, with effect from April 2011.

Assessing your abilities

Knowing what you have to offer a potential employer is an essential first step. Make a list of everything you have done, in both your formal career and ordinary life, including your outside interests. In particular, consider adding any practical or other skills, knowledge or contacts that you have acquired over the years. These could prove especially useful. If, for example, you have done a lot of public speaking, fundraising, committee work or conference organization, these would be excellent transferable skills that would make you attractive to a prospective employer. As a result of writing everything down, most people find that they have far more to offer than they originally realized. In addition to work skills, you should include your personal attributes and any special assets that would attract an employer. The list might include health, organizing ability, a good telephone manner, communication skills, the ability to work well with other people, use of a car and willingness to do flexible hours. Maturity can also be a positive asset.

Spend time working on your personal branding, how to market yourself and to whom – this will help you become much more focused and give you a clearer idea of what jobs might suit you. As a general rule when job hunting, the more accurate and targeted you can be in the application process, the more likely you are to succeed. If you intend to do something completely different, do your research carefully. Talking to other people helps. Friends, family, work colleagues or business acquaintances may have useful information. Whatever you decide to do, remember that with age and experience comes wisdom. You have the power to negotiate and you have the power to decide what you want to do next. Make sure the job you take is right for you.

Job counselling

If you're unsure how to start, job counselling could help. This is designed to identify your talents in a vocational sense, combined with practical advice on successful job-hunting techniques. Counsellors can assist with such essentials as writing a CV, preparing for an interview and locating job vacancies. They can also advise you on suitable training courses. There are many companies offering this service; a search on the internet will reveal them. Before you rush ahead, ask for recommendations from other people and don't sign up with a company unless you're sure they are right for you. You could ask to speak to one or two of their former clients to find out whether they found the service useful.

Training opportunities

Knowing what you want to do is one thing, but before starting a new job you may want to brush up existing skills or possibly acquire new ones. Most professional bodies have a full programme of training events, ranging from one-day seminars to courses lasting a week or longer. Additionally, adult education institutes run a vast range of courses or, if you are still in your present job, a more practical solution might be to investigate open and flexible learning, which you can do from home.

Open and flexible learning

Open and flexible learning is successfully helping to provide a greater range and flexibility of vocational education and training opportunities for individuals of all ages. In particular, it is designed to increase the scope for participants to learn at a time, place and pace best suited to their own particular circumstances. The following organizations offer advice and an excellent range of courses:

Adult Education Finder: **www.adulteducationfinder.co.uk**.

Home Learning College: **www.homelearningcollege.com**.

Home Learning Courses: **www.homelearningcourses.com**.

Learn Direct: **www.learndirect.co.uk**.

National Extension College: **www.nec.ac.uk**.

National Institute of Adult Continuing Education (NIACE):
   www.niace.org.uk.

Open and Distance Learning Quality Council (ODLQC):
   www.odlqc.org.uk.

Open University (OU): **www.open.ac.uk**.

IT skills

If you are considering a change in direction, some new qualifications may be advantageous. IT skills are essential, so make sure your skills are current. There are plenty of places to learn these skills, but here are a few websites for starters:

Affordable Training: **www.affordabletraining.co.uk**.

Computeach: **www.computeach.co.uk**.

Home and Learn: **www.homeandlearn.co.uk**.

National Skills Academy: **www.itskillsacademy.ac.uk**.

Help with finding a job

If you plan to work past retirement age, the best way to find the job you want is to start looking for a job while you still have one. Prospective employers may prefer applicants who are busy and actively working rather than those who have had a period of non-employment for whatever reason. However, whether you are hoping to go straight from one job to another, or have had an enforced period of not working, this should not affect the way you approach your job search. If you have been retired for some time and want to return to work, you might consider doing some voluntary work in the meantime (see Chapter 12). This would provide a ready answer to the inevitable interview question 'What have you been doing?'

When starting to look for work, make sure you tell your friends and acquaintances – and your present or recent employer – that you are in the job market. Many companies are happy to take on previous employees over a rush period or during the holiday season. If you are a member of a professional institute, talk to them and tell them of your availability. Institutes keep a register of members wanting work and, encouragingly, receive a fair number of enquiries from firms seeking qualified people for projects, part-time or temporary work or interim management. Often someone you know will be the perfect link between you and your next employer.

With so many vacancies being advertised online, it pays to have a CV and covering letter ready for submission straight away. Sign on to a select number of sites that will keep you posted about work opportunities. Check out where there are skills shortages and see if any of your transferable skills would help plug that gap. When applying for jobs, remember that enthusiasm counts. Sometimes being on the spot and available at the right time are the keys to success. Ask your colleagues, contacts and friends for their advice on which organizations could be worth approaching. If someone you know is willing to make an introduction, and act as referrer, this is far more likely to get you noticed.

The following websites have useful information:

Laterlife: **www.laterlife.com.**

Redundancy Expert: **www.redundancyexpert.co.uk.**

TAEN (Experts in Age & Employment): **www.taen.org.uk.**

Wise Owls: **www.wiseowls.co.uk.**

CV writing

Putting together a successful CV is not that difficult. There are some common sections you should cover. These include:

- personal and contact information;
- education and qualifications;
- work history and/or experience;
- relevant skills to the job in question;
- personal interests, achievements and hobbies;
- referees.

Presentation is key. It should be clear and carefully presented, the layout clean and well structured. The CV hotspot is the upper-middle area of the first page, so include your most important information there. The CV should be no more than two pages of A4; clear and concise, no waffle. Understand the job description and show the skills you have and how they are relevant or can be adapted to suit the position you're applying for. Tailor your CV to that role. Under the skills section of your CV, mention key skills that help you stand out from the crowd: such as communication skills, computer skills, team working, problem solving and any foreign languages you speak. Make the most of your interests, and your experience. Use assertive and positive language, emphasizing the skills you have gained from past work. Referees are important: one should be a previous employer, the other someone who can vouch for you personally.

To find sample CVs and how to write one, there are plenty of websites to look at. Try:

www.nationalcareersservice.direct.gov.uk/tools/cv;

www.prospects.ac.uk/how_to_write_a_cv;

www.learndirect.co.uk.

Interview technique

Top tips for a successful interview are:

- do your research;
- practise your answers;
- look the part;
- stay calm;
- ask questions.

You will need to know about the organization you are seeking to join, so do your research. List all the questions you expect to be asked, then rehearse your answers. Be prepared to say what you have done since leaving employment; whether your health is good; why you are interested in working for this particular employer; and, given the job requirements, what you think you have of special value to offer. Personal presentation matters, as does keeping calm. Be prepared to ask questions, including how much money is being offered. Be aware of what is a realistic salary in the current market. The following websites have advice on how to prepare for interviews:

CV Tips: **www.cvtips.com**.

Job Search News: **www.job-hunt.org**.

Useful reading

Preparing the Perfect CV (5th edition), *Preparing the Perfect Job Application* (5th edition) and *Successful Interview Skills* (5th edition), all by Rebecca Corfield and published by Kogan Page; website: **www.koganpage.com**.

Part-time openings

With the job market so competitive, many part-time or temporary assignments offer the perfect way into employment that may develop into full-time work in future. With the average job now lasting between 1.8 and 3 years, temporary or project-based professional and executive assignments that last a specific time are becoming increasingly common. People with specialist expertise are actively sought, so it is important to be aware of the growth areas in employment. Over one-fifth of all new jobs are now on a contract basis, the average being for six months or a year. Mature candidates have everything to gain here because of the greater turnover of jobs. Serial part-time or freelance work can easily develop into a full-time occupation. Many retired businesspeople take on two or three part-time jobs and then find themselves working as hard as they have ever done in their life. See:

Skilled People: **www.skilledpeople.com**.

TAEN (Experts in Age & Employment): **www.taen.org.uk**.

Wise Owls: **www.wiseowls.co.uk**.

Employment ideas

Consultancy

Have you thought of hiring yourself back to your former employer in a consultancy capacity? Consultancy, by definition, is not limited to a single client. By using your contacts judiciously, plus a bit of marketing initiative, it is quite possible to build up a steady list of assignments on the basis of your particular expertise. Marketing and organizational skills are always in demand, as are knowledge of IT, website design, accountancy, HR issues and public relations experience and fundraising. Small firms often buy in expertise as and when it is required. Many established consultancies retain a list of reliable associates – a sort of freelance register – on whom they call on an 'as needed' basis, to handle suitable assignments. Take a look at the following websites for suggestions:

Consulting UK: **www.consulting.co.uk**.

Institute of Consulting: **www.iconsulting.org.uk**.

Mindbench Management Consultancy: **www.mindbench.com**.

Interim management

Interim managers represent a huge growth area in recruitment over the past few years. An interim manager gives a company instant access to a 'heavyweight yet hands-on executive' with a proven track record to meet its needs. Typically hired for three to nine months, interim managers help organizations undergoing major change, implement critical strategies or plug a crucial management gap. Many of the best jobs go to those who have recently taken early retirement or been made redundant. Assignments could be full-time or involve just one or two days' work per week. For more information see:

Aim Recruitment Ltd: **www.aiminterims.co.uk**.

Executives Online: **www.executivesonline.co.uk**.

Interim Management Association (IMA):
www.interimmanagement.uk.com.

Interim Partners: **www.interimpartners.com**.

Openings via a company or other reference

Secondment from your current employer to another organization is something worth considering. This can be part-time for just a few hours a week or full-time for anything from a few weeks to two years. It can also often lead to a new career. Normally only larger employers are willing to consider the idea since, as a rule, the company will continue to pay your salary and other benefits during the period of secondment. If you work for a smaller firm it could still be worth discussing the suggestion, as employers benefit from the favourable publicity the company attracts by being seen to support the local community. See:

Business in the Community: **www.bitc.org.uk**.

Whitehall & Industry Group: **www.wig.co.uk**.

Public appointments

Opportunities regularly arise for individuals to be appointed to a wide range of public bodies, such as tribunals, commissions and consumer consultative councils. Many appointments are to local and regional bodies throughout the country. Some are paid but many offer an opportunity to contribute to the community and gain valuable experience of working in the public sector on a part-time, expenses-only basis. Public appointments vacancies at local and regional levels across the UK can be found on the website **www.gov.uk/public-appointments**.

Non-executive directorships

Many retiring executives see this as the ideal solution; however, these appointments carry heavy responsibilities made more onerous by recent legislation. If you are able and committed and have the necessary experience, see these websites:

First Flight Placements: **www.ffplacements.co.uk**.

NED Exchange: **www.nedexchange.co.uk**.

Non-Executive Directors' Club: **www.non-execs.com**.

Market research

In addition to the normal consultancy openings in marketing, there is scope for those with knowledge of market research techniques. The work covers a very broad spectrum, from street or telephone interviewing to data processing, designing questionnaires, statistical analysis and sample group selection. See these websites:

Market Research Society: **www.mrs.org.uk**.

National Centre for Social Research: **www.natcen.ac.uk**.

Paid work for charities

Although charities rely to a very large extent on voluntary workers (see Chapter 12), most charitable organizations of any size have a number of paid appointments. Other than particular specialists that some charities may require for their work, the majority of openings are for general managers or administrators, fundraisers and those with financial skills.

Anyone thinking of applying for a job in a charity must be in sympathy with its aims and style. Salaries in general are below the commercial rate. If possible, it is a good idea to work as a volunteer before seeking a paid appointment, as this will provide useful experience. The following organizations may help:

CF Appointments: **www.cfappointments.com**.
Charity JOB: **www.charityjob.co.uk**.
Charity People: **www.charitypeople.co.uk**.
Harris Hill: **www.harrishill.co.uk**.
ProspectUs: **www.prospect-us.co.uk**.
TPP Not for Profit: **www.tpp.co.uk**.
Working for a Charity: **www.wfac.org.uk**.

Sales

Almost every commercial firm in the country needs good sales staff. Many people who have never thought of sales could be excellent in the job because of their specialist knowledge in a particular field combined with their enthusiasm for the subject. There is always a demand for people to sell advertising space. Also, many firms employ demonstrators in shops or at exhibitions for special promotions. The work is temporary, and while pay is good, you could be on your feet for long periods of the day. If the idea of selling fires you with enthusiasm, there are many opportunities to tempt you. See:

Career Builder: **www.careerbuilder.co.uk**.
Employers Jobs: **www.employersjobs.co.uk**.

Tourist guide/holiday rep

Tourist guide work is something for extroverts, with stamina and a liking for people. It requires an academic mind, since you will need to put in some fairly concentrated study. While there are numerous possible qualifications, some are easier than others. Training for the coveted Blue Badge takes 15 months. The Blue Badge itself is no guarantee of steady work, and most tourist guides are self-employed. Opportunities are greatest in London, especially for those with fluency in one or more foreign languages. See:

Guild of Registered Tourist Guides: **www.britainsbestguides.org**.

You could sign on as a lecturer with one of the growing number of travel companies offering special interest holidays. To be eligible you need real expertise in a subject, the ability to make it interesting and have an easy manner with people. Pay is fairly minimal, although you may receive tips – plus of course the bonus of a free holiday. See:

Travel Job Search: **www.traveljobsearch.com**.
Travel Weekly: **www.jobs.travelweekly.co.uk**.

Other tourist work

If you live in a popular tourist or heritage area there is a whole variety of seasonal work, including jobs in hotels, restaurants, shops and local places of interest. Depending on the locality, the list might also include jobs as deckchair attendants, play leaders for children, caravan site staff, extra coach drivers and many others.

Teaching and training skills

If you have been a teacher at any stage of your career, there are a number of part-time possibilities, as listed below.

Coaching

With examinations becoming more competitive, demand has been increasing for former teachers with knowledge of the public examination system to coach youngsters in preparation for A and AS levels, GCSE and common entrance exams. Research local schools, search the internet or contact a specialist educational consultancy:

Gabbitas Education Consultants: **www.gabbitas.co.uk**.

Specialist subjects

Teachers are in demand for mathematics, physics, chemistry, technology and modern languages. People with relevant work experience and qualifications may be able to teach or give tuition in these subjects. A formal teaching qualification is required to teach in state-maintained schools. Before engaging with children, you will need a Disclosure and Barring Service (DBS) check (see later in this chapter, the section 'Caring for other people'). Retired teachers, linguists and others with specialist knowledge can earn good money from tutoring. See:

Further Education Jobs: **www.fejobs.com**.
Home Tutors: **www.hometutors.org.uk**.

English as a foreign language

There is an ongoing demand for people to teach English to foreign students. Opportunities are concentrated in London, but most cities that have universities offer language courses during the summer. Good English-language schools require teachers to have an initial qualification in teaching English to those who have a different first language. See:

British Council: **www.britishcouncil.org**.

Intensive Tefl Courses: **www.tefl.co.uk**.

Tefl Courses: **www.teflengland.co.uk**.

Working in developing countries

There are opportunities for suitably qualified people to work in developing countries in Africa, Asia, the Caribbean and the Pacific, on a semi-voluntary basis. Skills most in demand include civil engineering; mechanical engineering; water engineering; architecture; urban, rural and regional planning; agriculture; forestry; medicine; teaching English as a foreign language; maths; physics; and economics. All air fares, accommodation costs and insurance are usually covered by the organizing agency, and pay is limited to a 'living allowance' based on local levels. As a general rule, there is an upper age limit of 65 (VSO accepts volunteers up to 75), and you must be willing to work for a minimum of two years.

The following are the major agencies involved in this kind of work (more details are contained in Chapter 12):

International Service: **www.internationalservice.org.uk**.

Progressio: **www.progressio.org.uk**.

Skillshare International: **www.skillshare.org**.

Voluntary Service Overseas (VSO): **www.vso.org.uk**.

Publishing

Publishers regularly use freelance staff with appropriate experience for proofreading, copy-editing, design, typography, indexing and similar work as well as for writing specialist copy. See:

The Bookseller: **www.thebookseller.com**.

The Society for Editors and Proofreaders: **www.sfep.org.uk**.

Caring for other people

There are a number of opportunities for paid work in this field. If you are considering working with vulnerable people (young or old), you will be required to have a full Disclosure and Barring Service (DBS) check. This was formerly the Criminal Records Bureau (CRB) check. This is designed to protect those who need to rely on other people and to ensure that no one unsuitable is appointed to a position of trust if they are likely to abuse it. These checks are extremely thorough and can take several weeks or even months to process. Please be patient and as accurate as possible when asked to provide information by prospective employers, charities or not-for-profit organizations. For further information about DBS checks and why they are required, see the government website: **www.gov.uk** – Employing people (select the 'Recruiting and hiring' link).

Domestic work

A number of private domestic agencies specialize in finding temporary or permanent companions, housekeepers and extra-care help for elderly and disabled people or for those who are convalescent. Pay rates vary depending on which part of the country you live in and the number of hours involved. See:

Anchor Care: **www.anchor.org.uk**.

Consultus Care & Nursing Agency Ltd: **www.consultuscare.com**.

Country Cousins: **www.country-cousins.co.uk**.

Universal Aunts Ltd: **www.universalaunts.co.uk**.

The Lady magazine, published every Wednesday, has classified advertisements for domestic help.

Home helps and childminding

Local authorities sometimes have vacancies for home helps, to assist disabled or elderly people in their own home by giving a hand with the cleaning, light cooking and other chores. Ask your local social services department. If you already look after a grandchild during the day, you might consider caring for an additional couple of youngsters. You will need to be registered with the local social services department, which will explain all the requirements including details of any basic training – such as first aid – that you may first need to do.

Nursing

Qualified nurses are in great demand in most parts of the country and stand a good chance of finding work at their local hospital or through one of the many nursing agencies. Those with suitable experience, although not necessarily a formal nursing qualification, could apply to become a care support worker: Crossroads Care and The Princess Royal Trust for Carers have merged to form the leading carers' charity. See:

Carers Trust: **www.carers.org**.

Home sitting

Taking care of someone else's home while they are away on holiday or business trips is something that mature, responsible people, usually non-smokers with no children or pets, can do. It is a bit like a paid holiday, depending on the responsibilities and on the size of the house or flat. Food and travelling expenses are normally also paid. It is useful to have your own car. Firms specializing in this type of work include:

Absentia: **www.home-and-pets.co.uk**.

Homesitters Ltd: **www.homesitters.co.uk**.

Rest Assured House Sitters: **www.restassuredhousesitters.co.uk**.

Cashing in on your home interests

Cooking, gardening, home decorating, dressmaking and DIY skills can all be turned into modest money-spinners.

Bed and breakfast

Tourist areas, in particular, offer scope for taking in B&B visitors. However, unless you want to make a regular business of it, it is advisable to limit the number of guests to a maximum of five (over that number you would have to register as a business and be subject to health and safety, fire regulations, etc). To be on the safe side, contact the local environmental health officer who will advise you of anything necessary you should do. You should also register with your local tourist information centre. See Chapter 8, 'Letting rooms in your home' and 'Paying guests or lodgers'.

Cooking

Scope includes catering for other people's dinner parties, selling home-made goodies to local shops and cooking for corporate lunches. Other than top-class culinary skills, requirements are a large deep freeze, a car (you will normally be required to do all the necessary shopping) and plenty of stamina. Notify your friends, advertise locally and set up a website.

Gardening

Small shopkeepers and florists sometimes purchase flowers or plants direct from local gardeners, in preference to going to the market. Alternatively, you might consider dried flower arrangements or herbs, for which there has been a growing demand. However, before spending any money, check around to find out what the sales possibilities are. If you are willing to tend someone else's garden, the likelihood is that you will be inundated with enquiries. Spread the word among friends and acquaintances as well as local advertising.

Dressmaking, upholstery and home decorating

If you are happy to do alterations, the chances are that you could be kept busy from dawn to dusk. Many shops are desperate for people who sew. Likewise, many individuals and families would love to know of someone who could alter clothes, as well as offer skilled dressmaking. The same goes for curtains, chair covers and other soft furnishings. Approach firms selling materials for the home: they might be only too glad to put work out to you. If you spread the word among neighbours that you are available, or advertise locally, you may be surprised at the response.

Do your friends envy your ability to assemble flat-packed furniture, fix things that are broken or decorate your house? Why not start charging for DIY?

You can make money from any hobby – there is more about this in Chapter 10, Starting your own business.

Agencies and other useful organizations

Job hunting through agencies is very much a question of luck, but there is no need to be out of work for long if you are proactive. Work for the over-50s and -60s varies and, if you are seeking challenging opportunities, it might be worth checking the following websites:

Executive Stand-By: **www.esbpeople.co.uk**.

Prime 50 Plus: **www.prime50plus.co.uk**.

Skilled People: **www.skilledpeople.com**.

Chapter Twelve
Volunteering

If you think you're too small to make an impact, try going to bed with a mosquito in the room. BETTY REESE

Far from sitting at home twiddling their thumbs, 2,257,000 retirees over 60 volunteer for two or more charities. This information is from recent research carried out by the older people's charity, Royal Voluntary Service, formerly known as WRVS. (The name was changed to mark their 75th anniversary.) The findings show that even though many have no formal work commitments, millions of older people are 'portfolio volunteers', juggling many different volunteering roles with a variety of organisations. The research also provides an insight into why older people choose to volunteer. 83 per cent said it was because the work of the charity is very important, but most older people choose to volunteer because they need to have a purpose, while others are keen to keep learning. Overwhelmingly the research found that older people who volunteer are less depressed, have a better quality of life and are happier. Royal Voluntary Service supports over 100,000 older people each month to stay independent in their own homes for longer with tailor-made solutions. It has over 40,000 volunteers.

Source: **www.maturetimes.co.uk**

One way to define volunteering is to distinguish 'involvement' from 'commitment' and consider the difference between a chicken and a pig. While the chicken is involved in the production of an egg, the pig is committed to the making of bacon. And so with volunteers. While you were working and being paid a salary you were doubtless involved in your work. But once you begin volunteering you will join the army of people who are committed to the work they do to help others. There are interesting facts and figures to be found on the Institute for Volunteering Research website (**www.ivr.org.uk**). This is part of the NCVO (National

Council for Voluntary Organisations), which champions and strengthens volunteering and civil society. It has over 10,000 members, from the largest charities to the smallest community organizations. The most frequently cited reasons why people volunteer include:

- wanting to 'make a difference' to other people's lives;
- enjoying using their skills in new and valuable ways;
- feeling better both physically and mentally;
- supporting local activities and neighbourhood organizations;
- being a committed member of social and charitable projects;
- actively participating in democratic institutions – such as parish/ community councils, boards of school governors, neighbourhood watch;
- finding opportunities to help in education, sport, culture, leisure, conservation and the environment.

It is vital we celebrate and maximize the contributions of older people. Someone who is starting to volunteer at the age of 60 or just over could have 20 or more years of positive contribution to make. So if this appeals to you, why not give it some thought? There are thousands of opportunities – here are just a few suggestions.

Types of work

Clerical

Any active group is likely to need administrative help, from stuffing and labelling envelopes to organizing committees. This may involve a day or so a week or occasional assistance at peak times. Many smaller charities are desperate for help from individuals with IT expertise and accountancy experience.

Fundraising

Every voluntary organization needs money, and when donations are static or falling, more creativity and ingenuity are required to help bring in funds. Events are many and varied, but anyone with energy and experience of organizing fundraising events would be welcomed with open arms as a volunteer.

Committee work

This can cover anything from very occasional help to a virtually full-time commitment as treasurer or secretary. People with business skills or financial or legal backgrounds are likely to be especially valuable, and those whose skills include minute-taking are always in demand.

Direct work

Driving, delivering 'meals on wheels', counselling, visiting the house-bound, working in a charity shop, helping with a playgroup, respite care for carers: the list is endless and the value of the work incalculable. There are many interesting and useful jobs for those without special training. As regards time commitment, do as much as you feel comfortable with. Whether one morning per month or a certain number of hours per week, it is far better to be reliable than to over-promise and have to cancel or let people down. Equally, as with a paid job, before you start you should be absolutely clear about all the terms and conditions. Find out:

- what sort of work is involved;
- who you will be working with;
- what is expected;
- when you will be needed;
- if expenses are paid – if so, what for and how much.

Once you have all this mapped out you will find that voluntary work is not only rewarding in its own right but also allows you to make a real contribution to the community.

Should you consider working with vulnerable people (young or old) you will need to have a full DBS (formerly CRB) check. This was covered in Chapter 11 and applies to many jobs, both paid and unpaid. For further information about this see the government website: **www.gov.uk** – Employing people (select the 'Recruiting and hiring' link).

Choosing the right voluntary work

Once you've decided that you might take on some volunteering, next you will need to find out where the opportunities are in your local area and what particular outlet would suit your talents. You may have friends or neighbours who are already involved in volunteering locally. Asking their advice would be a start, as they may well have some good suggestions or know which organizations are in need of extra pairs of hands. However, if you don't know where to start, the organizations listed here are arranged in broad categories of interest. As there are literally thousands of voluntary groups – national and local – that need help in some way or other, it is impossible to include them all, or describe all their activities and volunteering opportunities. For a full list of charities you could search **www.charitychoice.co.uk**. The following websites are general national volunteering organizations and can act as signposts to help you learn more about them and how you can get involved:

National Council for Voluntary Organisations (NCVO): **www.ncvo.org.uk**.

REACH: **www.reachskills.org.uk**.

Volunteer Scotland: **www.volunteerscotland.net**.

Volunteering England: **www.volunteering.org.uk**.

Wales Council for Voluntary Action: **www.wcva.org.uk**.

General

The scope of the work of the following well-known charities is so broad that they almost justify a category to themselves:

British Red Cross: **www.redcross.org.uk**.

Citizens Advice Bureau: **www.citizensadvice.org.uk**.

Community Service Volunteers (CSV): **www.csv.org.uk**.

Lions Clubs International: **www.lionsclubs.org**.

RVS: **www.royalvoluntaryservice.org.uk**.

Toc H: **www.toch-uk.org.uk**.

Animals

Animal charities exist to protect animals from harm. Some are dedicated to stopping animal cruelty and others provide care for animals that have been neglected or mistreated. Animal conservation charities work hard to save endangered animals from extinction, for example by protecting their natural habitat, or putting a stop to animal poaching and illegal trade. Some animal charities have sanctuaries or wildlife parks where they rehabilitate rescued animals for release back into the wild. There are over 20 animal charities in the UK, all of whom require volunteers, so you can choose the type of animal you want to help. Some suggested websites:

Blue Cross: **www.bluecross.org.uk**.

Cats Protection: **www.cats.org.uk**.

Cinnamon Trust: **www.cinnamon.org.uk**.

Dogs Trust: **www.dogstrust.org.uk**.

Horse Trust: **www.horsetrust.org.uk**.

PDSA: **www.pdsa.org.uk**.

Pet Fostering Service Scotland: **www.pfss.org.uk**.

Pets As Therapy (PAT): **www.petsastherapy.org**.

RSPCA: **www.rspca.org.uk**.

Royal Society for the Protection of Birds (RSPB): **www.rspb.org.uk**.

World Society for the Protection of Animals (WSPA): **www.wspa.org.uk**.

Wildfowl & Wetlands Trust (WWT): **www.wwt.org.uk**.

Bereavement

There are a number of bereavement charities in the UK. To find specific charities, you could search **www.charitychoice.co.uk**, where you'll find dedicated child bereavement charities and grief counselling organizations. Here are some suggestions:

Cruse Bereavement Care: **www.cruse.org.uk**.

Grief Encounter: **www.griefencounter.org.uk**.

Winston's Wish: **www.winstonswish.org.uk**.

Children and young people

If helping children and young people is close to your heart, there are many UK-based charities involved with children and youths. By volunteering your time and skills, you can make a huge difference. The work done by this section of charities ranges from research, health and social care, disability, education, child protection, overseas aid to holidays and recreation. To see which ones exist, you could search **www.charitychoice.co.uk**. Here are just a few of them:

Action for Sick Children: **www.actionforsickchildren.org**.

Barnardo's: **www.barnardos.org.uk**.

Beanstalk (formerly Volunteer Reading Help): **www.beanstalkcharity.org.uk**.

Children's Society: **www.childrenssociety.org.uk**.

Children's Trust: **www.thechildrenstrust.org.uk**.

Girl Guiding: **www.girlguiding.org.uk**.

Marine Society and Sea Cadets: **www.ms-sc.org**.

NSPCC: **www.nspcc.org.uk**.

Save the Children: **www.savethechildren.org**.

Scout Association: **www.scouts.org.uk**.

UNICEF: **www.unicef.org.uk**.

Conservation

Should you be interested in promoting urban or rural conservation, there are several UK-based organizations concerned with the general issue of conservation. Others look at specific areas such as urban conservation, architectural conservation or rural development. For a list of charities in this sector, see **www.charitychoice.co.uk**. Here are some for starters:

Architectural Heritage Society of Scotland: **www.ahss.org.uk**.

Campaign to Protect Rural England (CPRE): **www.cpre.org.uk**.

Churches Conservation Trust (CCT): **www.visitchurches.org.uk**.

Friends of the Earth: **www.foe.co.uk**.

Greenpeace: **www.greenpeace.org.uk**.

Ramblers: **www.ramblers.org.uk**.

The Conservation Volunteers (TCV): **www.tcv.org.uk**.

The elderly

Are you interested in helping the elderly? The following charities cover assisted living, elderly care and welfare, and independent living – and will be happy to accept your assistance. If you want to help the aged by volunteering your time, search **www.charitychoice.co.uk**, or begin your research here:

Age UK: **www.ageuk.org.uk**.

Carers Trust: **www.carers.org**.

Carers UK: **www.carersuk.org**.

Contact the Elderly: **www.contact-the-elderly.org.uk**.

Independent Age: **www.independentage.org.uk**.

The family

There are a number of UK-based family support charities, each having a particular area of work. Perhaps you would like to find out about adoption and fostering, a poverty charity, a domestic violence charity or a group offering financial support for families – search for charities in this sector on **www.charitychoice.co.uk**, or start with these websites:

British Association for Adoption & Fostering (BAAF): **www.baaf.org.uk**.

Family Action: **www.family-action.org.uk**.

Marriage Care: **www.marriagecare.org.uk**.

Relate: **www.relate.org.uk**.

Shelter: **www.shelter.org.uk**.

Health and disability

There are many UK-based health charities. Is your interest in organizations supporting people with particular conditions – such as diabetes, heart disease, mental health or cancer charities? Or are you keen to support charities for disabled people? There are charities concerned with specific conditions, such as cerebral palsy or multiple sclerosis, and those providing care for the disabled. Whether you are looking for a specific charity, or wish to volunteer, search **www.charitychoice.co.uk**, or look at these websites:

Attend: **www.attend.org.uk**.

BackCare: **www.backcare.org.uk**.

British Deaf Association: **www.bda.org.uk**.

British Heart Foundation (BHF): **www.bhf.org.uk**.

Cancer Research UK: **www.cancerresearchuk.org**.

Diabetes UK: **www.diabetes.org.uk**.

Guide Dogs: **www.guidedogs.org.uk**.

Leonard Cheshire Disability: **www.leonardcheshire.org**.

Marie Curie Cancer Care: **www.mariecurie.org.uk**.

Mind: **www.mind.org.uk**.

Parkinson's UK: **www.parkinsons.org.uk**.

RDA (Riding for the Disabled Association): **www.rda.org.uk**.

RNIB (Royal National Institute of Blind People): **www.rnib.org.uk**.

St John Ambulance: **www.sja.org.uk**.

Scope: **www.scope.org.uk**.

Thrive: **www.thrive.org.uk**.

Heritage and the arts

There are numerous opportunities if you wish to volunteer in the culture and heritage charity sector. Whatever your specific interest in this area, there are many categories among the UK-based arts charities and national heritage organizations. Further information on charities in this sector can be found on **www.charitychoice.co.uk**, or via these websites:

Ancient Monuments Society: **www.ancientmonumentssociety.org.uk**.

Architectural Heritage Fund: **www.ahfund.org.uk**.

Archaeology for All: **www.new.archaeologyuk.org**.

English Heritage: **www.english-heritage.org.uk**.

National Trust: **www.nationaltrust.org.uk**.

SPAB (Society for the Protection of Ancient Buildings):
www.spab.org.uk.

The needy

Social welfare charities are always delighted to receive help. Whether you wish to volunteer with refugee charities, addiction charities or poverty charities, you can easily find the social welfare charity of greatest interest to you by searching on **www.charitychoice.co.uk**, or starting with these websites:

Elizabeth Finn Care: **www.elizabethfinncare.org.uk**.

Oxfam: **www.oxfam.org.uk**.

Salvation Army: **www.salvationarmy.org.uk**.

Samaritans: **www.samaritans.org**.

Shelter: **www.shelter.org.uk**.

Offenders and the victims of crime

If you are interested in helping ex-offenders' rehabilitation and victim support, a number of charities in this sector can be found by searching on **www.charitychoice.co.uk**, or start here with these websites:

CRI (Crime Reduction Initiatives): **www.cri.org.uk**.

Nacro: **www.nacro.org.uk**.

New Bridge: **www.newbridgefoundation.org.uk**.

SOVA (now part of CRI): **www.sova.org.uk**.

Victim Support: **www.victimsupport.org.uk**.

Politics

You may not immediately think of political parties in the context of voluntary work, but all of them use vast numbers of volunteer helpers. Between elections the help is mostly required with fundraising, committee work and staffing the constituency offices. At election time, activity is obviously intense. See the major parties' websites for details:

Conservative Party: **www.conservatives.com**.

Green Party: **www.greenparty.org.uk**.

Labour Party: **www.labour.org.uk**.

Liberal Democrats: **www.libdems.org.uk**.

Plaid Cymru: **www.plaidcymru.org**.

Scottish National Party: **www.snp.org**.

Social Democratic and Labour Party (SDLP): **www.sdlp.ie**.

UKIP: **www.ukip.org.uk**.

Ulster Unionist Party: **www.uup.org**.

Service personnel and veterans

Want to support armed and ex-services charities? Whatever your interest, you'll find lots of UK-registered organizations offering support for soldiers, sailors and airmen and women in this sector on **www.charitychoice.co.uk**, or you could start with the following:

ABF The Soldiers' Charity: **www.soldierscharity.org**.

Blind Veterans UK: **www.blindveterans.org.uk**.

Combat Stress: **www.combatstress.org.uk**.

Help for Heroes: **www.helpforheroes.org.uk**.

Royal Air Force Benevolent Fund: **www.rafbf.org**.

Royal Alfred Seafarers' Society: **www.royalalfredseafarers.com**.

Royal British Legion: **www.britishlegion.org.uk**.

SSAFA: **www.ssafa.org.uk**.

Work after work

Would you like to support organizations that are associated with commerce, trades and the professions? Or do you wish to get involved with employment charities, professional associations or groups concerned with apprenticeships? Search on **www.charitysearch.co.uk** to view the whole sector, or see below:

British Chambers of Commerce: **www.britishchambers.org.uk**.

National Enterprise Network: **www.nationalenterprisenetwork.org**.

Scottish Business in the Community: **www.sbcscot.com**.

Long-term volunteering

If you are thinking of volunteering in the long term, there are organizations that require such a commitment in the UK or abroad. These have a wide range of projects, some of which require specialist skills such as engineering or medicine; others essentially need people with practical qualities, common sense and enthusiasm. Each organization has a minimum period of service. General conditions are similar for all of them; travel is paid, plus a living allowance or salary that is based on local levels rather than on expatriate rates. Couples without dependant children are welcome, as long as both have the necessary skills. National Insurance contributions are provided, and a resettlement grant is paid on completion of the tour. If you are up to the challenge, it can be immensely rewarding.

Overseas

There are four main organizations for overseas volunteering: Voluntary Service Overseas (VSO), Skillshare International, Progressio and International Service, details of which have already been provided in Chapter 11 (Looking for paid work: 'Working in developing countries').

Volunteering abroad for the over-50s is often referred to as 'golden gapping'. It is gaining popularity among many 50- to 75-year-olds. Thousands of mature people have enjoyed gap years recently and the number is growing. If a life-changing experience and doing some voluntary work abroad before or just after you retire appeal to you, Gap Year Advice For All should be able to help; see website: **www.gapadvice.org**. (This is further described in Chapter 14, Holidays.)

In the UK

Although the organizations in this section are primarily concerned with schemes requiring volunteer help for between two weeks and six months, they would also welcome shorter-term help. See:

Sue Ryder Care: **www.sueryder.org**.

Vitalise: **www.vitalise.org.uk**.

Chapter Thirteen
Health

If you want a cure for a cold, put on two pullovers, take up a baton, poker or pencil, tune the radio to a symphony concert, stand on a chair, and conduct like mad for an hour or so and the cold will have vanished. It never fails. You know why conductors live so long? Because we perspire so much.

SIR JOHN BARBIROLLI

One of the most important things in retirement is to stay fit and healthy for as long as we can. So forget relaxing days, lounging about is not an option if we are to believe much of what we read. Sitting around watching too much TV in retirement can actually make us poorly and depressed. A recent study claims that finishing work is a major cause of declining physical and mental health. Researchers from the Institute of Economic Affairs and Age Endeavour Partnership have found that retirees are 40 per cent less likely to declare themselves in either 'very good' or 'excellent' health than those still working. One of the reasons for the decrease in health is due to retirees taking less exercise, particularly if they used to walk to work or had physically demanding jobs. There are some of us, however, who will happily spend more time in bed, get up late, read the paper, potter about a bit, have lunch and then take an afternoon nap, eschewing any but the mildest forms of exercise. Indeed, the actor Peter O'Toole, who died at the age of 81, was quoted as saying: 'The only exercise I take is walking behind the coffins of friends who took exercise.' But since increasing longevity has to be one of the wonders of the last century or so, it is vital that we do all we can to ensure that we have a 'healthy life expectancy'. None of us wants to spend years of our retirement dogged by ill-health.

There is a wealth of information available on how best to keep fit and healthy once we're over 50. The BBC's Dr Michael Mosley suggests that taking exercise, eating well, maintaining a healthy weight, keeping positive and staying mentally fit are five important rules we should adopt for a healthier lifestyle. Now perhaps is the time to reassess your lifestyle strategy, should you have one. It makes sense for all of us over-55s to look after ourselves and not take our health for granted.

Keep fit

Regular exercise is important throughout life, regardless of age, but it is particularly important for older people, including those with disabilities. Do not rush into unaccustomed exercise too quickly: regular exercise on a little-and-often basis is best. Small changes can make a big difference. But do consult your doctor before starting any exercise programme. Information on where you can find classes in your area is available online, in your local newspaper or library. The following organizations may also be able to help you:

Extend: **www.extend.org.uk**.

Fitness League: **www.thefitnessleague.com**.

Keep Fit Association: **www.keepfit.org.uk**.

Medau Movement: **www.medau.org.uk**.

Pilates

Pilates is an holistic exercise system designed to elongate, strengthen and restore the body balance. Exercises involve the whole body. Pilates is beneficial for everyone regardless of age, ability or fitness level. Find out about it at:

Pilates Foundation: **www.pilatesfoundation.com**.

Yoga

The practice of yoga helps to coordinate the breath, mind and body to encourage balance and promote feelings of relaxation and ease. There are a number of specialist organizations:

British Wheel of Yoga: **www.bwy.org.uk**.

Iyengar Yoga Institute: **www.iyi.org.uk**.

Yoga for Health and Education Trust (YHET):
   www.yoga-health-education.org.uk.

Yoga Village UK: **www.yogauk.com**.

Sensible eating

Healthy eating is important for the over-50s because it can improve your quality of life and help you to avoid diseases associated with ageing. A major reason for age-related weight gain is that the rate at which you burn calories in food and drink slows down with age. The extra calories turn into surplus body fat over time if you don't adjust your diet or exercise more. The best advice is to cut down on your dairy and meat intake, be aware of the amount of additional fats that are in your diet and don't cook with oils. The government offers the following advice on how to get the best from your diet:

- eat at least five portions of fruit and vegetables per day;
- base meals on starchy foods such as bread, potatoes, rice or pasta;
- drink plenty of water and cut out fizzy drinks;
- limit consumption of food and drink that are high in sugar or saturated fats;
- eat more fish – aim for two portions per week;
- drink less alcohol;
- limit salt intake to 6 grams per day;
- try not to skip meals, particularly breakfast.

Source: **www.gov.uk**

Weight loss programmes require commitment and can be challenging as they involve an ongoing change in lifestyle and eating habits, but they are successful for people who are prepared to stick to them. Here are two websites, should you want to kick-start a weight-loss regime:

Slimming world: **www.slimmingworld.com**.

Weightwatchers: **www.weightwatchers.co.uk**.

Keeping healthy in the heat

Although everyone loves sunshine, sometimes summer heat can catch you by surprise. According to the NHS, anyone over the age of 65 is in the 'high-risk' category for heat-related illness. Age UK offers some useful tips for staying cool in the heat:

- *Stay inside* during the hottest time of the day.
- *If you're travelling by car or public transport*, always take a bottle of water with you.
- *Use sunscreen lotion* of factor 15 or above.
- *Splash your face with cool (not very cold) water*, or place a damp cloth or scarf on the back of your neck to help you cool off.
- *Limit activities such as housework* and gardening to cooler times of the day.
- *Wear loose, lightweight, cotton clothing.*
- *Drink lots of fluids* and eat cold foods such as salad and fruit, which contain water.
- *If you have breathing problems or a heart condition*, your symptoms may be worse in the heat. Contact your GP for further advice.

Source: **www.ageuk.org.uk**

Food safety

The UK has more than 850,000 reported cases per year of people experiencing food poisoning, according to the FSA (Food Standards Agency). Don't assume that food poisoning comes only from eating out in restaurants and fast-food outlets. The FSA suggests that you are just as likely to get ill from food prepared at home. Follow these tips to reduce the risk of food poisoning at home:

- Wash your hands thoroughly with soap and water and dry them before handling food.
- Wash worktops before and after preparing food, especially if they've been touched by raw meat, poultry or eggs.
- Wash dishcloths and tea towels regularly and dry them before using them again. Bacteria thrive in dirty, damp cloths.

- Use separate chopping boards for raw food and ready-to-eat food.

- Inside or out of the fridge, keep raw meat away from ready-to-eat food such as salads, fruit and bread.

- Always cover raw meat and store on the bottom shelf of the fridge where it can't touch other foods or drip on them.

- Cook food thoroughly and ensure that it is piping hot all the way through.

- Keep your fridge below 5 degrees centigrade. By keeping food cold you stop food-poisoning bugs from growing.

- Cool leftovers quickly and store in the fridge or freezer. Any leftovers in the fridge should be used within two days.

- Respect 'use by' dates. Don't eat food that is past its date label.

You can find out more about food safety on **www.nhs.uk/Livewell/ homehygiene**.

Drink

Retirement is no reason for giving up pleasures. In moderate quantities alcohol can be an effective nightcap and can also help to stimulate a sluggish appetite. However, bear in mind that alcoholism is the third greatest killer after heart disease and cancer. Whereas most people are sensible and can control the habit themselves, others may need help. The family doctor will be the first person to check with for medical advice. But additionally, for those who need moral support, the following self-help groups may be the answer:

Al-Anon Family Groups UK & Eire: **www.al-anonuk.org.uk**.

Alcohol Concern: **www.alcoholconcern.org.uk**.

Alcoholics Anonymous: **www.alcoholics-anonymous.org.uk**.

Smoking

The ban on smoking in restaurants, bars and pubs and other designated areas has had an impact on helping people to cut down on smoking. Smokers are 20 times more likely to contract lung cancer and they are also at more serious risk of suffering from heart disease, chronic bronchitis and other ailments. Dozens of organizations concerned with health have information on giving up smoking. The following are helpful:

NCSCT (National Centre for Smoking Cessation and Training): **www.ncsct.co.uk**.

Quit: **www.quit.org.uk**.

Smokefree: **www.nhs.uk/smokefree**.

Smokeline (Scotland only): **www.canstopsmoking.com**.

Stop Smoking UK: **www.stopsmokinguk.org**.

Accident prevention

One of the most common causes of mishap is an accident in the home. In particular this is due to falling and incidents involving faulty electrical wiring. The vast majority of these could be avoided by taking normal common-sense precautions, such as repairing or replacing worn carpets and installing better lighting near staircases. For a list of practical suggestions, see 'Safety in the home', in Chapter 8. ROSPA (Royal Society for the Prevention of Accidents) has some excellent advice on this subject: see **www.rospa.com/home safety**.

If you are unlucky enough to be injured in an accident, whether in the street or elsewhere, you should contact National Accident Helpline, which has been helping people claim the compensation they deserve since 1993: **www.national-accident-helpline.co.uk**.

Aches, pains and other abnormalities

Age itself has nothing to do with the vast majority of ailments. Many people ignore the warning signs when something is wrong, yet treatment when a condition is still in its early stages can often cure it altogether, or at least help to delay its advance. The following should always be investigated by a doctor:

● any pain that lasts more than a few days;

● lumps, however small;

- dizziness or fainting;
- chest pains, shortness of breath or palpitations;
- persistent cough or hoarseness;
- unusual bleeding from anywhere;
- unnatural tiredness or headaches;
- frequent indigestion;
- unexplained weight loss.

Health insurance

According to a BUPA survey, the main reason that people in the UK choose private medical insurance (PMI) is to avoid superbugs such as MRSA, and to cut down on hospital waiting lists. Private medical insurance allows you to receive fast-track consultations and private treatment for short-term, curable medical problems. PMI can be a low-cost route to peace of mind, but policyholders often get a nasty shock when they reach retirement age, when their premiums start to rocket – just at the point when their income has reduced. However, switching to a cheaper scheme gets more difficult as we get older. Pre-existing medical conditions, including associated complaints, will normally be excluded when you take out a new policy.

The NHS has, generally, an excellent record in dealing with urgent conditions and accidents. However, it sometimes has a lengthy waiting list for the less urgent and more routine operations. By using health insurance to pay for private medical care you will probably get faster treatment, as well as greater comfort and privacy in hospital. Here are some organizations that provide cover:

AXA PPP Healthcare: **www.axappphealthcare.co.uk**.

BUPA: **www.bupa.co.uk**.

Exeter Family Friendly Society: **www.exeterfamily.co.uk**.

Saga: **www.saga.co.uk**.

SimplyHealth: **www.simplyhealth.co.uk**.

Help with choosing a scheme

With so many plans on the market, selecting the one that best suits your needs can be quite a problem. An independent financial adviser (IFA) or specialist insurance broker could advise you. See:

Association of Medical Insurance Intermediaries (AMII): **www.amii.org.uk**.

The Private Health Partnership: **www.php.co.uk**.

Private patients – without insurance cover

If you do not have private medical insurance but want to go into hospital in the UK as a private patient, there is nothing to stop you, provided your doctor is willing and you are able to pay the bills. The choice if you opt for self-pay lies between the private wings of NHS hospitals or hospitals run by charitable or non-profit-making organizations, such as:

BMI Healthcare: **www.bmihealthcare.co.uk**.

Nuffield Health: **www.nuffieldhealth.com**.

Health and medical tourism

Health and medical tourism is a growing area where you travel abroad to have your medical or health treatment, saving time and often over 50 per cent on the fees you would pay in the UK. It is an industry dating back to the ancient Greeks, who travelled to Epidauria for healing. It became popular in England in the 18th century when the spa towns sprang up, and people travelled across the country in search of healing mineral waters. In 2013 more than 75,000 people sought faster or cheaper alternatives outside the UK. Within the EU some treatments are available on the NHS, as long as you can prove that you are facing 'undue delay'. To find out more, here are a few websites:

Health Tourism Show: **www.healthtourismshow.com**.

Medical Tourist Company: **www.themedicaltouristcompany.com**.

Treatment Abroad: **www.treatmentabroad.com**.

Long-term care insurance (LTCI)

Following the 2014 Budget, which abolished any requirement to buy a pension annuity, there is one area of annuities that is becoming increasingly popular. This is as a way of paying for residential care. The principle is that someone going into care pays a lump sum; in return the insurer promises to pay an annual sum to the care home for as long as the annuitant lives there. There is an associated tax perk: provided the payment goes directly from the insurer to the care home no tax is paid. As with all annuities, the policyholder is effectively gambling that they will live long enough for the exercise to be worthwhile. The average age of someone taking out one of these plans is 85. In most cases, policies are bought by the children of those going into care, or other trusted family members who have been granted power of attorney to act on their behalf (see: **www.telegraph.co.uk/finance/personalfinance**).

There are three main providers of care annuities:

Partnership Assurance: **www.partnership.co.uk**.

Just Retirement: **www.justretirement.com**.

Friends Life: **www.friendslife.co.uk**.

If contemplating this option, it is wise to ask your IFA to recommend what would be your best choice. All LTCI products and services now come under the compulsory jurisdiction of the Financial Ombudsman Service and the Financial Services Compensation Scheme. If you choose to seek the advice of an IFA, refer to Chapter 6, where there is more information.

A useful booklet, *A Brief Guide to Long Term Care Insurance, Choosing the right option for you*, is available from Association of British Insurers (ABI): **www.abi.org.uk**.

A possible alternative to a conventional long-term care policy is *critical illness insurance*, which pays a lump sum if you are unfortunate enough to suffer from cancer or have a stroke.

Hospital care cash plans

These are inexpensive insurance policies, known as health cash plans, which provide cover for the cost of everyday health care. Claims are made after the customer has paid for the treatment and are usually reimbursed within a week. See British Health Care Association: **www.bhca.org.uk**.

Permanent health insurance (PHI)

PHI should not be confused with other types of health insurance. It is a replacement-of-earnings policy for people who are still in work and who, because of illness, are unable to continue with their normal occupation for a prolonged period and, in consequence, suffer loss of earnings. While highly recommended for the self-employed, many employees have some protection under an employer's policy. Either way, if you are close to retirement, PHI is unlikely to feature on your priority list.

Health screening

Health screening is a wise precaution. Most provident associations offer a diagnostic screening service to check general health and to provide advice on diet, drinking and smoking if these are problem areas. Screening services normally recommend a check-up every two years, and centres are usually available to members of insurance schemes and others alike. See:

BMI Healthcare: **www.bmihealthcare.co.uk**.

BUPA: **www.bupa.co.uk**.

National Health Service: **www.nhs.uk**.

National Health Service

Choosing a GP

If you move to a new area, the best way to choose your new GP is to ask for a recommendation. Otherwise, your local primary care trust or strategic health authority can assist, or you can search the NHS website: **www.nhs.uk**.

Points you may want to consider are: how close the doctor is to your home; whether there is an appointments system; whether it is a group practice and, if so, how this is organized. All GPs have practice leaflets, available at their premises, with details about their service. Having selected a doctor, you should take your medical card to the receptionist to have your name registered. This is not automatic as there is a limit to the number of patients any one doctor can accept. Also, some doctors prefer to meet potential patients before accepting them on their list. If you do not have a medical card, you will need to fill in a simple form.

Changing your GP

If you want to change your GP, you go about it in exactly the same way. If you know of a doctor whose list you would like to be on, you can simply turn up at his or her surgery and ask to be registered; or you can ask your local primary care trust, or health board in Scotland, to give you a copy of its directory before making a choice. You do not need to give a reason for wanting to change, and you do not need to ask anyone's permission.

NHS 111 service

NHS 111 is the new service that is being introduced to make it easier to access local NHS health care services in England. You can call 111 when you need medical help but it is not a 999 emergency. NHS 111 is available 24 hours per day, 365 days per year. Calls are free from landlines and mobiles.

People calling 111 can obtain health advice and information about local services such as out-of-hours GPs, walk-in centres, emergency dentists and 24-hour pharmacies. For further information see: **www.nhs.uk**.

Help with NHS costs

If you or your partner are in receipt of Income Support, income-based Jobseeker's Allowance or the Pension Credit Guarantee Credit, you are both entitled to help with NHS costs. For full information and advice see NHS Choices: **www.nhs.uk/nhsengland/healthcosts**. If you live in Scotland, see: **www.scotland.gov.uk/healthcosts**.

Prescriptions

Both men and women aged 60 and over are entitled to free NHS prescriptions. Certain other groups are also entitled to free prescriptions, including those on low income. If you are not sure if you qualify, you should pay for your prescription and ask the pharmacist for an NHS receipt form FP57, which tells you how to claim a refund. For further information, see leaflet HC11, 'Help with health costs', obtainable from some pharmacies and GP surgeries.

People who do not qualify for free NHS prescriptions but who require a lot of prescriptions could save money by purchasing a prescription prepayment certificate. A prepayment certificate will work out cheaper if you are likely to need more than four prescription items in three months, or more than 14 items in 12 months, as there is no further charge regardless of how many prescription items you require. See **www.nhs.uk/nhsengland/healthcosts** or, if you live in Scotland, **www.scotland.gov.uk/healthcosts**.

Going into hospital

Many patients are unaware that they can ask their GP to refer them to a consultant at a different NHS trust or even, in certain cases, help make arrangements for them to be treated overseas. Before you can become a patient at another hospital, your GP will need to agree to your being referred. Those likely to need help on leaving hospital should speak to the hospital social worker, who will help make any necessary arrangements. Help is sometimes available to assist patients with their travel costs to and from hospital.

If you go into hospital you will continue to receive your pension as normal. Your pension – as well as Employment and Support Allowance, Severe Disablement Allowance, Income Support and Pension Credit Guarantee Credit – will continue to be paid in full, without any reductions, for the duration of your stay. For further information, see leaflet GL12, 'Going into hospital?', obtainable from your GP, social security or Jobcentre Plus offices and NHS hospitals.

Complaints

If you wish to make a complaint about an NHS organization, you should contact them directly first. If you're not sure where to start or how to get in touch with an NHS body or independent regulator, here are some suggestions. The first stage is known as *local resolution*. If you are not satisfied with this, you can ask the NHS trust or strategic health authority for an *independent review*. The complaints manager will be able to tell you whom to contact about arranging this. If you are still dissatisfied after the independent review, then the Health Service Ombudsman (formerly known as the Health Service Commissioner) may be able to help. See the following websites:

NHS Choices: **www.nhs.uk/choiceinthenhs/rightsandpledges/ complaints.**

Parliamentary and Health Service Ombudsman for England: **www.ombudsman.org.uk.**

Public Services Ombudsman for Wales: **www.ombudsman-wales.org.uk.**

Scottish Public Services Ombudsman: **www.spso.org.uk.**

An alternative approach is to contact the independent advice centre that offers guidance to patients in the event of a problem with the health service:

Patients Association: **www.patients-association.com.**

Complementary and alternative medicine

Complementary and alternative medicines (CAM) are treatments that fall outside mainstream health care. A number of complementary and alternative treatments are typically used with the intention of treating or curing a health condition: for example, homoeopathy, osteopathy, acupuncture, chiropractic and herbalism. A treatment that is regarded as complementary is used alongside conventional medicine, whereas alternative medicine is used in place of conventional medicine. Here are some of the better-known organizations:

British Acupuncture Council (BacC): **www.acupuncture.org.uk.**

British Chiropractic Association: **www.chiropractic-uk.co.uk.**

British Homoeopathic Association: **www.britishhomeopathic.org.**

British Hypnotherapy Association: **www. hypnotherapy-association.org.**

General Osteopathic Council: **www.osteopathy.org.uk.**

International Nature Cure Society: **www.naturecuresociety.org.**

National Institute of Medical Herbalists: **www.nimh.org.uk.**

Eyes

It is advisable to have your eyes tested at least every two years. Regular sight tests can pick up many conditions and detect signs of other diseases, so it is a sensible precaution to do this. You will qualify for a free NHS sight test if you are aged 60 and over; if you live in Scotland; if you or your partner receive Income Support, Family Credit, income-based Jobseeker's Allowance, Pension Credit Guarantee Credit and are entitled to or named on a valid NHS Tax Credit exemption certificate or are named on a valid HC2 certificate. People with mobility problems, who are unable to get to an optician, can ask for a domiciliary visit to have their eyes examined at home. The going rate for private sight tests if you do have to pay is about £35. There is a voucher system for helping with the purchase of glasses or contact lenses for those on low incomes. People who are registered blind are entitled to a special tax allowance each year. For 2014/15 it is £2,230.

All the main banks will provide statements in Braille; several institutions offer large-print chequebooks or templates for chequebooks, as well as other facilities such as a taped version of their annual report. There is no extra charge for these services.

For matters relating to sight, see:

Royal National Institute of Blind People (RNIB): **www.rnib.org.uk**.

International Glaucoma Association: **www.glaucoma-association.com**.

Partially Sighted Society: **www.partsight.org.uk**.

BT: **www.bt.com/includingyou**.

British Wireless for the Blind: **www.blind.org.uk**.

Calibre Audio Library: **www.calibre.org.uk**.

Talking News Federation: **www.tnf.org.uk**.

Feet

Anyone who has experienced foot pain knows only too well how debilitating it can be. Over time it can become a significant health issue because if we can't walk properly, we are less likely to get out and about. People who suffer from diabetes or arthritis should get their feet checked regularly. There is a lot we can do to protect our feet and most problems can be treated successfully by a chiropodist or podiatrist. An annual foot check is recommended, but, unlike free sight tests for the over 60s, you will have to pay for a foot health check. You can find some good advice for 'fitter feet' on the Age UK website: **www.ageuk.org.uk**. The professional association for registered chiropodists and podiatrists has a list of over 10,000 private practitioners.

Society of Chiropodists and Podiatrists: **www.scpod.org**.

Hearing

In the UK alone there are 10 million people living with a hearing loss – one in six of the population; 6.3 million of them are of retirement age (65+). Being able to hear properly is important for a number of reasons: safety and awareness; conversation and interaction; enjoyment and entertainment. Because hearing works 'invisibly' it isn't always given as much attention as it should be. Changes happen so gradually that hearing loss can often go undetected. Signs to look out for are:

- not hearing the doorbell or a telephone ring;
- turning up the television too loud for the comfort of others;
- failing to hear people come into the room;
- misunderstanding what has been said in conversation;
- not speaking clearly or speaking in a monotonous tone;
- uncertainty about where sounds are coming from;
- difficulty in hearing at a distance or in public gatherings.

If you have noticed any of these, talk to your GP, who may refer you to an audiologist or hearing care professional. Friends and family can do a great deal to help those who are deaf or hard of hearing. One of the essentials is not to shout but to speak slowly and distinctly. You should always face the person, so that he or she can see your lips, and avoid speaking with your hand over your mouth or when smoking. Learning British Sign Language is another option. In case of real difficulty, write down your message. There are other specialist organizations that can give you a lot of help on hearing aids and other matters:

Action on Hearing Loss (the new name for RNID):
www.actiononhearingloss.org.uk.

British Deaf Association (BDA): **www.bda.org.uk**.

British Tinnitus Association (BTA): **www.tinnitus.org.uk**.

Hearing Link: **www.hearinglink.org**.

Sleep/insomnia

The importance of sleep increases as we get older. Lack of sleep can be serious, causing permanent loss of brain cells. New research shows that even having short naps can be life-saving. Sleep is a necessary biological function to keep us physically and emotionally well. A good night's sleep is restorative and refreshing: it helps us to function well the next day. Our 24-hour biological clock (known as the circadian rhythm) governs our sleep/wake cycle. Most people need about seven hours sleep per night in order to feel refreshed the next day. As we age, sleep patterns change: elderly people experience nocturnal awakening and early morning awakening. The prevalence of insomnia increases with age. Quality of sleep is more important than quantity. Sleep helps boost a healthy immune system, so sleep deprivation may be detrimental to health. If you have difficulties with sleeping, it is important to speak to your GP. There is some good advice to be found on the Age UK website:

www.ageuk/health&wellbeing/conditions&illnesses/insomnia.

Teeth

People in their 50s, 60s and 70s look much younger these days thanks to advances in medicine and a healthier diet and lifestyle. But one thing that can let down the older generation is discoloured or misshapen teeth. Everyone knows the importance of having regular dental check-ups. Dentistry is one of the treatments for which you have to pay under the NHS, unless you are on a very low income. If you or your partner is in receipt of Income Support, income-based Jobseeker's Allowance or Pension Credit, you are entitled to free NHS dental treatment. You may also receive some help if you are in receipt of the Working Tax Credit;

for details, see leaflet HC11. To avoid any nasty surprises when the bill comes along, it is important to confirm possible costs with your dentist before he or she treats you, and to check that you are being treated under the NHS. This also applies to the hygienist, should you need to see one. To find a dentist in your area, search NHS Choices: **www.nhs.uk**.

Prevention is always better than cure. If you want free, independent and impartial advice on all aspects of oral health, and free literature on a wide range of topics, including patients' rights, finding a dentist and dental care for older people, see British Dental Health Foundation: **www.dentalhealth.org**.

For those who like to be able to budget ahead for any dental bills, the best advice is to take out a dental health plan. One of the UK's leading dental payment plan specialists has over 6,500 member dentists and approximately 1.8 million patients across the UK – Denplan: **www.denplan.co.uk**.

Personal relationships

According to Relate chief executive, Ruth Sutherland, there are three pillars to a successful later life: health, financial security and good personal relationships. In a poll of 1,000 people over age 50 for Relate, more than 8 out of 10 believed that relationships are the most important requirement for a happy retirement. Retirement involves a major life-style change and, sadly, some couples feel as they get older that they have less in common than they once had. The debate about 'silver divorce' continues but it is not clear whether those divorcing tend to be the recently married or whether long-term partnerships are breaking down. There is no doubt that good-quality relationships are key to happiness and wellbeing in older age. Here are some organizations that can offer help and guidance:

Albany Trust: **www.albanytrust.org**.

Marriage Care: **www.marriagecare.org.uk**.

The Spark (formerly Scottish Marriage Care): **www.thespark.org.uk**.

Relate: **www.relate.org.uk**.

Relationships Scotland: **www.relationships-scotland.org.uk**.

Help for grandparents

Regular contact with grandparents has been shown to be of great benefit to grandchildren from birth onwards. Sadly it is difficult for grandparents to maintain close contact with their grandchildren should adult children divorce. While some divorcing parents work hard to avoid this happening, others deny grandparents access and sometimes sever the relationship completely. There are a number of organizations that have experience of advising grandparents and offer practical help and support should this be of concern to you. See:

Grandparents' Association: **www.grandparents-association.org.uk**.

Grandparents Plus: **www.grandparentsplus.org.uk**.

Gransnet: **www.gransnet.com**.

Depression

Findings from the English Longitudinal Study of Ageing show that women become more lonely and depressed with age, but men grow more content with their lives in retirement. Maybe men are happier once they stop working, whereas older women are more likely to feel lonely or be living alone. The research suggests that women affected by loneliness feel a greater sense of isolation when children leave home or when husbands, partners or friends are no longer around. Loneliness doesn't just make people depressed and unhappy, it has an effect on mental health and can contribute to cardiovascular disease, hypertension and dementia. Wealth is closely associated with all aspects of wellbeing, with more affluent individuals having fewer depressive symptoms and greater life satisfaction. However, depression in later life is a widely under-recognized and under-treated medical condition. Most forms of depression can be dealt with – regardless of the person's age – using medication, talking treatments or other interventions.

It can be difficult to diagnose depression in older people because it often occurs alongside other mental and physical illnesses. In addition, many older people do not seek help from their GP. It is important to seek help as early as possible. Here are some useful websites:

Depression Alliance: **www.depressionalliance.org**.

Mind: **www.mind.org.uk**.

Samaritans: **www.samaritans.org**.

Sane: **www.sane.org.uk**.

Some common disorders

The rest of this chapter deals with some of the more common disorders such as back pain and heart disease. If you are unfortunate enough to be affected, or have a member of your family who is, here are some organizations that provide information and support.

Aphasia

This is a condition that affects a person's ability to *communicate*, not their *intelligence*. Individuals who have suffered a stroke, a head injury or other neurological damage who have aphasia find it difficult to speak, read and write. The national charity that can help is: Speakability, **www.speakability.org.uk**.

Arthritis

This is joint inflammation: the two most common forms are *osteoarthritis* and *rheumatoid arthritis*. Osteoarthritis is characterized by gradually worsening symptoms, including sore or stiff joints, stiffness after resting (which improves with movement), and pain that worsens after activity or towards the end of the day. Rheumatoid arthritis is caused by the body attacking its own tissues, producing symptoms that vary but often involving pain, fatigue, and warm, swollen, inflamed-looking joints. Although arthritis is often thought of as an older person's complaint, it accounts for the loss of an estimated 70 million working days per year in Britain, and 10 million people suffer from it. Gout is another form of arthritic disorder: 1 in 40 people in Britain suffer from it, making us the gout capital of Europe. Caused by an excess of uric acid in the blood, which crystallizes in the joints and around organs, gout is agonizingly painful. You don't have to put up with the pain of arthritis, however, as there are a number of organizations that can help:

Arthritic Association: **www.arthriticassociation.org.uk**.

Arthritis Care: **www.arthritiscare.org.uk**.

Arthritis Research UK: **www.arthritisresearchuk.org**.

Back pain

Four out of five people suffer from back pain at some stage of their lives. Although in most cases it is nothing serious, and disappears spontaneously, the sheer number of people affected makes it a very costly condition, imposing considerable burdens on the individual and society. Simple measures can be taken to reduce the chances of developing back pain. While there are many different causes, doctors agree that much of the trouble could be avoided through correct posture, care in lifting heavy articles, a firm mattress, and chairs that provide support in the right places. For further information, see:

BackCare: **www.backcare.org.uk**.

Blood pressure

Having high blood pressure (hypertension) is not usually something you feel or notice. The only way to find out the level of your blood pressure is to have it measured. High blood pressure is the leading cause of strokes in the UK and can lead to heart attack and heart failure. One in three adults has high blood pressure but one-third of those will be completely unaware of it. Anyone over the age of 50 should keep a check on their blood pressure as it tends to rise with age. Post-menopausal women also see an increase in their blood pressure. The good news is that blood pressure can be successfully managed with medication and some simple lifestyle changes, such as:

- Watch your salt intake.
- Eat at least five portions of fruit and vegetables per day.
- Watch your weight.
- Cut down on alcohol.
- Take regular exercise.
- Laugh – watch a funny movie.
- Be sociable – lonely people often suffer from high blood pressure.

For further information see The Blood Pressure Association: **www.bloodpressureuk.org**.

Cancer

With continuing research and improved treatments more people suffering from cancer today can be expected to make a complete recovery. Early diagnosis can make a vital difference, and if you are offered the opportunity for screening or testing it is advisable to take advantage of it. There has been a lot of publicity recently on the 'last taboo cancer', since bowel cancer is the UK's second biggest cancer killer and 80 per cent of cases are people aged 60 and over. But it can be successfully treated in over 90 per cent of cases if caught early. It goes without saying that anyone with a lump or swelling, or unexplained tiredness or weight loss, should waste no time in having it investigated by a doctor.

There are now over 300 cancer charities in existence, each researching or focusing on a particular variant of the disease. Here are a few, but to find a list of all of them consult **www.charitychoice.co.uk**:

Beating Bowel Cancer: **www.beatingbowelcancer.org**.

Bowel Cancer UK: **www.bowelcanceruk.org.uk**.

Breast Cancer Care: **www.breastcancercare.org.uk**.

Cancer Research UK: **www.cancerresearch.org**.

Macmillan Cancer Support: **www.macmillan.org.uk**.

Marie Curie Cancer Care: **www.mariecurie.org.uk**.

Chest and heart diseases

Keeping your heart healthy, whatever your age, is the most important thing you can do to help prevent and manage heart disease. The earlier sections on smoking, diet, drink and exercise list some of the most pertinent 'dos and don'ts' that can help. Statistics reveal that UK death rates from coronary heart disease are among the highest in the world, killing almost 120,000 people per year, and coronary heart disease is responsible for one in five of all deaths. Although people tend to think of heart attacks as particularly affecting men, over four times as many women die from heart disease as from breast cancer. The following charity plays a leading role in the fight against diseases of the heart and circulation:

British Heart Foundation: **www.bhf.org.uk**.

Diabetes

Diabetes is a common lifelong health condition. There are 3.2 million people diagnosed with diabetes in the UK and an estimated 630,000 people have the condition but don't know it. Diabetes occurs when the amount of glucose in the blood is too high for the body to use properly. It can sometimes be treated by diet alone; sometimes pills or insulin may also be needed. There are two main types of diabetes: type 1 and type 2. It can be diagnosed at any age, although it is common in the elderly and especially among individuals who are overweight. For further information see:

Diabetes UK: **www.diabetes.org.uk**.

Independent Diabetes Trust: **www.iddt.org**.

Migraine

This is a chronic health condition that affects over 10 million people in the UK. It can involve severe head pains, nausea, vomiting, visual disturbances and in some cases temporary paralysis. Most of the time migraines are not a threat to your overall health but they can interfere considerably with your day-to-day quality of life. Migraines are more common in women but often become less severe and less frequent with age. The leading UK charity that funds and promotes research, holds international symposia and runs an extensive support service is:

Migraine Trust: **www.migrainetrust.org**.

Osteoporosis and menopause problems

Bone is a living tissue that reacts to increases in loads and forces by growing stronger. Maximum bone density and strength are achieved around the age of 30. They change throughout our lifetime, with new bone constantly replacing old bone. From the age of 35 our bones begin to weaken gradually as most of us become less active. For women, bone loss is usually most rapid during the first few years after menopause, during which time women's levels of the hormone oestrogen naturally decrease. This can lead to osteoporosis: a condition in which bones become so fragile that they can break very easily. The most common injuries from falls affect the spine, hip and wrist. One in two women (and one in five men) suffers from osteoporosis.

Age UK compiled a list of ways to boost bone health:

- Weight-bearing exercise is important to help keep your bones strong. Walking, tennis, aerobics and dancing strengthen your bones.

- Enjoy a balanced diet. Milk, cheese, yoghurt, baked beans, lentils and dried apricots are great sources of calcium.

- Taking a stroll in the summer sun (just 10 minutes will help) is a great way of absorbing vitamin D, which keeps bones healthy

- Avoid smoking. Smokers lose bone at a faster rate than non-smokers.

- Drink moderately.

The following websites may be useful:

Menopause Exchange: **www.menopause-exchange.co.uk**.

National Osteoporosis Society: **www.nos.org.uk**.

Women's Health Concern: **www.womens-health-concern.org**.

Stroke

Every year over 150,000 people in England alone suffer a stroke. A stroke is a brain injury caused by the sudden interruption of blood flow. Strokes are the largest cause of death after heart disease and cancer and a leading cause of adult disability. People over 65 are most at risk and it has recently been discovered that iron deficiency may lead to an increased risk of suffering a stroke. A stroke is unpredictable in its effects, which may include physical problems, depression, fatigue, and problems with memory, attention and communication. Prevention is similar to the avoidance of heart disease. A stroke has a greater disability impact than any other medical condition. Most people experience a faster period of recovery just after a stroke; this is followed by a longer period of slower rehabilitation.

If you come across someone who may be having a stroke, remember the word 'FAST'. This stands for face – arms – speech – time. Look out for:

- *Face*: if the face droops on one side, or cannot smile evenly.

- *Arms*: if the person cannot lift one or both arms and keep them up because of weakness or numbness.

- *Speech*: if speech becomes slurred or garbled, or if the person finds it difficult to talk.

- *Time*: if you see any of these symptoms and suspect a stroke, dial 999 immediately. A stroke is a medical emergency that requires immediate professional attention.

Source: **www.laterlife.com/features/strokes-iron-deficiency**

The Stroke Association is the only UK-wide charity solely concerned with combating stroke in people of all ages. See:

Stroke Association: **www.stroke.org.uk**.

Disability

Disability is covered in Chapter 15, so if you or someone in your family has a problem not mentioned here, you may look there to find the answer you need.

Chapter Fourteen
Holidays

> *Live all you can: it's a mistake not to. It doesn't so much matter what you do in particular, so long as you have your life. If you haven't had that, what have you had?*

Life is meant to be enjoyed. For lots of people this means taking as many holidays as possible, while health and finances permit. Holidays apparently are good for you: they boost the immune system. As a large number of common illnesses result from stress, a holiday that reduces stress will keep you healthier. If you take two or more holidays per year, you are less likely to suffer from depression than those who stay at home – and according to research from the State University of New York you'll live longer too. Frequent holidays can lower your risk of death from heart disease by around 25 per cent. Having time away from daily routines allows you to indulge in some self-reflection and self-discovery. Some people insist that they return from holiday nicer people. Going on holiday, it seems, is good for mind, body and spirit.

When Gatwick Airport announced the winner of the UK's Oldest Traveller competition a year or so ago, it was 101-year-old Fauja Singh who took the prize. His claim to fame is having completed nine marathons since he began competing when he was 89. So don't even begin to think you are too old to travel...

Maybe a holiday is just what you need to help you feel healthier and more relaxed. But what sort of trip appeals? Are you adventurous – do you enjoy going to far-flung places, off the tourist trail? Do you enjoy being pampered at luxury hotels or on cruise ships? Or do you prefer short breaks in Europe? Many people find that there is enough variety and choice within the UK itself, despite the uncertainty of the weather. The best holidays should be exciting and full of treasured memories. This year, perhaps you'll try something new that will provide unforgettable experiences.

The fact that you've retired makes very little difference to what you can do, or where you can go. Lots of people combine holidays with special interests, such as painting or music. There is ample opportunity for you to enrol for summer school, or exchange homes with someone in another country. You could sign up for a working holiday, such as a voluntary conservation activity, or home and pet sitting, for which you get paid. The choice is enormous. If you wish to go somewhere exotic, it is likely that the prices will be high. But if your budget is limited, with a bit of research you will find some holidays that are extremely reasonable in cost. Whether you are fit and active or require special care, there are plenty of options. Retirement is a time for experimentation, so don't think about your age being an issue – there's plenty of opportunity to embrace new experiences.

Top tips for the over-50s when planning overseas travel

Money Saving Expert offers great advice, which can be found on: **www.moneysavingexpert.com/travel/travel-tips**. But some other suggestions from travel experts are worth bearing in mind:

- Spend some time researching the best deals so you don't pay over the odds.

- Be sure to take out travel insurance – the cheapest is not always best – and do check the small print.

- If you are happy joining a group tour, do your research and find one that suits your age range and interests.

- If you're not tied down with commitments, late booking can yield great discounts.

- When looking for places to eat and drink at your destination, ask for recommendations for local or hidden gems.

- There are lots of opportunities for over-50s singles who enjoy travelling. A number of tour companies operate specific departures and don't charge hefty supplements.

- And, if you love travelling, have lots of holiday and travel experience, you could consider becoming a holiday rep. Did you know that over 20 per cent of all tour guides are 50 years old and over...

Since there are so many types of holidays to choose from, for ease of reference the entries here are listed under subheadings. To avoid repetition, the majority are featured only once, in the most logical place. At the end of the chapter, there is a general information section with brief details about insurance, concessionary fares and other travel tips.

Art and cultural appreciation

Cultural holidays offer a combination of visits to places of artistic, historic, musical and architectural interest, with lectures given by professional academics, writers and curators. They are carefully researched and provide high standards of customer service, including comfortable hotels and authentic restaurants. Here are a few to consider:

Abercrombie & Kent: **www.abercrombiekent.co.uk**.

Ace Cultural Tours: **www.aceculturaltours.co.uk**.

Cox and Kings: **www.coxandkings.co.uk**.

Kirker Holidays: **www.kirkerholidays.com**.

Martin Randall Travel: **www.martinrandall.com**.

Opera Tours Italy: **www.operatoursitaly.com**.

Specialtours: **www.specialtours.co.uk**.

Travel for the Arts: **www.travelforthearts.co.uk**.

UK festivals

There is a feast of music, drama, literature and the arts to be found annually all over Britain and you will find a number of lists printed in the national press (*Guardian*, *Telegraph* and *The Times*) giving information on the music, poetry, literary and arts festivals taking place throughout the year. To find out what is going on where, in your local area or any other part of the UK, contact the Arts Council or your regional Arts Council office. There are simply too many to list here, but the booklet *Go Away Great Britain – The Oldie's Guide to Britain through its Festivals* provides a comprehensive list: **www.theoldie.co.uk**.

Arts and crafts

For those who want to discover new skills, this section focuses on taking courses on such subjects as crochet, knitting, painting, basket making and jewellery making. Further suggestions are also given in Chapter 9 (Leisure activities). There are plenty of good residential arts and crafts holidays offered by a number of organizations. See:

Adult Residential Colleges Association (ARCA): **www.arca.uk.net**.

Field Studies Council: **www.field-studies-council.org**.

Marlborough College Summer School: **www.mcsummerschool.org.uk**.

Missenden Abbey: **www.missendenabbey-al.co.uk**.

The Crafts Council: **www.craftscouncil.org.uk**.

West Dean College: **www.westdean.org.uk**.

Coach holidays

You can choose from hundreds of coach holidays and short breaks to many popular destinations across Britain, Europe and Ireland. Before embarking on a lengthy coach tour, try a few shorter excursions to see how you cope with the journey. A couple of good websites to get you started are:

Find A Coach Holiday: **www.findacoachholiday.com**.

National Express: **www.nationalexpress.com**.

Other websites that offer good choices of coach holidays include:

www.grandukholidays.com;

www.nationalholidays.com;

www.shearings.com.

Historical holidays

Holidays with a particular focus on history are becoming increasingly popular. Last year saw a huge boom in historical tours commemorating the outbreak of the First World War. For those with a passion for historic locations there are a number of companies offering to 'keep the spirit alive' of what went on in times gone by. Memorable events need to be communicated to future generations and here are a few websites worth checking out:

Battlefield Tours: **www.battlefieldtours.co.uk**.

Commonwealth War Graves Commission: **www.cwgc.org**.

Holts Tours – Battlefields & History: **www.holts.co.uk**.

Military History Tours: **www.militaryhistorytours.co.uk**.

Remembrance Travel (formerly Poppy Travel):
   www.remembrancetravel.org.uk.

The Cultural Experience: **www.theculturalexperience.com**.

Learning holidays

There is a huge choice of learning holidays available to the discerning traveller: from teaching your dog to be a truffle hunter to learning to scuba dive in the Red Sea or trekking with Masai warriors. If you dream about enlarging the mind while enjoying a holiday, there is nothing you cannot learn if you do your research. Here are some companies that can help:

Centre for Alternative Technology: **www.cat.org.uk**.

Dana Holidays: **www.danaholidays.com**.

Denman College: **www.denmancollege.org.uk**.

Go Learn To: **www.golearnto.com**.

HF Holidays: **www.hfholidays.co.uk**.

Painting and Cooking in Italy: **www.paintinginitaly.com**.

Responsible Travel: **www.responsibletravel.com**.

SwimTreck: **www.swimtreck.com**.

Truffle Hunters Dog School: **www.trufflehuntersdogschool.com**.

Other people's homes

Living in someone else's home for free is one of the cheapest ways to enjoy a holiday. There are two ways of doing this: exchange your home with another person in this country or abroad, or become a home sitter and mind someone else's property while they are away.

Home exchange

With home-swap sites, you find a property you like and, if the owners also like yours, then you swap homes for a holiday. Some people even exchange their cars and pets. Here are some websites to look at:

Guardian Home Exchange: **www.guardianhomeexchange.co.uk**.

Happy Home Swap: **www.happyhomeswap.com**.

Home Base Holidays: **www.homebase-hols.com**.

Home Exchange: **www.homeexchange.com**.

HomeLink: **www.homelink.org.uk**.

Simply Home Exchange: **www.simplyhomeexchange.com**.

Home and pet sitting

Retired people are generally considered ideal home sitters: you provide a caretaking service and get paid for doing so. Duties variously involve light housework, plant watering, care of pets and sometimes tending the garden. Careful vetting of applicants is essential, as are first-class references. See:

Absentia: **www.home-and-pets.co.uk**.

Animal Angels: **www.animalangels.co.uk**.

Homesitters: **www.homesitters.co.uk**.

Trusted House Sitters: **www.trustedhousesitters.com**.

Overseas travel

Many big tour operators make a feature of offering special holidays designed for the over-55s. Also included here are companies that specialize in arranging cruises and packaged motoring holidays, and information on timesharing:

Explore Worldwide: **www.explore.co.uk**.

Relais du Silence: **www.relaisdusilence.com**.

Saga Holidays: **www.saga.co.uk/travel**.

Silver Travel Advisor: **www.silvertraveladvisor.com**.

Telegraph Travel: **www.telegraph.co.uk/travel**.

Travelsphere: **www.travelsphere.co.uk**.

Cruises

Some 2 million people in the UK take a cruise holiday every year – and that figure is rising. Some of the reasons that so many people enjoy them include: a cruise vacation represents good value; you can see multiple destinations but unpack only once; cruise ships come in all shapes and sizes; cruise vacations are easy to plan; it's social and there are activities and entertainments galore. Finding a cruise that suits you has never been easier. Certain destinations, such as Alaska, lend themselves to a seafaring experience; others can be reached only by ship. And it's hard to beat a cruise if you want a first taste of the islands of the Caribbean. If you are interested in finding out more, visit:

Cruise Critic: **www.cruisecritic.co.uk**.

The Cruise Show: **www.cruisingshow.com**.

Here are some top tips for cruising:

- *Avoid an inside cabin*: it will be cheaper because there is no natural light, but it plays havoc with your body clock.

- *Don't pay the brochure price*: protect yourself by booking your cruise through an ABTA agent.

- *Remember that prices usually include extras*: if you think the cost is high, remember that food and non-alcoholic drinks are included.

- *Watch out for on-board credit offers*: cruise lines tempt customers with on-board credit that can only be spent on the ship.

From among the mass of companies offering cruise travel advice and tours, here are just a few websites to look at. Start with:

Alastair MacKenzie's Travel Lists: **www.travel-lists.co.uk**.

Avalon Waterways: **www.avaloncruises.co.uk**.

Blue Water Holidays: **www.cruisingholidays.co.uk**.

Celebrity Cruises: **www.celebritycruises.co.uk**.

Cunard: **www.cunard.co.uk**.

Fred. Olsen Cruise Lines: **www.fredolsencruises.com**.

Hebridean Island Cruises: **www.hebridean.co.uk**.

Hurtigruten Norwegian Cruises: **www.hurtigruten.co.uk**.

NCL (Norwegian Cruise Line): **www.ncl.co.uk**.

Noble Caledonia: **www.noble-caledonia.co.uk**.

P&O Cruises: **www.pocruises.com**.

Princess Cruises: **www.princess.com**.

Regent Seven Seas Cruises: **www.rssc.com**.

Royal Caribbean International: **www.royalcaribbean.co.uk**.

SeaDream Yacht Club: **www.seadream.com**.

Silversea: **www.silversea.com**.

Six Star Cruises: **www.sixstarcruises.co.uk**.

Titan: **www.titantravel.co.uk**.

Viking River Cruises: **www.vikingrivercruises.co.uk**.

Voyages of Discovery: **www.voyagesofdiscovery.co.uk**.

Voyages to Antiquity: **www.cruisedirect.co.uk**.

Windstar Cruises: **www.windstarcruises.com**.

Cargo ship cruises

Seeing the world by cargo ship doesn't offer the trappings of a conventional cruise, but being aboard a freight ship as a paying passenger is like being in another world. Many carry up to 12 non-crew members on routes from a week to months long. Securing a berth can be complicated, and periods in port tend to be brief, but life on board is uneventful – perfect for reading and writing. Price, accommodation and facilities (gyms and pools) vary according to the size and type of vessel. See:

Cargo Ship Voyages: **www.cargoshipvoyages.com**.

Strand Voyages: **www.strandtravelltd.co.uk**.

The Cruise People: **www.cruisepeople.co.uk**.

Possibly the most unusual cruise in the world is on board one of the few Royal Mail ships still working. Take a relaxing voyage on RMS *St Helena* to one of the most remote, inhabited islands in the world – a magical voyage to the stunning South Atlantic island of St Helena, just a speck in the ocean, south of the equator. The ship sails there from South Africa, calling at various islands along the way. It's the world's best-kept travel secret. See website: **www.rms-st-helena.com**.

Motoring holidays abroad

A number of organizations, including in particular some ferry operators, offer packages for the motorist that include ferry crossings, accommodation and insurance. While these often provide very good value, some people prefer to make all their own arrangements in order to get exactly what they want. Here are some of the major operators:

AA: **www.theaa.com**.

Brittany Ferries: **www.brittany-ferries.co.uk**.

RAC: **www.rac.co.uk**.

Top tips for motoring abroad, if taking your own vehicle

- Have your car thoroughly serviced before you go.

- Make sure your GB sticker is clearly visible.

- Check with the Foreign and Commonwealth Office (FCO) for travel advice via their website (**www.gov.uk/government/organisations/foreign-commonwealth-office**).

- Make sure your European health insurance card (EHI) is valid.

- Fit headlight converters if driving in Europe.

- Get insured for medical and travel purposes for the countries you are visiting.

- Invest in a good guide book on your destination that advises on local customs and laws.

- Find out about speed limits and if you require any specific equipment.

- Does your breakdown cover provide roadside assistance while abroad?

- Make sure all documentation is easily available, should you need it.

- Take the following with you: a tool kit, the manual for your car, a rented spares kit, a fuel can, a mechanic's light that plugs into the cigarette lighter socket, at least one extra set of keys, and any extras required by local laws such as a reflective tabard and warning triangles.

- Always lock your car and park it in a secure place overnight (nearly 75 per cent of luggage thefts abroad are from cars).

Other sources of advice and services are:

Association of British Insurers: **www.abi.org.uk**.

Aria Assistance: **www.aria-assistance.co.uk**.

Green Flag: **www.greenflag.com**.

If instead of taking your own car you plan to hire a vehicle overseas, you will probably have to buy special insurance at the time of hiring the vehicle. Make sure that this is properly comprehensive (check for any excesses or exclusions) or, at the very least, it gives you adequate third-party cover. If in doubt, seek advice from the local motoring organization regarding essential requirements, and do not sign any documents unless you understand them.

How is your driving?

If you've recently travelled in a car and been frightened by a friend's driving, or you think you might be starting to scare others with your driving skills, it is simple enough to get yourself checked. The Institute of Advanced Motorists offers to assess anyone over 55 on their driving skills. It is sensible to take advantage of this exercise every few years or so in order to maintain confidence and be safe on the road.

If you are already a member of the Institute of Advanced Motorists, did you know that you are eligible to be insured to drive by IAM Surety?

One bonus feature is that this company will continue to insure you until the age of 120! New members are accepted up to the age of 85, but must be prepared to take an IAM assessment if over 79. For further information on both points, see: **IAM: www.iam.org.uk**.

Short breaks

One of the many benefits of being an older traveller is being able to take advantage of short-break holidays all year round, some of which offer special bargain prices in spring and autumn. British hotels have winter breaks from November to April, and overseas travel operators slash prices during the off-peak seasons. Here are just a few websites to look at:

Cities Direct: **www.citiesdirect.co.uk**.

Easy Breaks: **www.easy-breaks.com**.

Great Little Breaks: **www.greatlittlebreaks.com**.

Shortbreaks Ltd: **www.short-breaks.com**.

Superbreak: **www.superbreak.com**.

Travel 55: **www.travel55.co.uk**.

Timesharing

By signing a timeshare holiday contract, you agree to pay for a holiday year after year until the expiration of the contract. One timesharing formula involves buying points, which can then be exchanged for stays in selected accommodation. Another formula is long-term use of an accommodation unit extending over a specific period in the year. The same unit can then accommodate different vacationers every week of the year. Prices vary depending on the location, the size of the property, the time of year and the facilities of the resort. There are maintenance charges on top and you should always check that these are linked to some form of cost-of-living index, such as the RPI. Another useful point to check is that there is an owners' association linked to the property. These websites provide information and safeguards:

RCI Europe (Resort Condominiums International): **www.rci.com**.

Interval International: **www.intervalworld.com**.

RDO (Resort Development Organisation): **www.rdo.org**.

Existing owners wishing to sell their property should be on their guard against unknown resale agents contacting them and offering, in exchange for a registration fee, to act on their behalf. A telephone call to the RDO will establish whether the company is a member body. If not, leave well alone.

Holiday Property Bond

A uniquely flexible alternative to the fixed-week timeshare or villa ownership, the Holiday Property Bond (HPB) is a life assurance bond that invests, after product charges, in a combination of securities and carefully chosen holiday properties throughout the UK and Europe. Bondholders and their families and friends are entitled to use any HPB property at any time *rent free*. It is a privilege that they can pass on – without charge – to their children and grandchildren. HPB has been in existence for over 30 years and is one of the best-kept secrets in the holiday industry. For further information see:

Holiday Property Bond: **www.hpb.co.uk**.

Rail holidays

Taking the train is often cheaper than flying, and can even be cheaper than travelling by bus – and far less bumpy. If you fancy a holiday by rail, but without the hassle of poring over timetables and transfers, one of the following tour operators or agents may be able to help:

Danube Express: **www.danube-express.com**.

Erail: **www.erail.co.uk**.

French Travel Service: **www.f-t-s.co.uk**.

Golden Eagle Luxury Trains: **www.gwtravel.co.uk**.

Great Rail Journeys: **www.greatrail.com**.

Holidays By Rail: **www.holidaysbyrail.com**.

Planet Rail: **www.planetrail.co.uk**.

Rail Trail: **www.railtrail.co.uk**.

Railway Holidays: **www.railwayholidays.com**.

The Venice Simplon-Orient-Express: **www.orient-express.com**.

The Man in Seat 61: **www.seat61.com**.

Trainbreaks.com: **www.trainbreaks.com**.

Retreats

Retreat holidays are a great way to de-stress, de-tox and recharge your batteries. There are lots of different types: yoga, meditation, spiritual, and wellbeing retreats. If peace, quiet and contemplation are what you seek, this could be the ideal holiday for you. Here are some websites to consider:

The Good Retreat Guide: **www.thegoodretreatguide.com**.

The Retreat Company: **www.theretreatcompany.com**.

The Retreat Association: **www.retreats.org.uk**.

Self-catering and low-budget holidays

If you enjoy flexibility when on holiday, self-catering breaks come in all shapes and sizes. This type of holiday gives you the freedom to do whatever you want, whenever and wherever you want, and they are also excellent for those on a budget. Here are some websites:

Camping and Caravanning Club:
   www.campingandcaravanningclub.co.uk.

Cheap Holiday Cottages: **www.homeaway.co.uk**.

English Country Cottages: **www.english-country-cottages.co.uk**.

Farm Stay UK: **www.farmstay.co.uk**.

Group Stay UK: **www.groupstayuk.com**.

Landmark Trust: **www.landmarktrust.org.uk**.

Lowcostholidays: **www.lowcostholidays.com**.

National Trust Holiday Cottages: **www.nationaltrustcottages.co.uk**.

National Trust for Scotland: **www.nts.org.uk/holidays**.

Scottish Country Cottages: **www.scottish-country-cottages.co.uk**.

YHA (England and Wales) Ltd: **www.yha.org.uk**.

Sport

Holidays with on-site or nearby sporting facilities exist all over the country. The list that follows is limited to organizations that can advise you about organized residential courses or can offer facilities. For wider information, see Chapter 9, which lists some of the national sports associations.

Boating

The beauty of life aboard a boat is that you're not on a set holiday itinerary. There's no rushing to the next destination, unless you want to. Whether you choose to holiday abroad or in Britain, there loads of choice. If you're new to boating, it's akin to travelling in a cosy floating villa, with all the comforts of home – and each day you wake up in a beautiful new destination. See the following websites:

Beautiful Boating Holidays: **www.leboat.co.uk**.

Blakes: **www.blakes.co.uk**.

Hoseasons Boating Holidays: **www.hoseasons.co.uk**.

Royal Yachting Association (RYA): **www.rya.org.uk**.

Waterways Holidays: **www.waterwaysholidays.com**.

Cycling

Cycling holidays are fun and you do not need to be super fit to enjoy stunning views and scenery. If you wish to take to two wheels for your holiday, you can enjoy bike touring in many parts of the world. Depending on age, health and fitness it is advisable to choose suitable terrain for your level of expertise. There are many websites to look at; here are a few:

CTC Cycling Holidays: **www.cyclingholidays.org**.

Cycle Active: **www.cycleactive.com**.

Cycle Breaks: **www.cyclebreaks.com**.

Cycling for Softies: **www.cycling-for-softies.co.uk**.

Hooked on Cycling: **www.hookedoncycling.co.uk**.

Saddle Skedaddle: **www.skedaddle.co.uk**.

The Bike Bus: **www.bikebusuk.com**.

UK Cycling Holidays: **www.ukcyclingholidays.co.uk**.

Golf

There are some amazing holiday destinations for golf players. You may be looking for a short golf break with friends, organizing a full golf society break, or just looking to enjoy a golfing trip in the sun. Whether you wish to travel abroad, or play on a UK course, there is a destination or vacation to suit you. Here are a few websites that can help:

Glencor Golf: **www.glencorgolf.com**.

Golf Escapes: **www.golf-escapes.com**.

Golf Holidays.Com: **www.golfholidays.com**.

Longshotgolf: **www.longshotgolf.co.uk**.

The Golf Travel Company: **www.thegolftravelcompany.co.uk**.

Your Golf Travel: **www.yourgolftravel.com**.

Rambling

Rambling features on many special interest and other programmes as one of the options on offer. It is a relaxing holiday that many people enjoy. The latest offering from the tour company Ramblers Worldwide (see website listed below) is walking holidays for women only. This is not a new thing: Victorian women used to enjoy walking holidays without men but were urged to travel light. One eminent Victorian lady walker, Emily Lowe, is famous for saying, 'The only use of a gentleman in travelling is to look after the luggage.' Whatever you may think, here are some of the companies that specialize in rambling holidays:

ATG Oxford: **www.atg-oxford.co.uk**.

Exodus: **www.exodus.co.uk**.

Rambling Tours: **www.ramblingtours.co.uk**.

Ramblers Worldwide Holidays: **www.ramblersholidays.co.uk**.

Skiing

Why do people love skiing? Some reasons given: the speed is exhilarating; it is exercise without feeling it; the views in the mountains are amazing;

you get plenty of fresh air as well as physical and mental challenges. Whether you are a skier or snowboarder there are lots of organizations, tour operators and destinations to choose from:

Crystal Ski Holidays: **www.crystalski.co.uk**.

Disability Snowsport UK: **www.disabilitysnowsport.org.uk**.

Powder White: **www.powderwhite.com**.

Ski Club Great Britain: **www.skiclub.co.uk**.

Ski Collection: **www.skicollection.co.uk**.

Snow-wise: **www.snow-wise.com**.

VIP Ski: **www.vip-chalets.com**.

Tennis

The key ingredients of a good tennis holiday are: good weather, a great tennis venue and exceptional accommodation. There are a number of companies who offer tennis holidays to suit your needs, whether you are a single traveller, a family or a group of friends:

ActiveAway: **www.activeaway.com**.

Discovery Tennis: **www.discoverytennistours.com**.

Jonathon Markson Tennis: **www.marksontennis.com**.

Lawn Tennis Association (LTA): **www.lta.org.uk**.

Roger Walker Travel: **www.tennisholidays.co.uk**.

Wine tasting

Whatever the reason for your trip – romantic break, birthday or anniversary celebration, or group travel – wine tours are hugely popular holidays. The combination of an enjoyable holiday with great wine-tasting experiences is something that appeals to many people. Tours offer plenty of variety with visits, talks, convivial meals and free time for exploring as well as memorable tastings. See the following websites:

Arblaster & Clarke Wine Tours: **www.winetours.co.uk**.

Grape Escapes: **www.grapeescapes.net**.

Responsible Travel: **www.responsibletravel.com**.

Smooth Red: **www.smoothred.co.uk**.

Winetasting France: **www.winetastingfrance.com**.

Working holidays

There is scope for volunteers in innumerable organizations across the UK and the rest of the world. If you research carefully, you'll find that you can engage in a worthwhile project, see some of the world for free (almost), and have a great holiday at the same time. The other place to look for listings is in Chapter 12, Volunteering. See:

Helpx: **www.helpx.net**.

Crewseekers International: **www.crewseekers.net**.

National Trust Working Holidays: **www.nationaltrust.org.uk**.

TCV The Conservation Volunteers: **www.tcv.org.uk**.

Workaway.info: **www.workaway.info**.

Wwoof: **www.wwoof.net**.

Grown-up gappers

Who, or what, exactly is a 'grown-up gapper'? The answer is that they come in all shapes, sizes and varieties. What they all have in common is a sense of adventure, a desire to experience 'real' travel, see new places and broaden their horizons. You could be a career-break professional, someone whose kids have finally all flown the nest, or wishing to pack in as much excitement to your retirement as possible. Rather than sit at home, you may feel that now is the ideal opportunity to take the long-haul trips not possible previously. The top 10 destinations for the over-50s are: Australia, Canada, New Zealand, the United States, the Caribbean, Italy, the Seychelles, Ireland, Florida and the Maldives. If you think that escaping on a gap year could be fun and want the latest information and advice, see:

Gapadvice: **www.gapadvice.org**.

Inspired Breaks: **www.inspiredbreaks.co.uk**.

World Wide Experience: **www.worldwideexperience.com**.

Holidays for singles

Deciding to travel on your own can be a tough decision whatever your age. Many people do travel solo: some may be single, others not. If you are single, widowed, divorced or simply having to travel without your partner, you can enjoy being part of a group, or if that's not your thing, you can opt out. There are tour holidays, exploring holidays and relaxing escape holidays. Travelling alone need not be expensive: with single-traveller specialists firms there is no supplement to pay. There are a number of companies that specialize in organizing trips for solo holidaymakers:

Friendship Travel: **www.friendshiptravel.com**.

Just You: **www.justyou.co.uk**.

One Traveller: **www.onetraveller.co.uk**.

Solitaire: **www.solitairhols.co.uk**.

Solos: **www.solosholidays.co.uk**.

Travel One: **www.travelone.co.uk**.

Holidays for those needing special care

Everyone enjoys a holiday: it is one of life's greatest pleasures and a vital tonic to body, mind and spirit. The great news is that affordable, accessible and enjoyable holidays for the disabled are on the increase. More airlines, hotels and resorts are providing people with disabilities or mobility issues the opportunities to travel, enjoy holidays and see the world. Specially designed self-catering units are more plentiful and of a higher standard. Also, an increasing number of trains and coaches are installing accessible loos. An elderly or disabled person seeking a holiday needs to explain clearly what their care needs are, not only in terms of getting to and from but also with regard to accommodation requirements.

Travel and other information

If you need help getting on and off a train or plane, inform your travel agent in advance. Arrangements can be made to have staff and a wheelchair available to help you at both departure and arrival points. If you are travelling independently, you should ring the airline and/or local bus or train station and explain what assistance you require, together with details of your journey, so that facilities can be arranged at any interim points, should you need to change buses or trains. Some people take companions/carers with them. Organizations that can help you include:

Age UK: **www.ageuk.org.uk**.

Able Community Care. **www.uk-care.com**.

Accessible Travel & Leisure: **www.accessibletravel.co.uk**.

Can Do Holidays: **www.candoholidays.com**.

Choice Care Assisted Holidays: **www.choicecareservices.co.uk**.

Disabled Access Holidays: **www.disabledaccessholidays.com**.

Enable Holidays: **www.enableholidays.com**.

Holidays for the Disabled: **www.holidaysforthedisabled.com**.

Tourism for All: **www.tourismforall.org.uk**.

Vitalise: **www.vitalise.org.uk**.

Another source to contact is your local social services department. Some local authorities arrange holidays or give financial help to those in real need.

Touring in the UK

Why not plan to holiday within the UK and take advantage of the many beautiful places to visit, without the need of a passport? There are masses of choice, but a good place to start your research, if you are looking for hotels and accommodation in Britain, or are simply after UK travel, attractions or event information, is the following websites:

Discovering Britain: **www.discoveringbritain.org**.

Discover Northern Ireland: **www.discovernorthernireland.com**.

UK Tourist Attractions: **www.uktouristattractions.co.uk**.

Visit Britain: **www.visitbritain.com**.

Visit London: **www.visitlondon.com**.

Visit Scotland: **www.visitscotland.com**.

Visit Wales: **www.visitwales.com**.

Long-haul travel

It is advisable when booking long-haul flights to book through a specialist agent. They can almost always match, and sometimes undercut, the airlines' own best deals. They are geared to booking packages, which is normally cheaper than booking everything separately. The specialist organizations listed below can also offer a lot of practical information and help. Round-the-world air tickets are an excellent buy. Travel agents may also achieve savings by putting together routes using various carriers. Most airlines offer seasonal discounts that sometimes include a couple of nights' concessionary hotel stay, if you want to break your journey or visit another country at minimum extra travel cost. See the following websites:

Kuoni: **www.kuoni.co.uk**.

Trailfinders Travel Centre: **www.trailfinders.com**.

Virgin Holidays: **www.virginholidays.co.uk**.

Voyages Jules Verne: **www.vjv.com**.

WEXAS: **www.wexas.com**.

Visa and passport requirements and health and safety advice

It is vital that you check passport and visa requirements as well as any immunization guidelines for the countries you are travelling to (and through) as early as possible, as processing necessary documentation can take some time. As a starting point, you should ensure your passport has at least six months' validity beyond your length of stay as this is now a mandatory requirement for many countries around the world. The best website for up-to-the-minute travel advice for your destination and guidance on everything from health and immunization to passport and visa requirements is the Foreign & Commonwealth Office: **www.gov.uk/foreign-travel-advice**.

For information on tax and duty-free reliefs when bringing goods into the UK, see HM Revenue & Customs: **www.hmrc.gov.uk/customs**.

Insurance

It is a fact of life that people over 65 are more likely to have a pre-existing medical condition that needs to be declared and covered on their travel insurance. Despite this age group now having a much greater choice of holidays and travelling further afield, travel insurance for the over-65s tends to carry higher premiums, as insurers view them as higher risk because they are more likely to suffer health problems. When planning a trip it is important to focus on finding good, affordable cover. If you are travelling independently it is even more important to be properly insured, as you will not be protected by the normal compensation that the reputable tour operators provide to cover the event of a mishap. A useful book on this subject is *The Mature Guide to Travel Insurance*, published by Mature Times (see **www.maturetimes.co.uk**). To find out more about travel insurance options, take a look at the following websites:

Age UK: **www.ageuk.org.uk**.

American Express: **www.americanexpress.com**.

Avanti Travel Insurance: **www.avantitravelinsurance.co.uk**.

Insurance Choice: **www.insurancechoice.co.uk**.

Laterlife Travel Insurance: **www.laterlife.com**.

Onestop4:Insurance: **www.onestop4.co.uk**.

Saga: **www.saga.co.uk**.

Staysure: **www.staysure.co.uk**.

Top tips when buying holiday insurance

Your policy should cover you for:

- *medical expenses*, including hospital treatment and the cost of an ambulance, an air ambulance and emergency dental treatment, plus expenses for a companion who may have to remain overseas with you should you become ill;

- *personal liability cover*, should you cause injury to another person or property;

- *personal accident* leading to injury or death (check the small print, as some policies have reduced cover for older travellers);

- *additional hotel and repatriation costs* resulting from injury or illness;

- *loss of deposit or cancellation* (check what emergencies or contingencies this covers);

- *the cost of having to curtail your holiday*, including extra travel expenses, because of serious illness in the family;

- *compensation for inconvenience* caused by flight cancellations or other travel delays;

- *cover for baggage and personal effects* and for emergency purchases should your baggage be delayed;

- *cover for loss of personal money* and documents.

Before purchasing new insurance, check whether any of the above items are already covered under an existing policy. This might apply to your personal possessions and to medical insurance. Even if the policy is not sufficiently comprehensive for travel purposes, it will be better and cheaper in the long run to pay a small supplement to give you the extra cover you need than to buy a holiday insurance package from a tour operator. A cost-effective plan may be to extend any existing medical insurance to cover you while abroad. Then take out a separate policy (without medical insurance) to cover you for the rest of your travel needs. Two websites that provide good advice regarding the amount of cover you should be looking for in your travel insurance policy are:

The Association of British Insurers: **www.abi.org.uk**.

The Association of British Travel Agents (ABTA): **www.abta.com**.

Compensation for lost baggage

If the airline on which you are travelling loses or damages your baggage, you should be able to claim compensation up to a maximum value of about £850. (The figure may vary slightly up or down, depending on currency fluctuations.)

How to complain to an airline

If you have reason to complain about an airline and are not getting satisfaction, don't give up. Contact the Civil Aviation Authority (CAA) with full details of your complaint. The CAA can help in these circumstances.

Cancelled or overbooked flights

Denied Boarding, Cancellation and Delay Regulation sets out a number of rules on the level and nature of compensation and assistance to be provided to passengers in the event of their being adversely affected by overbooking, flight cancellation or long delay. The regulation applies to all flights operated within the European Economic Area (EEA), flights departing from airports in the EEA and flights arriving in the EEA from non-member states operated by Community carriers. For full details and information on this subject, see:

Air Travel Advisory Bureau (ATAB): **www.atab.org.uk**.

Aviation Consumer Advocacy Panel: **www.caa.co.uk**.

Medical insurance

This is one area where you should never skimp on insurance. Although many countries now have reciprocal arrangements with the UK for emergency medical treatment, these vary greatly in both quality and generosity. Some treatments are free, as they are on the National Health Service; others, even in some EU countries, may be charged for as if you were a private patient.

The Department of Health has advice for travellers. In particular you should get a European health insurance card (EHIC). This card entitles the holder to free or discounted medical treatment at state-run hospitals and GPs in any EEA (European Economic Area) country plus Iceland, Liechtenstein, Norway and Switzerland. But it is not insurance and will not, for instance, arrange for repatriation, nor pay for a hotel room if you have to extend your stay to look after a sick relative. Search European health insurance card on the NHS UK website: **www.nhs.uk**.

However, even the very best reciprocal arrangements may not be adequate in the event of a real emergency. For peace of mind, experts recommend cover of £1 million for most of the world and up to £2 million for the United States. Some policies offer higher or even unlimited cover.

Although theoretically there is no upper age limit if you want to take out medical insurance, some insurance companies are very difficult about insuring older travellers. If you are over 75, many request a note from a qualified medical practitioner stating that you are fit to travel, or require you to confirm that you are not travelling against medical advice. For further information, see Fit For Travel: travel health information for people travelling abroad from the UK (**www.fitfortravel.nhs.uk**).

Book through a reputable operator

It is essential that holidaymakers check to ensure that their travel agent or tour operator is affiliated to an association with strict regulations that its member companies must follow. No one can guarantee you against every mishap, but a recognized travel company plus adequate insurance should go a long way towards giving you at least some measure of protection. See Air Travel Advisory Bureau (ATAB): **www.atab.org.uk**.

Travel and other concessions

Buses, coaches, some airline companies and especially the railways offer valuable concessions to people of retirement age.

Trains

Some of the best-value savings that are available to anyone aged 60 and over are provided by train companies. These include:

Disabled Persons Railcard: **www.disabledpersons-railcard.co.uk**.

Family Friends Railcard: **www.familyandfriends-railcard.co.uk**.

Network Railcard: **www.railcard.co.uk**.

Senior Railcard: **www.senior-railcard.co.uk**.

Buses and coaches

Over 11 million people over 60 in the UK use buses for free travel around the country. Make the most of this while you can: it is reported that the government has plans to raise the eligible age gradually to 65. Bus passes are usually issued free by local authorities. For further information see the government website: **www.gov.uk/apply-for-elderly-person-bus-pass**.

Airlines

Several of the airlines offer attractive discounts to older travellers. The terms and conditions vary, with some carriers offering across-the-board savings and others limiting them to selected destinations. Likewise, in some cases the qualifying age is 60; in others, it is a couple of years older. A particular bonus is that concessions are often extended to include a companion travelling at the same time. Ask your travel agent or the airline at the time of booking what special discounts, if any, are offered.

Overseas

Many countries offer travel and other reductions to retired holidaymakers including, for example, discounts for entry to museums and galleries, day excursions, sporting events and other entertainment. As in Britain, provisions are liable to change, and for up-to-date information probably the best source to contact is the national tourist office of the country to which you are travelling. All EEA countries – as well as most lines in Switzerland – give 25 per cent reductions on international rail fares. These are available to holders of a Railplus Card who are purchasing international rail travel tickets, and are applicable to both first- and second-class travel.

Airport meet-and-greet services

With the number of 'meet and greet' parking services at UK airports on the increase, it can be hard to make a confident choice. While your vehicle is left at an airport at your own risk, the British Parking Association provides a few handy hints to follow when selecting a service:

- Is the member of staff that greets you wearing a uniform – and carrying an ID badge? If so, check the badge – does it match up with the company you think you're dealing with, in the location you're at?

- Are you doing business in a designated location – such as a stand at the airport or a kiosk in the vicinity of the airport? Not having premises is a sure-fire indication that something might not be right.

- Check where the company will be storing your car. Can they point out their storage facility? If it is off-site, which they usually are, can they tell you where it is, or show you a picture? Does the company own the storage facility?

- Ask whether the car park in which your car will be stored has the 'Park Mark'. The Park Mark® is given to car-parking facilities that have undergone an annual police assessment.

See the following websites:

British Parking Association: **www.britishparking.co.uk**.

Park Mark Safer Parking: **www.parkmark.co.uk**.

Tips for safe travelling

- Remember to pack any regular medicines you require: even familiar branded products can be difficult to obtain in some countries. In addition, take a mini first-aid kit with you. If you are going to any developing country, consult your doctor as to what pills (and any special precautions) you should take.

- An overdose of sun can be painful. In some countries it really burns, so take it easy, wear a hat and apply plenty of protective lotion.

- Be careful of the water you drink. Beware the water, ice, salads, seafood, ice cream and any fruit that you do not peel yourself. Always wash your hands before eating or handling food, particularly if you are camping or caravanning.

- Have any inoculations or vaccinations well in advance of your departure date. When flying, wear loose clothes and above all comfortable shoes, as feet and ankles tend to swell in the air.

- To avoid risk of deep vein thrombosis, which can be fatal, medical advice is to do foot exercises and walk around the plane from time to time. For long-haul travel especially, wear compression stockings and, another tip, unless advised otherwise by your doctor, take an aspirin before flying.

For more information and advice, see Safe Travel: **www.safetravel.co.uk**.

Chapter Fifteen
Caring for elderly parents

A reporter interviewing a 104-year-old woman asked:
'What do you think is the best thing about being 104?' She
replied: 'No peer pressure.' ANONYMOUS (FOUND ON THE INTERNET)

Did you know that there are certain places in the UK that are 'glad to be grey'? Figures from the Office for National Statistics (ONS) suggest that one such place is Christchurch in Dorset, which has a higher proportion of residents over the age of 65 (average age 69.8 years), than anywhere else in the UK. This is closely followed by Eastbourne in Sussex (average age 71.1 years). Clearly, in these places the old are in charge. With regard to elderly relatives, the ONS also reports that more than half a million 'very old' people (that is, aged 90 and over) were living in the UK in 2012. Out of the 13,350 centenarians living, 660 were aged 105 years and older, suggesting that there might indeed be some peer pressure in that age group after all. In the longevity league – that is, people living in the UK who are over 107 years of age – at the time of going to press, Ethel Lang from Barnsley, South Yorkshire, aged 114, is Britain's oldest person, born on 27 May 1900. She resisted a care home until she was 105, and enjoyed dancing until she was 107. And male readers should note that in the top 50 of this list, all but two are women. So much for the weaker sex... (**www.oldestinbritain.nfshost.com**).

What is really striking is that the term 'old' is now so vague as to be almost meaningless. No matter where you live, old age can stretch elastically across three, or even four, decades. There are a fast-growing number of multigenerational pensioner families, with recently retired children looking after their much older parents. While it is true that there are now more people over 65 in the UK than children under 15, rising life expectancy means older people are effectively 'younger', healthier and fitter than previous generations. As the entire country gets a little greyer each year, with increasing numbers of older people, we still have difficulty embracing our ageing population as a success story. All too often old age is seen as an enemy, when in fact from the point of view of many communities it is a big plus. It is the active pensioners who keep voluntary organizations running, local communities vibrant, and ensure that theatres, cinemas and other recreational places are full. Caroline Abrahams, charity director at Age UK, said: 'Nearly one in five people in our country will live to see their 100th birthday. The increase demonstrates the true worth of advances in medicine and the increasing effectiveness of preventative treatments' (**www.bbc.co.uk/news/magazine-27066299**).

The good news is that many of the elderly, given a bit of support in the community, stand a reasonable chance of remaining independent and living in their own homes for a long time. Old age may bring its challenges, but it doesn't necessarily spell a downward spiral to infirmity. The majority of people in their late 80s rate their health and quality of life as good, but there are certain key factors: having a cheerful outlook, remaining active and maintaining friendships. Indeed, the generation that lived through the Second World War is more content with life than the middle aged, a recent study has concluded. However, quality of life for those over 80 can deteriorate rapidly should they be faced with the combined effects of failing health, losing a spouse and isolation. On average, people in this age group are remarkably resilient, have a positive attitude to ageing, and look back with satisfaction on their life and achievements. Indeed the majority learn to be content with their lot. Age UK's '*love later life*' approach is aimed at encouraging people to think differently about getting older, and highlights how the charity can help more people to make the most of later life.

So is growing old getting easier? It should be. There are masses of information and advice available these days – however, much of it is confusing and contradictory. Do you know the story of the gentleman who visited his doctor to ask whether he was ready to go into a care home? The doctor said there was a simple test that would establish this. 'We fill a bathtub with water, then offer a teaspoon, a tea cup and a bucket and ask them to empty the bath.' 'I understand,' said the man. 'A normal person would use the bucket because it is bigger than the spoon or the teacup.' 'No,' replied the doctor, shaking his head. 'A normal person would pull out the plug. Now do you want a bed near the door or the window?'

The most often expressed wish by elderly people is that they remain independent and able to live in their own home for as long as possible. With assistance from friends, relatives or local care organizations, many should be able to do this. Should you become responsible for an elderly, frail or disabled relative, you are not alone. There are 6.5 million carers in the UK today (one in eight adults). You are doing valuable service. This unpaid care saves the state £119 billion a year (source: Carers UK: **www.carersuk.org**). One thing that is vital as people get older is attitude: remaining positive about their physical health, because it is good for their mental health as well. According to recent research, genetics accounts only for about one-quarter of what determines the length of life. This means that three-quarters of how well people age is dictated by factors that are within each individual's control, such as cheerful outlook, good nutrition and healthy lifestyle. If you are keen to help your parent, relative or friend remain well and happy for as long as possible, read the list of tips provided here.

Ten top tips for healthy ageing

- Looking on the brighter side of life is really important.
- Think ahead: stay curious and stay fit.
- Try to maintain a healthy immune system in older age.
- Be sociable: social isolation causes stress, which lowers immunity.
- Look after the eyes: good vision underpins independent living.
- Get regular health checks for risk factors of stroke and heart disease.
- Protect the skin you're in. Avoid excessive exposure to the sun.
- Use it or lose it. It's never too late to start strengthening muscles.
- To sleep or not to sleep? Managing sleep is vital to healthy ageing.
- Report any problems to your GP at an early stage: better late than never.

These tips are from an excellent booklet, *Improving Later Life*, which can be ordered from Age UK's website: **www.ageuk.org.uk/ improvinglaterlifebook**.

SOURCE: RiAF – Research into Ageing Fund

The main focus of this chapter is on helping the elderly to remain independent for as long as possible, until a care home or nursing home becomes necessary. Knowing what facilities are available and what precautions your parents can take against a mishap occurring is an important factor. Being aware of whom they can turn to in an emergency can make all the difference. There is now much greater awareness of the needs of the elderly, mostly in regard to the financial implications of funding older people's care. In line with this, many provisions for the elderly have improved enormously. It is possible to find out from your local authority what programmes operate in your area that can help. Ask your parents' GP where to start, such as obtaining an assessment from Adult Social Services.

It is well worth investing a bit of time finding out where help and support can be found and familiarizing yourself (on your parents' behalf) with how to source funding or access equipment and personal aids. A bit of time spent improving their home to make it easier to cope as they become more frail, and fine-tuning their social and support network, should make all the difference. If faced with the choice between moving parents to live with the family, or allowing them to continue to live on their own, the decision will depend on individual circumstances. But if safe to do so, 'staying put' is usually the preferred option.

Ways of adapting a home

Many elderly people will not require anything more complicated than a few general improvements. These could include better lighting, especially near staircases, a non-slip mat and grab rails in the bathroom, and safer heating arrangements. For some, a practical improvement might be to lower kitchen and other units, to place them within easy reach to make cooking less hazardous, also to raise sofas, beds or chairs to make it easier to get up and out of them. Another fairly simple option is to convert a downstairs room into a bedroom with en suite bath or shower, if managing the stairs is proving difficult. These and other common-sense measures are covered in more detail in Chapter 8. Should such arrangements not be sufficient, in the case of a physically handicapped or disabled person, more radical changes will usually be needed. This involves accessing help from the GP and local authority.

Local authority help

The state system is designed to support the elderly in their own home for as long as possible. Local authorities have a legal duty to help people with disabilities and, depending on what is required and the individual's ability to pay, may assist with the cost. The best advice is to approach their GP or contact the adult social services department direct. A sympathetic doctor will be crucial support at this stage, particularly if he or she has known the patient for some years and is familiar with their circumstances. The GP will be able to advise what is needed and supply any prescriptions, such as for a medical hoist, and will also be able to suggest which unit or department to approach, and make a recommendation to the housing department, should rehousing be desirable. If your parents can afford it, they will have to pay for the services they need themselves. If their income and savings are low, the council may pay part or all of the cost.

Local authority services

Social services departments (social work departments in Scotland) provide many of the services that people with disabilities may need, including:

- practical help in the home, perhaps with the support of a home help;
- adaptations to the home, such as a ramp for a wheelchair or other special equipment for your safety;
- meals on wheels;
- provision of day centres, clubs and similar;
- the issue of badges for cars driven or used by people with a disability (in some authorities this is handled by the works department or by the residents' parking department);
- advice about other transport services or concessions that may be available locally.

In most instances, you should speak to the social worker allocated to look after your elderly relatives, who will either be able to make the arrangements or point you in the right direction. He or she will also be able to tell you about any special facilities or other help provided by the authority.

Health care and specialist services

Local authorities employ a number of specialist helpers, variously based in the social services department or health centre, who are there to assist:

- *Social workers* are normally the first people to contact if your parents need a home help or meals on wheels, or have a housing difficulty or other query. Contact the local social services department or, in Scotland, the social work department.

- *Occupational therapists* have a wide knowledge of disability and can assist individuals via training, exercise or access to aids, equipment or adaptations to the home. Contact the local social services department.

- *Health visitors* are qualified nurses with a broad knowledge of health matters and other available services. Rather like social workers, health visitors can put your parents in touch with whatever specialized facilities are required. Contact is through the local health centre.

- *District nurses* are fully qualified nurses who will visit a patient in the home, change dressings, attend to other routine nursing matters, monitor progress and help with the arrangements if more specialized care is required. Contact is through the health centre.

- *Physiotherapists* use exercise and massage to help improve mobility and strengthen muscles, for example after an operation or to alleviate a crippling condition. They are normally available at both hospitals and health centres.

- *Medical social workers* (MSWs) (previously known as almoners) are available to consult if patients have any problems – whether practical or emotional – on leaving hospital. MSWs can advise on coping with a disablement, as well as such practical matters as transport, aftercare and other immediate arrangements. They work in hospitals, and an appointment should be made before the patient is discharged.

Council tax

If an elderly relative has a disability, they may be able to claim a reduction on their council tax. If they have a blue badge on their car, they may get a rebate for a garage. They should apply to the housing benefits officer, but different councils employ different officers to deal with this; see website: **www.gov.uk** – Disabled people.

Help with home repair and adaptations

Disabled facilities grant

This is a local council grant to help towards the cost of adapting a home to enable a disabled or elderly person to live there. It can cover a wide range of improvements to help the occupants manage more independently. This includes widening doors and installing ramps, improving access to rooms and facilities (such as stairlifts or a downstairs bathroom), a suitable heating system, adaptation of heating or lighting controls to make them easier to use. Provided the applicant is eligible, currently a mandatory grant may be available of up to £30,000 in England, £25,000 in Northern Ireland and £36,000 in Wales. See website: **www.gov.uk** – Disabled people.

Home improvement agencies (HIAs)

Home improvement agencies and the charity Care & Repair help elderly, disabled and otherwise vulnerable people to make adaptations to the homes they own. They are supported by the government and local authorities, and are not-for-profit organizations. There are around 200 home improvement agencies in England covering over 80 per cent of local authorities. For HIAs in the UK, see:

Foundations: **www.foundations.uk.com**.

Care and Repair Cymru: **www.careandrepair.org.uk**.

Care and Repair Scotland: **www.careandrepairscotland.co.uk**.

Other organizations that can help include:

Age UK: **www.ageuk.org.uk**.

British Red Cross: **www.redcross.org.uk**.

Assist UK: **www.assist-uk.org**.

CAE (Centre for Accessible Environments): **www.cae.org.uk**.

DEMAND (Design & Manufacture for Disability): **www.demand.org.uk**.

Disability Wales/Anabledd Cymru: **www.disabilitywales.org**.

DLF (Disabled Living Foundation): **www.dlf.org.uk**.

REMAP: **www.remap.org.uk**.

Alarm systems

Alarm systems for the elderly are often life savers: the knowledge that help can be summoned quickly in the event of an emergency is reassuring to the elderly or disabled and their carers and families. Some alarm systems allow people living in their own homes to be linked to a central control, or have a telephone link, enabling personal contact to be made. Others simply signal that something is wrong. Sometimes a relative or friend who has been nominated will be alerted. Your parents' local authority social services department will have information. See website: **www.gov.uk**.

A number of organizations offer alarm systems, medical alerts and other devices. Some useful websites include:

Aidcall: **www.aidcall.co.uk**.

Callsafe: **www.callsafe.org**.

Careline UK: **www.carelineuk.com**.

DLF (Disabled Living Foundation): **www.dlf.org.uk**.

Helpline: **www.helpline.co.uk**.

Community alarms

Telephone alarm systems operated on the public telephone network can be used by anyone with a direct telephone line. The systems link into a 24-hour monitoring centre and the individual has a pendant that enables help to be called even when the owner is some distance from the telephone. Grants may be available in some cases to meet the costs.

Age UK Personal Alarm Service: **www.ageuk.org.uk**.

SeniorLinkEldercare: **www.seniorlinkeldercare.co.uk**.

Main local authority services

Quite apart from any assistance with housing, local authorities supply a number of services that can prove invaluable to elderly people. The two most important are meals on wheels and home helps. Additionally, there are social workers and various specialists concerned with aspects of health care (already mentioned above). Since the introduction of Community Care, local authority social services departments have taken over all responsibility for helping to assess and coordinate the best arrangements for individuals according to their particular requirements. Other organizations that may offer home help include the British Red Cross and Age UK (websites already listed above).

Meals on wheels

The meals at home (meals on wheels) service is run by local councils or other voluntary organizations, but is available in England and Wales only. The purpose is to deliver ready-made meals to individuals in their own homes. Different arrangements apply in different areas. For further information, contact the local social services department or see website: **www.gov.uk** – Meals at home services. The original meals on wheels provider is the Royal Voluntary Service, which delivers over 2 million meals per year to people who have difficulty with shopping, carrying food home or cooking for themselves: **www.royalvoluntaryservice.org.uk**.

Community care services

For help in the home, the first step is to contact your parents' local council's social services department for an assessment of their needs. A social care assessment takes place in their home and they should not be charged for this. There is a lot of information on how to access these services available on the Age UK website: **www.ageuk.org.uk/home-and-care**. See also website: **www.gov.uk** – Disabled people.

Good neighbour schemes

A number of areas of the country have an organized system of good neighbour schemes. In essence, these consist of volunteers agreeing to act as good neighbours to one or several elderly people living close by.

Depending on what is required, they may simply pop in on a daily basis to check that everything is all right, or they may give more sustained assistance such as providing help with dressing, bathing, shopping or preparing a light meal. For more information see the Royal Voluntary Service website: **www.royalvoluntaryservice.org.uk**.

Key voluntary organizations

Voluntary organizations complement the services provided by statutory health and social services in making life easier for elderly people living at home. The range of provision varies from area to area but can include:

- lunch clubs;
- holidays and short-term placements;
- day centres and clubs;
- friendly visiting;
- aids such as wheelchairs;
- transport;
- odd jobs and decorating;
- gardening;
- good neighbour schemes;
- prescription collection;
- advice and information;
- family support schemes.

The particular organization providing these services depends on where your parents live, but the best place to get advice is the local Citizens Advice Bureau. These are the key agencies:

Age UK: **www.ageuk.org.uk**.

Age Scotland: **www.ageuk.org.uk/scotland**.

Age Wales: **www.ageuk.org.uk/cymru**.

Age Northern Ireland: **www.ageuk.org.uk/northern-ireland**.

Disability Wales: **www.disabilitywales.org**.

Update (Disability Information Scotland): **www.update.org.uk**.

Care Information Scotland: **www.careinfoscotland.co.uk**.

Centre for Individual Living, Northern Ireland: **www.cilbelfast.org**.

British Red Cross: **www.redcross.org.uk**.

St John Ambulance: **www.sja.org.uk**.

Royal Voluntary Service: **www.royalvoluntaryservice.org.uk**.

Other sources of help and advice include:

CSRF (Civil Service Retirement Fellowship): **www.csrf.org.uk**.

Disability Rights UK: **www.disabilityrightsuk.org**.

Jewish Care: **www.jewishcare.org**.

Transport

Difficulty in getting around is often a major problem for elderly and disabled people. In addition to the facilities run by voluntary organizations already mentioned, there are several other very useful services:

Forum of Mobility Centres: **www.mobility-centres.org.uk**.

London Taxicard: **www.londoncouncils.gov.uk/services/taxicard**.

Motability: **www.motability.co.uk**.

Driving licence renewal at age 70

All drivers aged 70 are sent a licence renewal form to have their driving licence renewed – for free. The entitlement to drive will need to be renewed by the DVLA; the new licence will normally be valid for three years. See website: **www.gov.uk/renew-driving-licence-at-70**.

Holidays

Many people in their 70s and 80s who still enjoy an active lifestyle travel across the world, go on activity holidays and visit wonderful places in the UK and abroad without any more difficulty than anyone else. They will find plenty of choice on where to go on holiday in Chapter 14, including information about how to obtain assistance at airports and railway stations. However, some elderly people need special facilities if a stay away from home is planned. A number of organizations can help:

Accessible Travel and Leisure: **www.accessibletravel.co.uk**.

Can be done: **www.canbedone.co.uk**.

Disability Holidays Guide.com: **www.disabilityholidaysguide.com**.

Enable holidays: **www.enableholidays.com**.

Tourism for All: **www.tourismforall.org.uk**.

Voluntary organizations

A number of the specialist voluntary organizations run holiday centres or provide specially adapted self-catering accommodation. In some cases, outings and entertainment are offered; in others, individuals plan their own activities and amusement. Guests requiring assistance usually need to be accompanied by a companion, although in a few instances care arrangements are inclusive. Most of the organizations can advise about the possibility of obtaining a grant or other financial assistance. See:

Holidays for all: **www.holidaysforall.org.uk**.

Holiday with Help: **www.holidayswithhelp.org.uk**.

Vitalise: **www.vitalise.org.uk**.

The *Disabled Travellers' Guide*, published by the AA, lists a wide choice of holiday venues where disabled travellers can go in the normal way but with the advantage of having special facilities provided. Downloadable in pdf format, it gives information on holiday accommodation suitable for disabled individuals and their families, together with advice on travelling in Europe. See website: **www.theaa.com**.

Lasting power of attorney

A lasting power of attorney (LPA) is a legal document that allows the donor to appoint people, known as attorneys, to make decisions on their behalf. It could be used when the donor becomes unable to make his/her own decisions. There are two types of LPA: health and welfare, and property and financial affairs. To make an LPA, the person has to be over 18 and have mental capacity; it allows the donor to choose one or more people to make decisions for them. The health and welfare LPA covers daily routine (what to eat and wear), medical care, moving into a care home and life-sustaining treatment. The property and financial affairs LPA covers paying bills, collecting benefits, selling property.

The right time to draw up an LPA is while an individual is in full command of his or her faculties, so that potential situations that would require decisions can be properly discussed and the donor's wishes made clear. If an elderly person you care about is considering setting up an LPA, it is advisable that they consult both their GP and the family solicitor. For further information see: **www.gov.uk/power-of-attorney**.

Living-in help

Temporary

Elderly people living alone may not be able to cope very well with managing their homes or caring for themselves. In the event of an emergency, or if you have reason for concern, engaging living-in help can be a godsend. Most agencies are expensive, but in the event of a real problem they represent excellent value for money. A more unusual and interesting longer-term possibility is to recruit the help of a community service volunteer.

Community service volunteers (CSVs)

CSV is the UK's leading training and volunteering charity, training over 12,000 young people and adults each year. They provide practical assistance in the home and also offer companionship. For more information contact your parents' local social services department, or see CSV: **www.csv.org.uk**.

Agencies

The agencies listed below specialize in providing temporary help, rather than permanent staff. Fees are normally paid by private funding but, depending on individual circumstances, public financial assistance may be available. See:

Bunbury Care Agency: **www.bunburyagency.com**.

Consultus Care & Nursing Agency Ltd: **www.consultuscare.com**.

Country Cousins: **www.country-cousins.co.uk**.

Live-In Support: **www.live-insupport.co.uk**.

The Care Agency: **www.thecareagency.co.uk**.

For a further list of agencies, see *The Lady* magazine, or search the internet under the headings 'nursing agencies' or 'care agencies'.

Nursing care

If one of your parents needs regular nursing care, their GP may be able to arrange for a community or district nurse to visit him or her at home. This will not be a sleeping-in arrangement but simply involves a qualified nurse calling round when necessary. If they need more concentrated home nursing there are many specialist agencies that can arrange hourly, daily or live-in nurses on a temporary or longer-term basis. Fees and services vary considerably. Private health insurance can sometimes be claimed against part of the cost, but this is generally only in respect of qualified nurses. Your local health centre or social services department should be able to give you names and addresses of local agencies, or search the internet under the heading 'nursing agencies'.

Permanent

There may come a time when you feel that it is no longer safe to allow one of your parents to live entirely on his or her own. One possibility is to engage a companion or housekeeper on a permanent basis. Many domestic agencies supply housekeeper-companions. Alternatively, you could advertise in the most widely read publication for these kinds of posts. See *The Lady* magazine: **www.lady.co.uk**.

Permanent help can be provided by agencies, which will supply continuous four-weekly placements. This is an expensive option, and the lack of continuity can at times be distressing for elderly people, particularly at the staff changeover point. Contact the agencies listed above to see how they can assist.

Flexible care arrangements

One of the problems for many elderly people is that the amount of care they need is liable to vary according to the state of their health. There are other relevant factors, including, for example, the availability of neighbours and family. Whereas after an operation the requirement may be for someone with basic nursing skills, a few weeks later the only need may be for someone to act as a companion. Under normal circumstances it may be as little as simply popping in for the odd hour during the day to cook a hot meal and check all is well. Here are a few agencies that offer a flexible service:

Christies Care: **www.christiescare.com**.

Cura Domi – Care at Home: **www.curadomi.co.uk**.

Miracle Workers: **www.miracle-workers.co.uk**.

UKHCA (United Kingdom Home Care Association): **www.ukhca.co.uk**.

Although any of these suggestions can work extremely well for a while, with many families it may sooner or later come down to a choice between residential care and inviting a parent to live with you. Sometimes, particularly in the case of an unmarried son or daughter or other relative, it is more practical to move into the parent's (or relative's) home if the accommodation is more suitable.

Emergency care for pets

For many elderly people a pet is a very important part of their lives. It provides companionship and fun as well as stimulating them into taking regular outdoor exercise. Because pets usually have shorter life spans than us, some may have planned for this event. But what if your elderly loved ones become ill or incapacitated, or dies first? To ensure that their beloved pet will continue to receive care should something unexpected happen, it is vital to plan ahead. The following organizations will be able to help under these circumstances:

Blue Cross: **www.bluecross.org.uk**.

Cats Protection: **www.cats.org.uk**.

Cinnamon Trust: **www.cinnamon.org.uk**.

Dogs Trust: **www.dogstrust.org.uk**.

National Animal Welfare Trust: **www.nawt.org.uk**.

Pet Fostering Service Scotland: **www.pfss.org.uk**.

Practical help for carers

Carers Week is a UK-wide annual awareness campaign. Its aim is to improve the lives of carers and the people they care for. It takes place annually, in June, and celebrates and recognizes the outstanding contribution that the country's 6.5 million carers make every single day of the year. Carers Week is made up of a group of nine charities, who have joined forces to promote the role of carers in our society. For more information about the support available, see: **www.carersweek.org**.

If your elderly relative is still fairly active – visits friends, does his or her own shopping, or enjoys some hobby that gets him or her out and about – the strains and difficulties involved in caring for them may be fairly minimal. This applies particularly if your parent is moving in with you and your home lends itself to creating a granny flat, so everyone can retain some privacy and your parent can continue to enjoy maximum independence. However, when this is not possible, as in the case of an ill or very frail person, far more intensive care may be required. It is important to know what help is available and how to obtain it. The many services provided by local authorities and voluntary agencies, described earlier in the chapter, apply as much to an elderly person living with a family as to one living alone. If there is nothing there that solves a particular problem you may have, one of the following organizations may be able to help:

Age UK: **www.ageuk.org.uk**.

British Red Cross: **www.redcross.org.uk**.

Carers Trust: **www.carers.org**.

Independent Age: **www.independentage.org**.

Royal Voluntary Service: **www.royalvoluntaryservice.org.uk**.

Most areas have respite care facilities to enable carers to take a break from their dependants from time to time. A particularly welcome aspect of respite care is that many schemes specially cater for, among others, elderly people with dementia.

Holiday breaks for carers

There are various schemes to enable those with an elderly relative to go on holiday alone or simply to enjoy a respite from their caring responsibilities. A number of local authorities run *fostering schemes*, on similar lines to child fostering. There may be a charge, or the service may be run on a voluntary basis (or be paid for by the local authority). Some voluntary organizations arrange *holidays for older people* in order to give relatives a break. Different charities take responsibility according to the area where you live: the Citizens Advice Bureau, volunteer centre or social services department should know whom you should approach.

Another solution is a *short-stay home*, which is residential accommodation variously run by local authorities, voluntary organizations or private individuals, catering specifically for elderly people. The different types of home are described under the heading 'Residential care homes' further on in this chapter. For information about local authority provision, ask the social services department. If, as opposed to general care, proper medical attention is necessary, you should consult your parent's GP. Many hospitals and nursing homes offer short-stay care arrangements as a means of relieving relatives, and a doctor should be able to help organize this for you.

Benefits and allowances

There are benefits and allowances available to those with responsibility for the care of an elderly person and/or to elderly people themselves. If you are caring for someone, the government website is the place to turn to for the latest and widest range of online public information. It is the gateway for government advice. There is a section for carers covering support services and assessments, carer's rights, working and caring, carer's allowance and much more, and includes information for disabled people. See website: **www.gov.uk** – Disabled people.

Entitlements for carers

Home responsibilities protection

This is a means of protecting your state pension if you are unable to work because of the need to care for an elderly person. For further details, see under 'The state pension' at the start of Chapter 3, or look at the following websites:

www.gov.uk;

www.hmrc.gov.uk;

www.nidirect.gov.uk.

Carer's Allowance

If you spend at least 35 hours a week caring for someone who is getting Attendance Allowance or the middle or highest rate of the Disability Living Allowance care component, you may be able to claim Carer's Allowance. You cannot get this if you are already getting the state pension or work and earn over £100 per week. See: **www.gov.uk/carers-allowance**.

Entitlements for elderly or disabled people

Attendance Allowance

This is paid to people aged 65 or over who are severely disabled, either mentally or physically, and have needed almost constant care for at least six months. (They may be able to get the allowance even if no one has actually given them that help.) An exception to the six months' qualifying period is made in the case of those who are terminally ill, who can receive the allowance without having to wait. There are two rates of allowance: £54.45 or £81.30 per week. See: **www.gov.uk/attendance-allowance**.

Personal Independence Payment

In April 2013, the Department for Work and Pensions (DWP) introduced a new benefit called Personal Independence Payment (PIP) which gradually replaces Disability Living Allowance for eligible disabled people aged between 16 and 64. It is made up of two parts, a daily living component and a mobility component. There are two rates – standard and enhanced. For more information on the changes, and eligibility criteria, see: **www.gov.uk/pip**.

Cold Weather Payment

If your elderly relative is in receipt of certain benefits, he/she may be eligible for a Cold Weather Payment. These are made when the local temperature is either recorded as, or forecast to be, an average of zero degrees Celsius or below, over seven consecutive days. The amount paid is £25. Those eligible should receive it without having to claim. For more information, see website: **www.gov.uk/cold-weather-payment**.

Winter Fuel Payment

This is a special annual tax-free payment of between £100 and £300 given to all households with a resident aged 60 and over. See: **www.gov.uk/winter-fuel-payment**.

Free off-peak bus travel

People over the age of 60 and also disabled people can travel free on any bus service in the country. See Chapter 14, section on 'Travel and other concessions'.

Free TV licence

Anyone aged 75 or over is eligible for a free TV licence for their main address. There are currently almost 4 million free TV licences in force – and with some 4.9 million adults over the age of 75 living in the UK, TV Licensing is encouraging those able to claim the concession to apply online: **www.tvlicensing.co.uk**.

Financial assistance

A number of charities give financial assistance to elderly people in need. Some of these may have been listed in earlier sections but are also relevant here:

Counsel and Care: **www.counselandcare.org.uk**.

Elizabeth Finn Care: **www.elizabethfinncare.org.uk**.

Guild of Aid for Gentlepeople: **www.turn2us.org.uk**.

Independent Age: **www.independentage.org.uk**.

RABI (Royal Agricultural Benevolent Institution): **www.rabi.org.uk**.

SSAFA Forces Help: **www.ssafa.org.uk**.

For many people, one of the main barriers to getting help is knowing which of the many thousands of charities to approach. There are free services that help older people in genuine financial need to receive the support that may be available to them from a variety of charitable sources. These are provided by:

Charity Search: **www.charitysearch.org.uk**.

Turn2Us, part of Elizabeth Finn Care: **www.turn2us.org.uk**.

Useful reading

For other sources of financial help, ask at your library, or search online for *A Guide to Grants for Individuals in Need*, published by the Directory of Social Change (**www.grantsforindividuals.org.uk**).

Independent Age is a support community for thousands of older people across the UK and the Republic of Ireland. Their helpful publication, *Wise Guide – Life-improving advice for the over-65s*, is the practical elderly person's handbook. See: **www.independentage.org**.

Age UK guides and factsheets are aimed at keeping elderly people up to date with home and care information. Guides are short and easy to digest, giving a comprehensive overview of a subject. Factsheets are longer, more detailed and aimed at professionals. See: **www.ageuk.org.uk/ publications**.

Special accommodation

When is the right time for elderly relatives to consider moving into specialist housing? Usually before they need it, so that the right research into the various options can be done without a rush. It is unwise to wait until they cannot manage on a day-to-day basis without help.

Specialist housing comes in many guises: 'sheltered housing', 'housing with care', 'retirement housing', 'retirement villages'. Not all will be available in all parts of the UK, but one thing that all these alternatives have in common is that they all offer self-contained flats or bungalows within a community of older people. The first question to ask is whether your elderly relatives will be happy living in a community. Many people decide to move because they feel isolated, particularly after the death of a spouse. But living alongside others is not easy, and getting to know people can be difficult, particularly when health problems or disabilities get in the way.

It is important to find out what care and support are available, as in extra care housing some personal help may be included in the basic costs. In sheltered or retirement housing you would need to organize care for your relatives from a home care agency from outside. Housing providers and the local council should give advice on arranging extra help and how to afford it. In terms of costs, whatever your relative's financial circumstances, it is essential to get accurate information about the charges in retirement housing. Charges typically include: rent or the cost of buying the lease, service charges, and the cost of additional care and support. Some leaseholders have to pay towards a sinking fund (for major repairs) or may be liable for exit charges.

Even if your parents own their own home and have never considered claiming benefits, it is sensible to get advice on their eligibility. It may make all the difference to what they can afford, and help meet the costs. Disability benefits such as Attendance Allowance are not means-tested. Pension Credit, Housing Benefit and help with council tax are means tested but can help with the costs of housing, support and care.

In terms of whether to rent, buy or part-own, choice may be restricted by financial circumstances, what's available in the area, and the rules of the housing providers. Some former house owner-occupiers when switching to renting find they are glad they had, giving them more disposable income. Renting also makes it easier to leave if the scheme or accommodation becomes unsuitable for them (or their partner) and allows them to feel more in control. Retirement property leases can be complex documents, so it is important that your relatives understand what is involved in the lease – in particular any fees that might have to be paid should the property be sold in the future. If in doubt, always ask questions.

Much research on this subject has been carried out by the Joseph Rowntree Foundation; see: **www.jrf.org.uk**. For further information on retirement housing options, First Stop Advice is an independent, impartial and free service provided by the national charity Elderly Accommodation Counsel (EAC). See website: **www.firststopcareadvice.org.uk**.

Retirement village life

Retirement villages are opening up across the country: they are typically built around a central hub, containing a health club, swimming pool, GP surgery, village hall and café bar. The village comprises houses and apartments that can be bought or rented, designed to accommodate the needs of older people. Lifts can be installed and come equipped with floor-level showers and grab rails. There are also domiciliary care services that can be bought in, if and when necessary. Retirement villages give the sense of a self-contained community – a kind of university campus for pensioners.

Sheltered housing

There are many different types of sheltered housing schemes. Some will have a scheme manager (a warden) who lives on-site or off-site, and all should provide 24-hour emergency help through an alarm system. Each scheme usually has between 20 and 40 self-contained flats or bungalows, but there will often be communal areas. If residents require more support, extra-care sheltered housing may be available.

Sheltered housing for sale

Good developments are always sought after and can require you to join a waiting list. There are many companies offering sheltered housing for sale; some also provide personal care services as an adjunct to their retirement home schemes. Flats and houses are usually sold on long leases (99 years or more) for a capital sum, with a weekly or monthly service charge to cover maintenance and resident support services. Should a resident decide to move, the property can usually be sold on the open market, either through an estate agent or through the developer, provided the prospective buyer is over 55 years of age. Although the rights of sheltered housing residents have been strengthened over the years, you would nevertheless be strongly recommended to get any contract or agreement vetted by a solicitor before proceeding. For further information see:

Elderly Accommodation Counsel: **www.eac.org.uk**.

Retirement Homesearch: **www.retirementhomesearch.co.uk**

Rented sheltered housing

This is normally provided by local authorities, housing associations and certain benevolent societies. As with accommodation to buy, quality varies. Local authority housing is usually only available to people who have resided in the area for some time. There is often an upper and lower age limit for admission, and prospective tenants may have to undergo a medical examination, since as a rule only those who are physically fit are accepted. Should a resident become infirm or frail, alternative accommodation will be found. Apply to the local housing or social services department or via a housing advice centre.

Housing associations supply much of the newly built sheltered housing. Both rent and service charges vary around the country. In case of need,

Income Support or Housing Benefit may be obtained to help with the cost. The Citizens Advice Bureau and housing departments often keep a list of local housing associations. There are hundreds to choose from; here are just a few:

Abbeyfield: **www.abbeyfield.com**.

Anchor: **www.anchor.org.uk**.

Girlings: **www.girlings.co.uk**.

Hanover: **www.hanover.org.uk**.

Jewish Community Housing Association Ltd: **www.jcha.org.uk**.

Southern Housing Group: **www.shgroup.org.uk**.

Benevolent societies

These are charitable organizations that help a particular group of people in need. Here are just a few:

Housing&Care 21: **www.housingandcare21.co.uk**.

Royal Alfred Seafarers' Society: **www.royalalfredseafarers.com**.

Royal British Legion: **www.britishlegion.org.uk**.

SSAFA Forces Help: **www.ssafa.org.uk**.

Alternative ways of buying sheltered accommodation

For those who cannot afford to buy into sheltered housing, either outright or through a mortgage, there are a variety of alternative payment methods, as set out below.

Shared ownership and 'Sundowner' schemes

Part-ownership schemes are now offered by a number of developers. Would-be residents, who must be over 55 years, part-buy or part-rent with the amount of rent varying according to the size of the initial lump sum. Residents can sell at any time, but they only recoup that percentage of the sale price that is proportionate to their original capital investment, with no allowance for any rental payments made over the intervening period.

'Investment' and gifted housing schemes

Some charities and housing associations operate these schemes, for which a capital sum is required, to obtain sheltered accommodation.

Investment schemes work as follows. The buyer puts in the larger share of the capital, usually 50 to 80 per cent, and the housing association puts in the remainder. The buyer pays rent on the housing association's share of the accommodation and also service charges for the communal facilities.

Gifted housing schemes differ in that an individual donates his or her property to a registered charity, in return for being housed and cared for in his or her own home. The attraction is that the owner can remain in his or her own property with none of the burden of its upkeep. However, it is advisable to consult a solicitor before signing anything, because such schemes have the big negative of reducing the value of the owner's estate, with consequent loss for any beneficiaries. See: Age UK: **www.ageuk.org.uk/giftedhousing**.

Almshouses

Most almshouses are endowed by a charity for the benefit of older people of reduced means who live locally or have a connection with a particular trade. There are now over 1,700 groups of almshouses, providing homes for over 35,000 people. Although many of these properties are of considerable age, most of them have been modernized and new ones are being built. Rents are not charged, but there will be a maintenance contribution towards upkeep and heating.

Almshouses do not provide the same security of tenure as some other tenancies, so it is advisable to check with a lawyer exactly what the beneficiary's rights are. There is no standard way to apply for an almshouse, since each charity has its own qualifications for residence. For more information see: Almshouse Association: **www.almshouses.org**.

Salvation Army homes

The Salvation Army owns and operates care homes for elderly people in various parts of the UK, offering residential care for men and women unable to manage in their own homes. See: **www.saha.org.uk**.

Granny flats

A granny flat or annexe is a self-contained unit attached to a family house. A large house can be converted or extended for this purpose, but planning permission is needed. Enquire at your local authority planning department. Some councils, particularly new towns, have houses to rent with granny flats.

Extra-care schemes

A number of organizations that provide sheltered accommodation also have extra-care sheltered housing, designed for those who can no longer look after themselves without assistance. Although expensive, it is cheaper than most private care homes and often more appropriate than full-scale nursing care. A possible problem is that tenants of some of these schemes do not have security of tenure and, should they become frail, could be asked to leave if more intensive care were required. Among the housing associations that provide these facilities are Housing 21, Hanover Housing Association, Anchor and Abbeyfield (see the details listed earlier in this chapter).

Homesharing – a new idea

Homesharing is a new concept in the UK, offering an alternative to residential or live-in care. It is similar to taking in a lodger, but with a focus for those in later life to be able to do this safely and maximizing the benefits for both parties. Where an elderly person has a spare room in their house, renting that room to a young person will bring them companionship, income through rent and a situation where they benefit from help around the house. For more information see My Ageing Parent: **www.myageingparent.com**.

Community care

The much-awaited reform of the long-term care system has been brought forward by a year to 2016 and the cap on payments is to be set at £72,000. From 2016, this will be the amount that people must pay towards their long-term care needs, with the state stepping in to pay the rest. This will not prevent people having to sell their homes to meet the cost of their own care, experts warn, as the cap will cover only nursing, not residential costs and food. Individuals will still have to find the money for residence fees.

It is anticipated that nearly 70 per cent of men and some 85 per cent of women over the age of 65 will need care at some time. Frailty in old age is quite different from actual illness, where elderly people are entitled to receive free treatment under the National Health Service. While some older people can afford to retire in comfort, and others are confident and optimistic about how they will end their days, it is very sad when relatives have to sell their loved ones' property so that they can afford to pay for their growing care needs in their later years.

Care homes

If your parents need to move into a care home, the state may help with the cost. The rules are complex and only a brief outline is given here. For more information, the local council is the point of contact. If moving into a nursing home is a continuation of NHS treatment that your parents have been having for an illness – for example he or she is discharged from hospital direct to a home – this should be paid for by the NHS. However, this is a grey area and you may have to be persistent to get their costs met in this way.

If they do not qualify for NHS continuing care, they may still qualify for some state help with care home fees, provided that their means are low and their needs assessment found that this was the best option for them. If their capital (savings and other assets) are above a set threshold, they will have to pay for themselves. If their capital is less, their local council may pay part or, if their capital is below the lower threshold, the full amount. Moving into a care home is a big decision, whether you are doing it yourself or for a loved one. Here are some suggestions before taking the decision:

- Is a care home really needed? Get advice on the housing options.

- What type of care home is wanted? Some offer accommodation and help with personal care; other care homes offer nursing care as well as the basic help.

- How to find a care home? Think of it like buying a house: you need to get a feel for what is out there before making a decision. Personal recommendations are important.

- How much will it cost? There is a lot of difference in care home fees. If the local council is paying, it will set a maximum cost that it will contribute. If the costs are higher, a relative or friend will need to top up that amount. If your parents are self-funding, make sure they can afford the fees.

Residential care homes (care homes registered to provide personal care)

There may come a time when it is no longer possible for an elderly person to manage without being in proper residential care. In a residential care home, sometimes known as a 'rest home', the accommodation usually consists of a bedroom plus communal dining rooms, lounges and gardens. All meals are provided, rooms are cleaned, and staff are at hand to give whatever help is needed. Homes are run by private individuals (or companies), voluntary organizations and local authorities. All homes must have been inspected by the Care Quality Commission (CQC) to ensure minimum standards. *An unregistered home should not be considered.* It is very important that the individual should have a proper chance to visit it and ask any questions. Before reaching a final decision, it is a good idea to arrange a short stay to see whether the facilities are suitable and pleasant.

Moving from one care home into a new care home can be a highly distressing experience for an elderly person who has become attached to the staff and made friends among the other residents, so making an enquiry about long-term plans for the home is prudent. Though a move can never be totally ruled out, awareness of whether the home is likely to remain a going concern could be a deciding factor when making a choice.

Private homes

Private care homes are often converted houses, taking up to about 30 people. As more companies move into the market, the homes can be purpose-built accommodation and may include a heated swimming pool and luxury facilities. The degree of care varies. If a resident becomes increasingly infirm, a care home will normally continue to look after him or her if possible. It may, however, become necessary at some point to arrange transfer to a nursing home or hospital. Fees vary enormously.

Voluntary care homes

These are run by charities, religious bodies or other voluntary organizations. Eligibility may be determined by age, background or occupation, depending on the criteria of the managing organization. Income may be a factor, as may general fitness, and individuals may be invited to a personal interview before acceptance onto the waiting list. Priority tends to be given to those in greatest need. Homes are often in large converted houses, and fees vary depending on locality.

Local authority homes

These are sometimes referred to as 'Part III accommodation', and admission will invariably be arranged by the social services department. If someone does not like the particular accommodation suggested, he or she can turn it down and ask the department what other offers might be available. Weekly charges vary around the country. In practice, individuals are charged only according to their means.

Nursing homes (care homes registered to provide nursing care)

Nursing homes provide medical supervision and fully qualified nurses, 24 hours a day. Most are privately run, with the remainder being supported by voluntary organizations. All nursing homes in England must be registered with the Commission for Social Care Inspection, which keeps a list of what homes are available in the area. In Wales, the inspectorate is called the Care Standards Inspectorate for Wales, and in Scotland it is called the Scottish Commission for the Regulation of Care.

Private

These homes normally accommodate between 15 and 100 patients. Depending on the part of the country, charges vary. Some fees rise depending on how much nursing is required. For information about nursing homes in the UK, contact the following:

Elderly Accommodation Counsel: **www.eac.org.uk**.

RNHA (Registered Nursing Home Association): **www.rnha.co.uk**.

UKHCA (United Kingdom Home Care Association Ltd):
www.ukhca.co.uk.

Voluntary organizations

These normally have very long waiting lists, and beds are often reserved for those who have been in the charity's care home. Voluntary organizations that run care homes include:

Careways Trust: **www.carewaystrust.org.uk**.

Friends of the Elderly: **www.fote.org.uk**.

IndependentAge: **www.independentage.org**.

Jewish Care: **www.jewishcare.org**.

Costs of care

Free nursing care

NHS continuing health care (NHS CHC) is a package of health and social care funded solely by the NHS when a patient's need for care is primarily due to their need for health care. This financial contribution is paid directly to the care home. There is a downloadable fact sheet giving information relating to this, found on the Age UK website: **www.ageuk.org.uk/health-wellbeing**.

Financial assistance for residential and nursing home care

Under the community care arrangements, people needing to go into a residential or nursing home may receive help from their local authority social services department. As explained earlier, the department will make the arrangements direct with the home following its assessment procedure, and will seek reimbursement from the person towards the cost, according to set means-testing rules. For further information:

Citizens Advice Bureau: **www.citizensadvice.org.uk**.

Elderly Accommodation Counsel: **www.eac.org.uk**.

Funding care

A major worry for many elderly people going into residential care is the requirement to sell their own home to cover the costs. While this may still eventually be necessary, the rules have been made slightly more flexible to allow a short breathing space for making decisions. Planning for care is essential now that we are all living longer, and there are different types of care to consider: in the home, in residential care and in nursing care. The funding aspect is complex. The starting point is to see what the local authority can provide. Beyond that, careful planning is required so that best use is made of your parents' income and assets. Some organizations offer advice and information for carers; see:

Care & Quality Commission: **www.cqc.org.uk**.

Home Instead Senior Care: **www.homeinstead.co.uk**.

Solicitors for the Elderly: **www.solicitorsfortheelderly.com**.

Further information

Key sources of information about voluntary and private homes are: *Charities Digest* (available in libraries, housing aid centres and Citizens Advice Bureaux) and the *Directory of Independent Hospitals and Health Services* (available in libraries). *Charities Digest* also includes information about hospices. Here are some other sources of advice not previously listed:

Action on Elder Abuse: **www.elderabuse.org.uk**.

R&RA (Relatives & Residents Association): **www.relres.org**.

Some special problems

A minority of people, as they become older, suffer from special problems that can cause great distress. Because families do not like to talk about these problems, they may be unaware of what services are available and so may be missing out on practical help and sometimes also on financial assistance.

Hypothermia

Elderly people tend to be more vulnerable to the cold. If a person's body temperature drops below a certain level this can be dangerous, because one of the symptoms of hypothermia is that sufferers no longer actually feel cold. Instead, they may lose their appetite and vitality and may become mentally confused. British Gas, electricity companies and the Solid Fuel Association are all willing to give advice on how heating systems can be used more efficiently and economically. It is also worth checking that elderly parents are on the correct tariff when it comes to utility bills. Some utility providers have reduced charges for elderly people who are in receipt of certain benefits. Check out the following:

- British Gas Energy Trust (incorporating the Scottish Gas Energy Trust) awards grants to individuals in need of help with their utility bills. See: **www.britishgasenergytrust.org.uk**.

- Npower runs a Health through Warmth scheme to help ill and vulnerable people in England and Wales to heat and insulate their homes. See **www.npower.com/health_through_warmth/**.

- Age UK produces a useful guide on how to keep warm during the winter months. Details of how to obtain a copy of 'Winter wrapped up' is available on their website: **www.ageuk.org.uk/ getinvolved/spread-the-warmth/**.

Elderly and disabled people in receipt of Income Support may receive a Cold Weather Payment to help with heating costs during a particularly cold spell. Those eligible should receive the money automatically. In the event of any problem, ask at your social security office. In an emergency, such as a power cut, contact the Citizens Advice Bureau or Age UK. Every household with someone aged 60 or older will get an annual tax-free Winter Fuel Payment of £200–£400. See website: **www.gov.uk** – Winter Fuel Payment.

Incontinence

Bladder or bowel problems can cause deep embarrassment to sufferers as well as inconvenience to relatives. The problem can occur in an elderly person for all sorts of reasons, and a doctor should always be consulted, as it can often be cured or at least alleviated by proper treatment. To assist with the practical problems, some local authorities operate a laundry service that collects soiled linen, sometimes several times per week. Talk to a health visitor or district nurse (at the local health centre), who will be able to advise about this and other facilities. For more information, see:

B&BF (Bladder and Bowel Foundation):
www.bladderandbowelfoundation.org.

Dementia

The loss of short-term memory in older age that can terrify us with thoughts of impending Alzheimer's is not necessarily the precursor to dementia. It is an altogether more benign and general phenomenon. There are two types of memory: 'retrospective' and 'prospective'. The first deals with remembering what we did in the past and the second with what we have to do in the future. As people age there is a lot more past than future, so failure to remember things in the immediate past or near future is not unsurprising. However, sometimes an elderly person can become confused or forgetful, suffer severe loss of memory or have violent mood swings and at times be abnormally aggressive. It is important to consult a doctor as soon as possible. If dementia is diagnosed, there is ongoing research into finding a cure and there are some treatments that can delay the progression of some forms of dementia.

The most common type of dementia is Alzheimer's disease, which is usually found in people aged over 65. Approximately 24 million people worldwide have dementia, of which the majority of cases (over 60 per cent) are due to Alzheimer's. Clinical signs are characterized by progressive cognitive deterioration, together with a decline in the ability to carry out common daily tasks, and behavioural changes. The first readily identifiable symptoms of Alzheimer's disease are usually short-term memory loss and visual–spatial confusion. This advances to loss of familiar and well-known skills, such as recognition of objects and people.

The Alzheimer's Show, in association with the Alzheimer's Society, takes place each year in London and Manchester. It is the UK's only dedicated exhibition and conference for families and professionals caring for someone with dementia (see **www.alzheimersshow.co.uk**). People with dementia are still people – and the Alzheimer's Society recommends the following tips:

- Always treat the person with respect and dignity.
- Be a good listener and communicator.
- Remember that little things mean a lot.

Sources of help and support for people with dementia and their carers are:

Alzheimer Scotland: **www.alzscot.org**.

Alzheimer's Society: **www.alzheimers.org.uk**.

Chapter Sixteen
No one is immortal

"You can spend your whole life trying to be popular, but the size of the crowd at your funeral will still be dictated by the weather.   UNNAMED AMERICAN FOOTBALL COACH

Is the thought of the 'end game' something you can cope with? Are you prepared for death, having recorded your end-of-life wishes? This chapter is not about indulging in morbid thoughts, more a reminder that forward planning is advisable and helpful. For some people it can be difficult to have open discussions about end-of-life choices, and not everyone wants to. As far as famous last words go, it is interesting to note that Voltaire (the 18th-century French writer, historian and philosopher) on his deathbed was invited by his priest to renounce the devil. To which he replied: 'This is no time to be making new enemies.'

Facing up to the end of our life is not easy, although we all know it's inevitable. However, being prepared and making plans will ensure that your wishes and preferences are known to others, enabling those responsible for you to make the right decisions on your behalf if you are unable. According to a recent report, 'Divided in Dying', from the charity Compassion in Dying, almost half of those who have lost someone close to them through a short or long illness feel that the person died badly. In the case where the dying person had recorded their end-of-life wishes, relatives and friends are more likely to report that they had a good death. Compassion in Dying believes that the report reinforces the importance of advance planning, and the charity helps people to know and understand their legal rights at the end of life (**www.compassionindying.org.uk**).

To have a 'good end of life' means that conditions have been created for individuals to face the end of their life in comfort and dignity, with the right persons nearby. It starts with good communication. Anyone at any age can start preparing for this. As part of the plan people often explore their thoughts, feelings and preferences regarding some of the following issues:

- preferred place of care;
- advance decision to refuse treatment (ADRT);
- lasting power of attorney (LPA);
- wills;
- funeral arrangements;
- tissue donation.

You can include in your advance care plan anything that is important to you. Nothing is too trivial. You can add anything that reflects your beliefs and values and how you like things to be done. Talking openly to trusted friends, family, health care professionals or spiritual advisers can be helpful. It is essentially a matter of making sure everyone who needs to know does, and that your wishes are clearly recorded. This could involve a legal document, such as a living will or an advance directive about medical treatment. We all know that we should write a will, but it is one of those things that many people never get around to. It is estimated that 53 per cent of the population die intestate. Not writing a will might mean chaos and money problems for your family or dependants after you've gone. A great deal of heartbreak and real financial worry could be avoided if everyone was brave enough to broach the subject of dying before it is too late. At the earliest and most appropriate moment, if you can have an honest and open discussion with your family about mortality, it could potentially save huge amounts of trouble later on.

Wills

Planning what happens to your money and possessions after your death helps to ensure that your survivors are financially secure and that the people you want to inherit from you do so. When you retire, there are big changes to your finances as well as to the rest of your life. It is important, then, to review how your survivors would manage financially if you were to die. Would, in fact, your money and possessions (your 'estate') be passed on as you would wish? (Your estate is everything you own at

the time you die, including your share of any joint possessions, less everything you owe.)

Three out of 10 people aged 65 and over die without having made a
will. This is called dying 'intestate'. A will is, in its simplest form, a set of
instructions about how your estate should be passed on. If you don't
have a will, the law makes these decisions for you. This could mean that
the wrong people inherit; your home might have to be sold to split the
proceeds and your survivors could have extra work and stress. There are
five rules of making a will:

- The person making the will must be of sound mind.
- The will must be properly executed.
- The will must be correctly witnessed.
- Be clear about what or how much you want to leave and to
  whom.
- Remember to update your will as your life circumstances change.

Having a will is especially important if you live with an unmarried partner,
have remarried, need to provide for someone with a disability, own a
business, own property abroad, or your estate is large (ie over the inheritance tax threshold). A will is a legal document that sets out your wishes
clearly and unambiguously. Although you can write your own will, it is
safer to get a solicitor to do it.

Laws of intestacy

Under the intestacy laws:

- your husband, wife or civil partner and your own children are
  favoured; this includes a former partner if you are only separated
  rather than divorced;
- an unmarried partner and stepchildren have no rights;
- your husband, wife or civil partner does not automatically get the
  whole of your estate;
- possessions, including your home, may have to be sold to split the
  proceeds between your heirs;
- if you have no partner or children, more distant relatives inherit;
- if you have no relatives, the state gets the lot.

Making a will

You have three choices: you can do it yourself, you can ask your bank to help you, or you can use a solicitor or a specialist will-writing practitioner.

Doing it yourself

Home-made wills are not generally recommended, but provided your affairs are simple, it is possible to make one. You need to set out: who you want to benefit from your will; who should look after any children under 18; who is going to sort out your estate and carry out your wishes after death (your executor); what happens if the people you want to benefit die before you. Two witnesses are needed, and beneficiaries cannot witness a will, nor can the spouses of any beneficiaries. If making your own will, it is sensible to have it checked by a solicitor or by a legal expert from the Citizens Advice Bureau. (You should get legal advice if your will is not straightforward.) For individuals with sight problems, RNIB has some helpful advice. See: **www.rnib.org.uk**.

Banks

Advice on wills and the administration of estates is given by the trustee companies of most of the major high-street banks. In particular, the services they offer are to provide general guidance, to act as executor and to administer the estate. They will also introduce clients to a solicitor and keep a copy of the will – plus other important documents – in their safe, to avoid the risk of them being mislaid. Additionally, banks (as with solicitors) can give tax planning and other financial guidance, including advice on inheritance tax. Some banks will draw up a will for you.

Solicitors and will-writing specialists

Solicitors can draw up your will, act as executors and administer your estate. Like banks, they will also retain a copy of your will in safekeeping (most will not charge for storing a will). If you do not have a solicitor, your friends may be able to recommend one, or ask at the Citizens Advice Bureau. The Law Society can also provide you with names and addresses; see: **www.lawsociety.org.uk**.

Alternatively, if you simply want help in writing a will, you could consult a specialist will-writing practitioner. The best approach is to contact one of the following organizations:

The Society of Will Writers: **www.willwriters.com**.

Trust Inheritance: **www.trustinheritance.com**.

The Will Bureau: **www.thewillbureau.co.uk**.

Charges

A basic will costs around £150. However, if your affairs are complicated, it could be considerably more. Always ask for an estimate before proceeding. Remember that professional fees normally carry VAT. Many solicitors will give you a fixed-fee estimate for a will. The fees for will-writing practitioners are broadly in line with those of solicitors.

Age UK Legal Services offers legal advice and support , and this service is available free of charge to anyone of retirement age: **www.ageuk.org.uk**.

Executors

The person who sorts out your property when you die and carries out the instructions in your will is your executor. You can choose whoever you like to do this, but it is important to get the right person. It must be someone over the age of 18. Many people choose their spouse, civil partner or one of their children to be their executor. It is wise to choose two executors: one family member and one professional, such as a solicitor or accountant. It must be someone you trust, and someone who is good at dealing with paperwork. The duties of an executor are many. They might have to deal with the sale of your property so that the people who inherit the proceeds get the most money they can. They must ensure that the correct amount of inheritance tax or capital gains tax gets paid. Family disagreements over how the assets of the deceased are distributed can be fraught. The executor should have the capability to stay calm when dealing with disgruntled family members over the contents of a will.

When choosing an executor of a will, the following points are worth bearing in mind:

- A spouse as a sole executor is not the best choice, especially if both husband and wife are elderly.
- It is advisable not to appoint benefactors as an executor in case others claim there is a conflict of interests.
- The chosen person should be informed of the decision and must agree to accept the role.

- Legally, the executor must be over 18, of sound mind and not in prison when the executor decision is made.

- If conflicts within the family are likely to be a factor, it may be worthwhile appointing more than one executor, or even hiring a professional executor.

- If a family member is chosen, he or she should have the time to carry out all the duties. This can be difficult if the executor does not live in the same part of the country.

Other points

Wills should always be kept in a safe place – and their whereabouts known. You must tell your executor where it is. The most sensible arrangement is for the solicitor to keep the original, and for you and your bank to have a copy each. A helpful initiative devised by the Law Society is a mini-form, known as a personal assets log. This is for individuals drawing up a will to give to their executor or close relatives. It is, quite simply, a four-sided leaflet with space to record essential information: name and address of solicitor; where the will and other important documents, for example share certificates and insurance policies, are kept; the date of any codicils and so on. Logs are obtainable from most solicitors.

Wills need updating in the event of any important changes of circumstances: such as a divorce, remarriage or the birth of a grandchild. An existing will normally becomes invalid in the event of marriage or remarriage and should be replaced. Any changes must be by codicil (for minor alterations) or by a new will, and must be properly witnessed. The inheritance tax threshold is £325,000 for the 2014/15 tax year. If your estate is likely to exceed this amount, it is wise to review your will regularly. Partners who wish to leave all their possessions to each other should consider including a 'survivorship clause' in their wills, as an insurance against the intestacy rules being applied were they both, for example, involved in the same fatal accident. Legal advice is strongly recommended here.

If you have views about your funeral, it is sensible to write a letter to your executors explaining your wishes and to lodge it with your will. If you have any pets, you may equally wish to leave a letter filed with your will explaining what arrangements you have made for their immediate and long-term welfare. Over the years there has been increased interest in advance decision making. For those who would like more information on this matter, there are a number of organizations that can help:

Compassion in Dying: **www.compassionindying.org.uk**.

Dignity in Dying: **www.dignityindying.org.uk**.

Dying Matters: **www.dyingmatters.org**.

Say It Once: **www.sayitonce.info**.

If you would be willing to donate an organ that might help save someone else's life, you could indicate this in your will or alternatively obtain an organ donor card. These are available from most hospitals, GP surgeries and chemists.

Inheritance tax points

Inheritance tax (IHT) is a tax on money or possessions you leave behind when you die, and on some gifts you make during your lifetime (see Chapter 4). There are two main aims to planning inheritance: to make sure your estate is divided as you wish; and to minimize the amount of tax paid on the estate. The particular inheritance planning strategies you adopt will depend largely on your personal intentions and circumstances.

Some ways of reducing IHT include: making tax-free gifts in your will. Bequests to charity and whatever you leave to your spouse or civil partner are tax free. Nearly 75 per cent of people give to charity during their lifetime, but only 7 per cent include a charitable legacy in their will. The government has changed the tax law reducing the inheritance tax payable on estates that give at least 10 per cent to charity. It is called Legacy 10, and anyone who does this will have the remainder of their estate taxed at 36 per cent instead of the usual 40 per cent IHT tax rate.

Charities have welcomed the move, as have many will-writers. Existing wills can be amended by codicil to include the 10 per cent provision, providing the wording is precise enough to make the donor's wishes clear, yet not mention exact amounts because they won't know the size of their eventual estate. There is, however, no advantage to people with estates below the inheritance tax threshold.

Examples of IHT-free gifts:

- Gifts you make during your lifetime:
  - up to £3,000 a year of any gifts (or £6,000 if you did not use last year's allowance);
  - £250 a year to any number of people;
  - gifts on marriage up to £5,000 if you are a parent of the bride or groom and smaller sums for anyone else;
  - gifts that form a regular pattern of spending from your income;
  - gifts for the maintenance of your family;
  - gifts to any person, provided you survive for seven years after making the gift.
- Gifts you make during your lifetime or on death:
  - gifts to your husband, wife or civil partner (in most cases);
  - gifts to charities.

Useful reading

Will Information Pack, from Age UK; see: **www.ageuk.org.uk**. *How to Write Your Will* (the complete guide to structuring your will, inheritance tax planning, probate and administering an estate), by Marlene Garsia, published by Kogan Page; see: **www.koganpage.com**.

Provision for dependent adult children

A particular concern for parents with a physically or mentally dependent son or daughter is what plans they can make to ensure his or her care when they are no longer in a position to manage. There is no easy answer, as each case varies according to the severity of the disability or illness, the range of helpful voluntary or statutory facilities locally, and the extent to which they, as parents, can provide for their child's financial security in the long term. While social services may be able to advise, parents thinking ahead might do better to consult a specialist organization experienced in helping carers in this situation in order to explore the possible options available to them. Useful addresses are:

Carers UK: **www.carersuk.org**.

Carers Trust: **www.carers.org**.

Parents concerned about financial matters such as setting up a trust or making alternative provision in their will would also be advised to consult a solicitor or accountant.

Money and other worries – and how to minimize them

Many people say that the first time they really think about death, in terms of what would happen to their nearest and dearest, is after the birth of their first baby. As children grow up, requirements change, but key points that anyone with a family should consider – and review from time to time – include life insurance and mortgage protection. Both husbands and wives should have life insurance cover. If either were to die, not only would the partner lose the financial benefit of the other's earnings, but the partner would also lose immeasurably in other ways.

Most banks and building societies urge homeowners to take out mortgage protection schemes. If you die, the loan is paid off automatically and the family home will not be repossessed. Banks also offer insurance to cover any personal or other loans. This could be a vital safeguard to avoid leaving the family with debts.

Funeral plans

Funeral costs are a major worry for many people. To avoid this anxiety a funeral plan is a way of paying for a future funeral today. How they work: you pay either a lump sum or instalments to the plan provider, or to a funeral director. The money is invested either into a trust fund with trustees, or in an insurance policy: the money is then used to pay for the funeral whenever that is. The aim is to safeguard your money until it is needed, and to pay for the funeral you've planned. Because trust funds and insurance policies are already regulated, the money you pay into these funds is protected by compensation arrangements.

Plan providers can register with the Funeral Planning Authority (FPA) if they agree to meet its rules and code of conduct. You can find a list of registered plan providers from The Funeral Planning Authority: **www.funeralplanningauthority.com**.

If you take out a funeral plan, make sure you have a written record of the arrangements and keep it safe. You should receive a plan confirmation. Your next of kin should be informed that you have already paid for your funeral and what the details are. Check to see that the plan provider has a clear complaints procedure and is a member of the FPA. Members must follow its standards when dealing with you and when considering any complaints.

The following organizations offer funeral plans:

Age UK: **www.ageuk.org.uk**.

Co-operative Funeral Care: **www.co-operativefuneralcare.co.uk**.

Dignity Caring Funeral Services: **www.dignityfunerals.co.uk**.

Golden Charter: **www.golden-charter.co.uk**.

Perfect Choice Funeral Plans: **www.perfectchoicefunerals.com**.

Those in receipt of Income Support, Pension Credit, Housing Benefit or Council Tax Benefit may qualify for a payment from the Social Fund to help with funeral costs. For details of eligibility and how to claim, see website: **www.gov.uk** – Bereavement benefits.

Dealing with a death

A very real crisis for some families is the need for immediate money while waiting for the estate to be settled. At least part of the problem can be overcome by couples having a joint bank account, with both partners having drawing rights without the signature of the other being required. Sole-name bank accounts and joint accounts requiring both signatures are frozen. For the same reason, it may also be a good idea for any savings or investments to be held in the joint name of the couple. Additionally, any financial and other important documents should be discussed together and understood by both parties. Both partners need to know where important papers are kept.

When someone dies, the bank manager should be notified as soon as possible so that he or she can assist with the problems of unpaid bills and help to work out a solution until the estate is settled. The same goes for the suppliers of essential services: gas, electricity, telephone and so on. Unless they know the situation, there is a risk of services being cut off if there is a delay in paying the bill. Add, too, any credit card companies, where if bills lie neglected the additional interest could mount up alarmingly.

Normally, you must register the death within the first five days (eight in Scotland). Your local registrar can be found on the government website: **www.gov.uk**. You will need to take to the registrar's office the medical certificate issued by the doctor who attended the death and, if possible, the deceased's medical card, birth certificate and any marriage or civil partnership certificate. The registrar will give you:

- a certificate allowing cremation or burial to go ahead; give this to the funeral director you appoint;
- a certificate to give to the Jobcentre Plus or the Pension Service, if the deceased had been getting state benefits or pensions;
- a leaflet with details of bereavement benefits that you may be able to claim;
- one or more death certificates, for which there is a fee. You normally need to send a death certificate to each provider of pensions, life insurance, savings and investments that the deceased had. It is cheaper to buy extra certificates straight away than later.

For more information on what to do after a death, see the government website: **www.gov.uk**.

Registering a death is upsetting, and dealing with a death involves more paperwork and phone calls than a family wants to deal with at such a time. A new scheme, the Tell Us Once service, means that people need make just one appointment with their local registrar, who can then advise 28 different services of the changed circumstances, including all state pensions and benefits through the Department for Work and Pensions, and HMRC, passports, driving licences, council tax, local library, Blue Badge and social services. See: **www.gov.uk/after-a-death/**.

Another available service to help you after a loved one has died is that of reducing the amount of direct mail to the deceased. Originally launched in the UK in 2000, this service has since expanded into France and Canada. Coming to terms with the loss of a loved one takes time; receiving direct mail bearing the name of the deceased is often painful and unnecessary. For more information see:

The Bereavement Register: **www.the-bereavement-register.org.uk**.

Useful reading

Tips from Widows by Jan Robinson, is a great help. It is about before death, when death occurs and the months and years after death. Practical and emotional tips are dealt with succinctly. When trying to survive as a bereaved person, this little book enables you to cope that much better. See: **www.tipsfromwidows.co.uk**.

What to Do after a Death is a free booklet available from any social security office; and also *Planning for a Funeral*, a free fact sheet from Age UK; website: **www.ageuk.org.uk**.

State benefits and tax

Several extra financial benefits are given to widowed people. Most take the form of a cash payment. However, there are one or two tax and other points that it may be useful to know.

Benefits paid in cash form

There are three important cash benefits to which widowed people may be entitled: Bereavement Payment, Bereavement Allowance and Widowed Parent's Allowance. These have replaced the former widow's benefits, as all benefits are now payable on equal terms to men and women alike. To find out more information see website: **www.gov.uk** – Bereavement benefits. You will be given a questionnaire (BD8) by the registrar when you register the death. It is important that you complete this, as it acts as a trigger to speed up payment of your benefits.

Bereavement Payment

This is a tax-free lump sum of £2,000, paid as soon as people are widowed, provided that: the widowed person's spouse had paid sufficient NI contributions; the widowed person is under state retirement age; or, if over state retirement age, the widowed person's husband or wife had not been entitled to retirement pension.

Bereavement Allowance

Bereavement Allowance is for those aged between 45 and state pension age who do not receive Widowed Parent's Allowance. It is payable for

52 weeks and, as with widow's pension before, there are various levels of payment: the full rate and age-related allowance. Receipt in all cases is dependent on sufficient NI contributions having been paid.

Full-rate Bereavement Allowance is paid to widowed people between the ages of 55 and 59 inclusive. Age-related Bereavement Allowance is for younger widows or widowers who do not qualify for the full rate. Bereavement Allowance is normally paid automatically once you have sent off your completed form BB1, so if for any reason you do not receive it you should enquire at your social security office. In the event of your being ineligible, owing to insufficient NICs having been paid, you may still be entitled to receive Income Support, Housing Benefit or a grant or loan from the Social Fund. See website: **www.gov.uk** – Bereavement benefits.

Widowed Parent's Allowance

This is paid to widowed parents with at least one child for whom they receive Child Benefit. The allowance is usually paid automatically. If for some reason, although eligible, you do not receive the money, you should inform your social security office.

Retirement pension

Once a widowed person reaches state retirement age, he or she should receive a state pension in the normal way. An important point to remember is that a widow or widower may be able to use the late spouse's NICs to boost the amount he or she receives. See leaflet RM1, Retirement – a guide to benefits for people who are retiring or have retired.

Problems

Both pension payments and bereavement benefits are dependent on sufficient NICs having been paid. Your social security office will inform you if you are not eligible. If this should turn out to be the case, you may still be entitled to receive Income Support, Housing Benefit, Council Tax Benefit or a grant or loan from the Social Fund. If you are unsure of your position or have difficulties, ask at the Citizens Advice Bureau, which will at least be able to help you work out the sums and inform you of your rights. See website: **www.citizensadvice.org.uk**.

Particular points to note

Most widowed people's benefits are taxable. However, the £2,000 Bereavement Payment is tax free, as are pensions paid to the widows or widowers of armed forces personnel. Widowed people will normally be able to inherit their spouse's additional pension rights if they contributed to SERPS (see the note below) and/or the second state pension (S2P), or at least half their guaranteed minimum pension, if their spouse was in a contracted-out scheme. Additionally, where applicable, all widowed people are entitled on retirement to half the graduated pension earned by their husband or wife.

Women in receipt of widow's pension who remarry, or live with a man as his wife, lose their entitlement to the payment unless the cohabitation ends, in which case they can claim it again. If a woman is aged over 60, the fact that she is living with a man will not affect her entitlement to a retirement pension based on her late husband's contribution record. Widows and widowers of armed forces personnel whose deaths were a direct result of their service are now entitled to keep their armed forces attributable pension for life, regardless of whether they remarry or cohabit.

Tax allowances

Widows and widowers receive the normal single person's tax allowance of £10,000 and, if in receipt of Married Couple's Allowance, are also entitled to any unused portion of the allowance in the year of their partner's death.

Advice

Many people have difficulty in working out exactly what they are entitled to and how to claim it. The Citizens Advice Bureau is always very helpful. Additionally, Cruse and the National Association of Widows (see below) can assist you.

Organizations that can help

People deal with bereavement in various ways. For some, money problems seem to dominate everything. For others, the hardest thing to bear is the loneliness of an empty house. For older people who have been part of a couple for decades, widowhood creates a great gulf where for a while there is no real sense of purpose. Many widowed men and women go through a spell of feeling enraged against their partner for dying. Talking to other people who know the difficulties from their own experience can be a tremendous help. The following organizations not only offer opportunities for companionship but also provide an advisory and support service:

Cruse Bereavement Care: **www.cruse.org.uk**.

The National Association of Widows: **www.widows.uk.net**.

Many professional and other groups offer a range of services for widows and widowers associated with them. These include:

The Civil Service Retirement Fellowship: **www.csrf.org.uk**.

The War Widows Association of Great Britain: **www.warwidows.org.uk**.

Many local Age UK groups offer a counselling service. Trade unions are often particularly supportive, as are Rotary Clubs, all the armed forces organizations and most benevolent societies.

Useful resources and contacts

Benefits advice

Advice NI (Northern Ireland), tel: 028 9064 5919, website: **www.adviceni.net**.

Age UK, Tavis House, 1–6 Tavistock Square, London WC1H 9NA, tel: 0800 169 6565, website: **www.ageuk.org.uk**.

Citizens Advice Bureau – to find your local office see website: **www.citizensadvice.org.uk**; or for self-help: **www.adviceguide.org.uk**.

Citizens Advice Scotland, website: **www.cas.org.uk**.

Entitled To – to identify what benefits you may be eligible for: **www.entitledto.co.uk**.

Government benefits adviser, website: **www.gov.uk/benefits-calculators**.

Money Advice Scotland, tel: 0141 572 0237, website: **www.moneyadvicescotland.org.uk**.

Turn2us – to identify potential sources of funding for those facing financial difficulty: **www.turn2us.org.uk**.

Debt

Advice NI/ Debt Action NI tel: 0800 917 4607, website: **www.debtaction-ni.net**.

Citizens Advice Bureau – free independent debt advice in England, Wales and Northern Ireland, website: **www.citizensadvice.org.uk**.

Citizens Advice Scotland, website: **www.cas.org.uk**.

Money Advice Service – Debt Test: tel: 0300 500 5000 **www.moneyadviceservice.org.uk**.

Money Advice Scotland, tel: 0141 572 0237, website:
www.moneyadvicescotland.org.uk.

National Debtline, tel: 0808 808 4000, website:
www.nationaldebtline.co.uk.

Step Change Debt Charity: tel: 0800 138 1111, website:
www.stepchange.org.

Disabilities

Age UK, tel: 0800 169 665, website: **www.ageuk.org.uk**.
In Wales contact: 0800 169 6565; in Northern Ireland contact:
0808 808 7575; in Scotland contact: 0845 125 9732.

Action for Blind People – charity providing practical help and support.
Tel: 0303 123 9999, website: **www.actionforblindpeople.org.uk**.

Action on Hearing Loss (formerly RNID) – provides advice
and support for people who are deaf or hard of hearing.
Tel: 0808 808 0123, website: **www.actionforhearingloss.org.uk**.

Disability Benefits Centre: **www.gov.uk/disability-benefits-helpline**;

- Disability Living Allowance (DLA) tel: 0345 712 3456.

- Attendance Allowance (AA) tel: 0345 605 6055.

- Personal Independence Payment (PIP) tel: 0345 850 3322.

- Carer's Allowance Unit: tel: 0345 608 4321, website:
  www.gov.uk/carers-allowance-unit.

Pension Credit, tel: 0345 606 0265, website:
www.gov.uk/pension-credit.

Winter Fuel Payment Helpline, tel: 08459 151515, website:
www.gov.uk/winter-fuel-payment.

Energy-saving advice and grants

ACT ON CO2 Advice Line, tel: 0800 512 012.

Energy Efficiency Advice Centres, tel: 0300 123 1234, website:
www.energysavingtrust.org.uk.

National Energy Action (NEA) – a national charity that helps people on low incomes to heat and insulate their homes: tel: 0191 261 5677, website: **www.nea.org.uk**.

NEST (Wales Fuel Poverty Scheme), tel: 0808 808 2244, website: **www.nestwales.org.uk**.

Home Energy Scotland – Energy Assistance Packages, tel: 0808 808 2282, website: **www.scotland.gov.uk**.

Warm Homes Scheme (Northern Ireland), tel: 0800 988 0559, website: **www.warm-homes.com**.

Funeral and inheritance tax planning

Bereavement Register, tel: 0800 082 1230, website: **www.the-bereavement-register.com**.

Funeral Planning Authority Ltd, PO Box 123, Rye, Sussex, TN31 9EG, tel: 0845 601 9619, website: **www.funeralplanningauthority.com**.

HMRC Probate and Inheritance Tax Helpline: tel: 0300 123 1072, website: **www.hmrc.gov.uk/inheritancetax/**.

For inheritance tax advice

STEP – Society of Trust and Estate Practitioners, Artillery House (South), 11–19 Artillery Row, London SW1P 1RT, tel: 020 7340 0500, website: **www.step.org**.

To register a death

General Register Office (England and Wales), website: **www.gro.gov.uk**;

Scotland: **www.gro-scotland.gov.uk**;

Northern Ireland: **www.nidirect.gov.uk/general-register-office-for-northern-ireland**.

To obtain a copy of the government booklet: 'What to do after a death': England and Wales:

website: **www.gov.uk** – Death and bereavement;

Scotland: **www.scotland.gov.uk**;

Northern Ireland: **www.nidirect.gov.uk**.

Health and health care

NHS Low Income Scheme – provides full or partial help with health costs if you are on a low income. Tel: 0845 850 1166, website: **www.nhs.uk/healthcosts**.

Free prescriptions and other health benefits in the UK – free leaflet: HC11 'Help with Health Costs' from your GP or pharmacies, website: **www.nidirect.gov.uk/get-help-covering-health-costs/**.

In Scotland, Northern Ireland and Wales prescriptions are free.

For Scotland: free booklet HCS2 'Help with health costs', website: **www.scotland.gov.uk/Publications**.

Prescription pre-payment certificates (England). Tel: 0300 330 1341, website: **www.nhsbsa.nhs.uk/HealthCosts/2131.aspx**.

Health Scotland provides information to promote healthy living for people living in Scotland. Tel: 0131 536 5500, website: **www.healthscotland.com**.

Holidays

To apply for a European Health Insurance Card (EHIC) Pick up a form at the Post Office or tel: 0300 330 1350, website: **www.nhs.uk/NHSEngland/Healthcareabroad/EHIC**.

House and home

For details about local domestic energy assessors see EPC Register; website: **www.epcregister.com**.

The Energy Saving Trust has a network of Energy Efficiency Advice Centres (ESAS) offering free, impartial, expert advice. Their aim is to help consumers reduce their energy use, save money and help the environment. Contact: 0300 123 1234, website: **www.energysavingtrust.org.uk**.

Home Heat Helpline is a free national helpline offering access to grants for free home insulation and reduced or 'social' tariffs from energy suppliers. Tel: 0800 33 66 99, website: **www.homeheathelpline.org.uk**.

To find an independent surveyor/valuer

Royal Institute of Chartered Surveyors, website: **www.rics.org/uk/**.

For protection

The Property Ombudsman scheme provides an independent review service for buyers or sellers of UK residential property in the event of a complaint. To fill in a consumer enquiry form, see website: **www.tpos.co.uk**.

Help for the elderly

Elderly Accommodation Counsel, 3rd Floor, 89 Albert Embankment, London SE1 7TP, tel: 0800 377 7070, website: **www.eac.org.uk**; or **www.firststopadvice.org.uk**; or **www.housingcare.org.uk**.

Independent Age, 6 Avonmore Road, London W14 8RL.
Tel: 0800 319 6789, website: **www.independentage.org**.

NAPA – National Association for Providers of Activities for Older People offers stimulating activities for older people. Tel: 020 7078 9375, website: **www.napa-activities.co.uk**.

RoSPA – Royal Society for the Prevention of Accidents – promotes safety and prevention of accidents at work and in the home, and provides information on home safety. Tel: 0121 248 2000, website: **www.rospa.com**.

TPS – The Telephone Preference Service: you can register your phone number with the telephone preference service by calling their registration line: 0845 070 0707 or you can do this online at **www.tpsonline.org.uk**.

Home improvement agencies

England – Foundations, tel: 0845 864 5201, website: **www.foundations.uk.com**.

Wales – Care & Repair Cymru, tel: 0300 111 3333, website: **www.careandrepair.org.uk**.

Scotland – Care & Repair Forum Scotland, tel: 0141 221 9879, website: **www.careandrepairscotland.co.uk**.

Northern Ireland – Fold Housing Association, tel: 028 9042 8314, website: **www.foldgroup.co.uk**.

Help for tenants

Association of Retirement Housing Managers (ARHM): c/o EAC, 3rd Floor, 89 Albert Embankment, London SE1 7TP. Tel: 020 7463 0660, website: **www.arhm.org**.

Leasehold Advisory Service; tel: 0207 383 9800, website: **www.lease-advice.org**.

Landmark Leasehold Advisory Services Ltd – specializes in providing legal services to residential leaseholders of England and Wales; see website: **www.landmarklease.com**.

Department for Communities and Local Government – for advice on leasehold legislation and policy, tel: 0303 444 0000, website: **www.gov.uk/government/organisations/department-for-communities-and-local-government**.

Independent financial advice

To find an independent financial adviser

Unbiased.co.uk, website: **www.unbiased.co.uk**.

Institute of Financial Planning, One Redcliff Street, Bristol, BS1 6NP. Website. **www.financialplanning.org.uk**.

Personal Finance Society (PFS), website: **www.findanadviser.org**.

Financial Conduct Authority (formerly the FSA), 25 The North Colonnade, Canary Wharf, London E14 5HS, tel: 0800 111 6768, website: **www.fca.org.uk**.

Financial Ombudsman Service, South Quay Plaza, 183 Marsh Wall, London E14 9SR, tel: 0300 123 9123 or 0800 0234 567, website: **www.financial-ombudsman.org.uk**.

Financial Services Compensation Scheme, 10th Floor, Beaufort House, 15 St Botolph Street, London EC3A 7QU. tel: 0800 678 1100, website: **www.fscs.org.uk**.

MyLocalAdviser: **www.mylocaladviser.co.uk**. For financial advisers in your area.

SOLLA – Society of Later Life Advisers, tel: 0845 303 2902; website: **www.societyoflaterlifeadvisers.co.uk**.

To find a stockbroker

See London Stock Exchange website: **www.londonstockexchange.com**, or

The Wealth Management Association (WMA) website: **www.thewma.co.uk**.

To find equity release providers

Equity Release Council incorporating SHIP standards: 3rd Floor, Bush House, North West Wing, Aldwych, London WC2B 4PJ, tel: 0844 669 7085, website: **www.equityreleasecouncil.com**.

To find a tax adviser

Chartered Institute of Taxation, 1st Floor, Artillery House, 11–19 Artillery Row, London SW1P 1RT. tel: 0844 579 6700, website: **www.tax.org.uk**.

Insurance

Association of British Insurers, 51 Gresham Street, London EC2V 7HQ. Tel: 020 7600 3333 for advice and information on insurance: website: **www.abi.org.uk**.

Association of Medical Insurance Intermediaries (AMII), Suites 21–24, The North Colchester Business Centre, 340 The Crescent, Colchester CO4 9AD, tel: 01206 848 443, website: **www.amii.org.uk**.

To check whether you have enough buildings insurance: The ABI/ BCIS Residential Rebuilding Costs calculator can be found on the RICS website: **www.bcis.co.uk**.

To check a car's insurance group: **www.carpages.co.uk**; or CTC: **www.checkthatcar.com**.

British Insurance Brokers Association (BIBA), to find an insurance broker, Consumer Helpline: 0870 950 1790, website: **www.biba.org.uk**.

Legal

To find a solicitor

Law Society, 113 Chancery Lane, London WC2A 1PL,
tel: 0207 320 5650, website: **www.lawsociety.org.uk**.

Law Society of Scotland, 26 Drumsheugh Gardens, Edinburgh EH3
7YR, tel: 0131 226 7411, website: **www.lawscot.org.uk**.

Law Society of Northern Ireland, 96 Victoria Street, Belfast BT1
3GN, tel: 028 9023 1614, website: **www.lawsoc-ni.org**.

Civil Legal Advice (CLA). To check whether you are eligible for
legal aid and free legal advice from qualified legal advisers.
Tel: 0345 345 4345. See website: **www.gov.uk/civil-legal-advice**.

Solicitors for Independent Financial Advice (SIFA), is the trade body
for solicitor financial advisers. Its membership now also includes
accountancy IFAs as members. Tel: 01372 721 172, website:
www.sifa.co.uk.

For Complaints about a legal adviser: see Legal Ombudsman.
Tel: 0300 555 0333. See Website: **www.legalombudsman.org.uk**.

Making a will

Institute of Professional Will Writers, tel: 0345 257 2570, website:
www.ipw.org.uk.

Power of attorney

Office of the Public Guardian (England and Wales), PO Box
16185, Birmingham B2 2WH. Tel: 0300 456 0300, website:
www.justice.gov.uk – Office of the Public Guardian.

Office of the Public Guardian, Scotland, tel: 01324 678 300,
website: **www.publicguardian-scotland.gov.uk**.

Office of Care and Protection, Northern Ireland, tel: 028 9032 8594,
website: **www.courtsni.gov.uk**.

Leisure

Free digital TV channels

Freeview, website: **www.freeview.co.uk**.

Freesat. Tel: 0845 313 0051, website: **www.freesat.co.uk**.

Free bus travel

England and Wales, your local council or website: **www.gov.uk/ apply-for-elderly-person-bus-pass**.

Scotland, your local council or website: **www.transportscotland.gov.uk/ public-transport/concessionary-travel**.

Northern Ireland, your local council or website: **www.nidirect.gov.uk/ free-bus-travel-and-concessions**.

Cheap rail and coach travel

Rail travel in the UK, buy a Senior Railcard in UK from rail stations or some travel agents, or tel: 08448 71 40 36, website: **www.senior-railcard.co.uk**.

Rail travel in Europe: Rail Europe Ltd, tel: 08448 48 58 48, website: **www.raileurope.co.uk**.

For cheap coach travel: National Express, tel: 08717 81 81 81, website: **www.nationalexpress.com**.

Money

For information and advice on money matters: Money Advice Service: 0300 500 5000, website: **www.moneyadviceservice.org.uk**.

To trace lost savings: get a claim form from any bank or building society, library or Citizens Advice, or see website: **www.mylostaccount.org.uk**.

To trace lost investments: Unclaimed Assets Register, tel: 0844 481 81 80, website: **www.uar.co.uk**.

Internet comparison sites:

www.comparethemarket.com;

www.confused.com;

www.gocompare.com;

www.moneyfacts.com;

www.moneysupermarket.com;

www.which.co.uk/switch;

www.uswitch.com.

Pensions

State Pension Forecasting website:
www.gov.uk/state-pension-statement.

The Pension Service for any query regarding State Pension, if you live in the UK, tel: 0845 606 0265. If you are within four months of your state pension age and have not received your claim pack and you live in the UK: tel: 0800 731 7898.

If you live abroad, The International Pension Centre, Pension Service 11, Mail Handling Site A, Wolverhampton, WV98 1LW. Tel: 0191 218 7777, website: **www.gov.uk/international-pension-centre**

To check your State Pension age: website: **www.gov.uk** – State pension.

Pension Tracing Service, Pension Service 9, Mail Handling Site A, Wolverhampton, WV98 1LU. Tel: 0845 6002 537, website: **www.gov.uk/find-lost-pension.**

Pensions Advisory Service for any help understanding your pension rights, tel: 0845 601 2923, website: **www.pensionsadvisoryservice.org.uk.**

Pensions Ombudsman website: **www.pensionsombudsman.org.uk.**

Pension Protection Fund (PPF), Renaissance, 12 Dingwall Road, Croydon, Surrey, CR0 2NA. Tel: 0845 600 2541, website: **www.pensionprotectionfund.org.uk.**

Money Advice Service has comparison tables, if you wish to shop around for an annuity, see 'annuity and pensions comparison tables' on their website: **www.moneyadviceservice.org.uk**.

Service Personnel & Veterans Agency Service – to claim a war widow or widower's pension, tel: 0808 1914 218, website: **www.veterans-uk.info**.

SOLLA – Society of Later Life Advisers, tel: 0845 303 2909, website: **www.societyoflaterlifeadvisers.co.uk**.

Savings and investments

To find a credit union

ABCUL – Association of British Credit Unions Ltd, tel: 0161 832 3694, website: **www.abcul.org**.

Ace Credit Union Services, tel: 0191 276 3737, website: **www.aceus.org**.

Scottish League of Credit Unions, tel: 0141 774 5020, website: **www.scottishcu.org**.

UK Credit Unions, tel: 01706 214 322, website: **www.ukcu.coop**.

To compare savings accounts

Money Advice Service, tel: 0300 500 5000, website: **www.moneyadviceservice.org.uk** – comparison tables.

To find out about investment funds

Unit trusts and open-ended investment companies: IMA – Investment Management Association, tel: 020 7831 0898, website: **www.investmentfunds.org.uk**.

Investment trusts: AIC – Association of Investment Companies, tel: 0207 282 5555, website: **www.theaic.co.uk**.

Life insurance funds: Association of British Insurers, tel: 0207 600 3333, website: **www.abi.org.uk**.

Ethical investments: Ethical Investment Research Service, tel: 0207 840 5700, website: **www.eiris.org**.

To report suspected investment scams

If you spot a scam or have been scammed, report it and get help.
Contact **Action Fraud,** the UK's national fraud and internet
crime reporting centre on 0300 123 2040, or online at
www.actionfraud.police.uk or the police in your area.

Tax

Free help with tax problems if your income is low

Tax Aid, for help in understanding UK tax. Tel: 0345 120 3779,
website: **www.taxaid.org.uk.**

Tax Help for Older People, Unit 10, Pineapple Business Park,
Salway Ash, Bridport, Dorset DT6 5DB, tel: 0845 601 3321, or
01308 488 066, website: **www.taxvol.org.uk.**

For tax help and advice

ATT – Association of Taxation Technicians, 1st Floor,
Artillery House, 11–19 Artillery Row, London SW1P 1RT,
tel: 0207 340 0551, website: **www.att.org.uk.**

ACCA – Association of Chartered Certified Accountants,
29 Lincoln's Inn Fields, London WC2A 3EE, tel: 020 7059 5000,
website: **www.acca.global.com.**

CIOT – Chartered Institute of Taxation, 1st Floor, Artillery House,
11–19 Artillery Row, London SW1P 1RT. tel: 0844 579 6700, or
0207 340 0550, website: **www.tax.org.uk.**

ICAEW – Institute of Chartered Accountants in England and Wales,
PO Box 433, Chartered Accountants' Hall, Moorgate Place,
London EC2R 6EA, tel: 020 7920 8100, website: **www.icaew.co.uk.**

CAI – Chartered Accountants Ireland, Chartered Accountants
House, 47–49 Pearse Street, Dublin 2, Republic of Ireland,
tel: 00353 1 637 7200, website: **www.charteredaccountants.ie.**

ICAS – Institute of Chartered Accountants of Scotland, CA House,
21 Haymarket Yards, Edinburgh EH12 5BH, tel: 0131 347 0100,
website: **www.icas.org.uk.**

HM Revenue & Customs for local enquiry centres, see website **www.hmrc.gov.uk**. For your local tax office, see your tax return, other tax correspondence or check with your employer or scheme paying you a pension.

Contact the Adjudicator's Office for information about referring a complaint. The adjudicator acts as a fair and unbiased referee looking into complaints about HMRC, including the Tax Credit Office, the Valuation Office and the Office of the Public Guardian and the Insolvency Service. The Adjudicator's Office, PO Box 10280, Nottingham, NG2 9PF. Tel: 0300 057 1111. See website: **www.adjudicatorsoffice.gov.uk**.

If you have received an HMRC-related phishing/bogus e-mail, please forward it to the following e-mail address and then delete it: **phishing@hmrc.gsi.gov.uk**.

HMRC helplines

Income tax helpline: 0300 200 3300.

National Insurance enquiries: 0300 200 3500.

Capital gains tax: 0300 200 3300.

Self-assessment: 0300 200 3310.

Tax credit helpline: 0345 300 3900.

Volunteering

To find out about how to volunteer across the UK

REACH: **www.reachskills.org.uk**.

Volunteer Now (Northern Ireland): **www.volunteernow.co.uk**.

Volunteer Scotland: **www.volunteerscotland.net**.

Volunteering England: **www.volunteering.org.uk**.

WCVA – Wales Council for Voluntary Action: **www.wcva.org.uk**.

Leading volunteering organizations

British Red Cross: **www.redcross.org.uk**.

Citizens Advice Bureau: **www.citizensadvice.org.uk**.

Community Service Volunteers (CSV): **www.csv.org.uk**.

Lions Clubs UK: **www.lionsclubs.co/**.

Royal Voluntary Service: **www.royalvoluntaryservice.org.uk**.

Toc H: **www.toch-uk.org.uk**.

Checks for volunteering

DBS Disclosure Service (formerly CRB – Criminal Records Bureau and ISA – Independent Safeguarding Authority): Tel: 0870 90 90 811, website: **www.gov.uk** – Disclosure and barring service.

Work

To find out about rights at work

ACAS – Advisory, Conciliation and Arbitration Service, tel: 0300 123 1100, website: **www.acas.org.uk**.

Labour Relations Agency (N Ireland), tel: 028 9032 1442, website: **www.lra.org.uk**.

Jobcentre Plus (Great Britain), tel: 0345 604 3719, new applications helpline: 0800 055 6688, website: **www.gov.uk/contact-jobcentre-plus**.

Jobs and Benefits Office (Northern Ireland), tel: 0300 200 7822, website: **www.nidirect.gov.uk/jobs-and-benefits-offices**.

National Careers Service (UK), tel: 0800 100 900, website: **https://nationalcareersservice.direct.gov.uk**.

Skills Development Scotland, tel: 0800 917 8000, website: **www.skillsdevelopmentscotland.co.uk**.

Careers Wales, tel: 0800 028 4844, website: **www.careerswales.com**.

PCG – Professional Contractors Group: tel: 0208 897 9970, website: **www.pcg.org.uk**.

REC – Recruitment and Employment Confederation,
tel: 020 7009 2100, website: **www.rec.uk.com**.

To register a new business

HM Revenue & Customs (HMRC), newly self-employed helpline:
0300 200 3505, website: **www.hmrc.gov.uk/startingup/help-support**.

Companies House, tel: 0303 1234 500, website:
www.companieshouse.gov.uk.

HMRC Business Education & Support Team provides free training
events aimed at start-up businesses and on how to run a payroll:
www.hmrc.gov.uk/startingup/help-support.

Organizations providing free or subsidized help

Government resources

www.gov.uk contains the government's online resource for businesses.
Regional or country-specific support is also available at:

Regional help – **www.nationalenterprisenetwork.org**.

Northern Ireland – at **www.nibusinessinfo.co.uk**.

Scotland – at **www.business.scotland.gov.uk**.

Wales – at **www.business.wales.gov.uk**.

Other resources

StartUp Britain – an initiative of the CFE (Centre for Entrepreneurs)
– will help you find information about starting a business and
contains offers and discounts available to new business start-ups:
www.startupbritain.org.

PRIME (The Prince's Initiative for Mature Enterprise) helps people over
the age of 50 set up in business for themselves: **www.prime.org.uk**.

Index

NB: page numbers in *italic* indicate figures or tables

Also available from **Kogan Page**

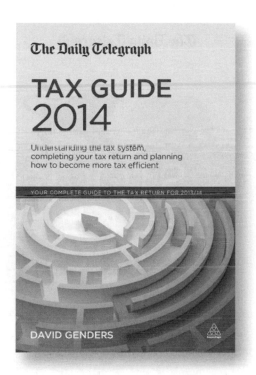

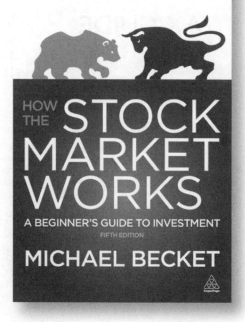